D1171184

YOU CAN GO HOME AGAIN

Also by Nora Johnson

FLASHBACK

PAT LOUD: A WOMAN'S STORY

LOVE LETTER IN THE DEAD LETTER OFFICE

A STEP BEYOND INNOCENCE

THE WORLD OF HENRY ORIENT

YOU CAN GO HOME AGAIN

An Intimate Journey

NORA JOHNSON

DOUBLEDAY & COMPANY, INC.
GARDEN CITY, NEW YORK
1982

Grateful acknowledgment is made to the following for permission to reprint their copyrighted material:
From *Farewell to Arabia* by David Holden. Copyright © 1966 by David Holden. Used by permission of the publisher, Walker & Company.
Excerpt from "American Culture in Saudi Arabia" that appeared in *Transactions* (March 1956) by Solon T. Kimball. Used by permission of the New York Academy of Sciences.
Excerpt from *Looking Back Over My Shoulder* by Lawrence Barnes. Used by permission of the author.
Excerpts from articles by Bill Gilbert that originally appeared in *The Bennington Banner*. Copyright © 1971 by Bill Gilbert. Used by permission of the Bennington Banner Publishing Corporation and by the author.
Interview with Bej Tewell. Used by permission of the author.
Interview with Marcel Grignon. Used by permission of the author.
Interview with Bill Taylor. Used by permission of the author.
Interview with Lawrence Barnes. Used by permission of the author.
Excerpt from "Housing Troubles in the Suburbs Grow . . ." by Richard Madden appearing in the New York *Times*. Copyright © 1981 by The New York Times Company. Reprinted by permission.
Excerpt from "Suburbia: End of the Golden Age" appearing in the New York *Times Magazine* by William Kowinski. Copyright © 1980. Used by permission of Sterling Lord Agency, Inc.
Letter to the Editor of the Mamaroneck *Daily Times* from M. L. Berridge. Used by permission of the author.
Letter to the Editor of the Mamaroneck *Daily Times* from Patricia Gould O'Brien. Used by permission of the author.
Letter to the Editor of the Mamaroneck *Daily Times* from Claudia McDonnell. Used by permission of the author.
Excerpt from *The Story of Dorset*, by Zephine Humphrey (1st edition 1924). Used by permission of the Charles E. Tuttle Co. Copyright 1924.
Excerpt from an article appearing in *Human Behavior* magazine, May 1979, by Robert Kanigel. Used by permission of the author.

Library of Congress Cataloging in Publication Data

Johnson, Nora.
You can go home again.

1. Johnson, Nora—Homes and haunts. 2. Authors, American—20th century—Biography. I. Title.
PS3519.O2834Z469 818'.5409 [B]
AACR2
ISBN: 0-385-15856-4
Library of Congress Catalog Card Number 82-2973

Printed in the United States of America
First Edition

To my mother

YOU CAN GO HOME AGAIN

When I was nine or ten, my friend Sarah and I often spent cold, rainy afternoons playing "In My Mansion" to escape our less than satisfactory childhoods. Our two mansions were alike except for a few small details. Mine stood on a piece of property the size of Delaware, which I thought tasteful—anything larger would have been vulgar. There I lived in an enormous mansion with many rooms and many servants, alone except for a few pets who lived in solid gold doghouses and diamond-studded birdcages. I slept in a bed the size of a city block covered with satin sheets, and the floors were carpeted with mink. In the mansion was a comic-book room, where every comic book ever published was neatly stacked and where a Coke machine was placed next to a comfortable armchair.

Far off at the edge of my property was a small, simply furnished house where my parents lived. Their privileges depended entirely on good behavior, but on the whole I kept them poor enough to stay out of mischief. Once a week or so they were allowed to come and visit me, to stay for dinner if I felt they deserved it. If my mother looked too shabby I gave her a new dress, for which she would weep with gratitude, and my father would say, "There, there, dear" (which to my knowledge he never said in his life). On Christmas they could come for the day. But if they crossed me—if they ever dared tell me what to do?

Even farther off at the edge of my property was . . . I can hardly write it, and it makes me so guilty that I must point out that this was *Sarah's* idea, and I only went along with it with great misgivings. Discreetly hidden behind tall trees was the torture yard and the Glass Mountain, in the top of which we deposited any parent who got out of line—Sarah with delight, I with terrified giggles. Within the Glass Mountain were the Chinese Water Torture, where water dropped slowly on the victim's head until he/she went mad; the Grinding Gears, the Fingernail Pick, the Eyeball Popper, the Backbone Stretcher, the Stomach Nail, and so forth. We sat outside and watched the steadily disintegrating parent whose final remains fell out of a small chute at the bottom. Of course this was the ultimate punishment. For smaller transgressions there were milder correctives—electric shocks, dousings with ink, and tickling machines, or we might amuse ourselves by shooting silver bullets an inch to the right of their heads.

I—we all—still have a mansion, less crude, more media-influenced, but in some primitive way the same.

Though I live by choice in the city, home is a rambling country house in some place where there is snow on the ground. There are fireplaces and many bookcases and deep carpeting everywhere. There are enough surfaces to dump things on when you walk in, plenty of hall tables and benches and cleared desks. There are big, bright lamps next to chairs and at the ends of sofas. Paintings hang in the halls, candles burn in hurricane lamps. The kitchen can only have been born in the head of a fifties bride—copper pots hanging from hand-hewn beams, a fireplace, a big round oak table where I serve the food I have cooked. For cook I do, though washing up and other chores are done by silent, faceless servants.

Though I can scarcely sew on a button, my dream house is a showplace of handicrafts, all created by me. Knitted afghans in burning colors hang over the backs of sofas, ceramic pots with herbs growing in them sit on sunny windowsills, chairs have needlepoint seats. Finds from my travels (real or imagined) are everywhere—pre-Islamic tiles are embedded in the bathroom floor and I sip my tea from French porcelain cups. I have become a perfect shopper, when the truth is I could stuff warehouses with the bargains that were left behind.

The other people who live in my house are unspecific, attractive, and obedient; they set me off without taking over. When I go into my paneled study to work, they run the house and never interrupt, then greet me with joy when I emerge. The guests who visit my house exclaim over my perfect taste and clever workmanship. They sit charmingly but unobtrusively at the dinner table, they flow out of the living room onto the terrace during parties, they neatly occupy a dormered guest room. They are interesting but not quite as interesting as I am, and they make jokes that are not quite as funny as mine. They never stay too long.

Very little about either of my mansions (and they have certain similarities) resembles the nineteen or twenty homes—if that is what they were—where I have lived in the forty-nine years of my life. Their choice and arrangement have always been at least partly determined by those other people who, in my imagination, I prefer to make into obedient robots—my mother, my father, my husband, my children. I have never lived alone, but even if I did I would choose the colors for the walls and hang the pictures thinking of other people and how they would see me when they came into my house, as though my house were a museum of my personality, a scale of my moral worth. Don't I, when I go into other people's houses, draw the most sweeping conclusions about them; don't I subject their decor to the most severe critical judgment? I hardly do it consciously, but aren't they offering it up for view, like a road map of their very souls? Even people with all-white apartments and indirect lighting are saying that they want to say nothing, that home to them is a stark backdrop only. But they are making a statement about themselves as definite as those who live amid a clutter of old photographs, china figurines, and butterfly collections.

We are sensitive about our homes, possibly more than about anything else. We are quicker to scrutinize the most intimate aspects of our own and our friends' lives than to say what we think of their apartments. I would sooner tell certain close friends that they look like hell or to suggest a therapist or a new lover than say what I really think of the place they live in—that nerve is too close to the surface. But how could they cover the couch in orange motel material, put that dreadful statue on the bookshelf, or leave that roachy stack of newspapers in the corner? How can these cries go unanswered? They assault my aesthetic sense—but then my house and furniture might be crying out too, saying things I don't hear. I blame its defects on the children—the battered chairs, the frayed slipcovers, the perpetual clutter—but I know, and everybody who walks through my door knows, that the children are only my excuse. It's me that's on trial, my taste, my judgment, my waste and penury and caution and extravagance, my very worth, in fact. For I made this place, I confirm it every day I live in it. I'm the one who chose these timid colors and painted the oak claw-legged table, who hung this odd collection on the wall and put a steel file cabinet in the corner and hasn't yet bought curtains.

It's strange that we care at all when other things are obviously more important. What matters is to be brave and honest and loving and hardworking and sensitive. But our homes are not values so much as they are private statements strangely magnified, the embodiments of fantasies. To the extent that we give ourselves to the creation of the stage set where we live, so much will our fantasies be on exhibit, in large dimension, every day for years, old dreams frozen in space, passing ephemeral notions blown up like garish parade balloons.

If they are ugly, we will be said to lack taste. But taste is only somebody else's judgment of what we were at some other time, what we hoped to be—or possibly still do. And since our fantasies are so delicate, so personal, and so crucial, since they enable us to live our tedious lives, to have them scorned is almost unbearable. "My God, how could you have painted that table?" cries a cruel friend. "Are you crazy? That's oak. Have it stripped down." But I painted that table in the sixties, early in my second marriage, as a ritual bridal act. That old table was going to match my new apartment and my new life. I bought an antiquing kit, which was what you did at the time, and *antiqued* it, to make the old look new and then older—or rather *finished*. You finished everything then. Unfinished things were *raw* (now they're natural).

I was going to seal up everything, cover up everything, including my own raw past life. I turned everything into something else. I even painted silver candelabra with gold paint. I finished chairs to match the table. I slipcovered everything . . . I slipcovered the couch in taxicab yellow; people flinched when they looked at it. Was that lack of taste? No, it was testimony to the fact that my new husband and I couldn't agree on anything—that already, unknown to us, we were locked into a struggle for power. I brought swatches home from stores; he didn't like any of them. I brought home more swatches, dozens of them—he hated them all. So I ordered taxicab yellow and a hideous jungle print—take that, I said to him, and to myself too. That's what you get. And we both hated the slipcovers on the furniture.

Of course it had been a mistake to cover everything up. But I like having that round table to remind me of what I was then and what I was doing at the time, as a kind of object lesson. I see myself doing it and it reminds me of my hope and my folly—like the Glass Mountain in which I truly thought I could dispose of my parents, or that huge empty mansion where I thought I would be happy alone with my comic books.

We are all profoundly affected by the places where we live, often without even realizing it. Their problems and paradoxes become our own, changing us and making us part of them. When we leave, the memories of their rooms and streets stay in our minds like ghosts, or the voices of old lovers. It may take years to understand how a place where we have lived has changed us. But it always does.

I know, looking back, that I have loved certain places as profoundly as I have loved certain people, and in much the same way. The feelings can be charted like a romance—euphoric anticipation, the dream of a perfect life, the excitement of the strange streets and the precious discoveries as we explore and claim the new place; then the slow-gathering fear of closeness which sometimes turns to angry disappointment at the inevitable failings, and then, possibly, the decision to move out. For no house, town, or city can live up to our expectations, as no person can, and the commitment to make a place home is as deep and exacting as the commitment to another person.

When we say that we don't like to live in a certain place, what we mean is that for a multitude of reasons, we don't like ourselves when we are there, that the chemistry of that place clashes with our own and makes us feel unimportant, insignificant, or frustrated. Sometimes the reasons are logical, but more often they are subtle and profound—certain streets or rooms remind us of other places where we have been unhappy, or confused, or felt unloved, and these old ghosts prevail. For rather than being rational beings, we are in fact subject to our own fantasies, and we invest the places where we live with a lifetime of images about *home* and what it should be like; and the towns, cities, and houses where we live become, in fact, products of those fantasies, laden with more hopes, myths, and expectations than they can ever possibly deliver.

To Americans, the very term *home* is intense and reverberating, thick with images and dreams. Traditionally a nation of wanderers, we long for the quiet house on the quiet street, the very community roots that we are so quick to leave when their obligations become stifling. Our profound ambivalence about a sense of place reflects the fact that, most of the time, we have never had one, for we all came from somewhere else. Our nation was founded on that most pervasive of fantasies, the American Dream, and most of what has happened to us has had to do with its possibilities and failures.

We blame places for our unhappiness as surely as we blame our parents, our spouses, or our children for disappointing us, particularly if those people took us to the place that didn't work out. We identify places where we live with the person who took us there—a town with the marriage that ended there, a city with the father who left home to move there—and try to go back to them, re-create them elsewhere, or erase them from conscious memory.

The more we move around, the more we imagine some ultimate home where everything will work out. As a nation we move often in our search for that place, to the city, to the suburbs, to a country farm, or to some place far away that will better our life. We have more than ever a persistent nostalgia, recurrent throughout our history, for some simple and quiet home where we can recapture long-lost values swept away by social change—simplicity, permanence, closeness to the land where we can spring roots and stop running.

American writers have always been haunted by a strong sense of place—or the searing effects of its absence—so much so that it is probably the single theme they have in common.

The locales in the fiction of the last century (Hawthorne's Salem, Alcott's Concord, Thoreau's Walden, Irving's New York, Cooper's "West," Mark Twain's Mississippi River, Henry James's U.S.-versus-Europe dichotomy) are pronounced and influential, and later certain fictive places—Lewis's Gopher Prairie, Sherwood Anderson's Winesburg, Faulkner's Yoknapatawpha, John O'Hara's Pottstown, Cheever's Shady Hill—become in fact characters themselves, significant forces that cause people to behave in certain ways. Conversely, there is a vagabond literature—Melville, Mark Twain, Kerouac—and an expatriate literature—Henry James, T. S. Eliot, Fitzgerald, Hemingway—that considers the alienation that comes from rootlessness, always with the consciousness of place. American fiction has seldom risen above its (regional) roots (as European fiction is more inclined to do) into some larger realm of universal human values—for our values *are* our roots, or lack of them; unlike Europe, we created our own nation, we created ourselves. The two themes of movement, of new beginnings, of self-creation, and that of nostalgic longing for the lost past are twin threads in our literature and a dichotomy in our cultural life. Here are the last lines of Fitzgerald's great novel: "[The dream] was already behind him, somewhere back in that vast obscurity beyond the city, where the dark fields of the republic rolled on under the night. Gatsby believed in the green light, the orgiastic future that year by year recedes before us . . . So we beat on, boats against the current, borne back ceaselessly into the past."

So continually do we beat on that we have gouged into the loveliness of our country, strewing urban ugliness far beyond city borders and littering roadsides with mass-produced service accommodations that have turned regional diversity into a nationwide sameness, where Texas is indistinguishable from New Hampshire, where even the same tired food is served in all fifty states. Communities have suffered from the lack of commitment to them by people who don't stay long, and we have hurt ourselves by doing so. We have become, in a sense, a "nation of strangers," as Vance Packard calls us—cold and lonely migrants who live nowhere, who have no clan or group, who live on some social fringe while the communities where we live rot from lack of care. We have turned our backs on our own need to belong somewhere, under the misapprehension that belonging to a place, or to another person, or to a group, will limit our self-fulfillment; and are only now beginning to understand that it is in such commitments that we can truly become fulfilled. The loner who lives nowhere for very long, loves no one, belongs to no group or clan is hardly fulfilled, but an empty shell whose untested feelings wither and dry up for lack of those human contacts that keep us responsive and alive. Without limits or boundaries, we have nothing to test ourselves against, to measure ourselves, try ourselves, fight, negotiate, or compromise. If anything goes, there is no human drama, only the terrible boredom and meaninglessness that comes out of the absence of risk and reward, those slow hard lessons that teach us, with infinite slowness, why we are here.

But out of the debris of all this is coming a new awareness, a slowing down, a search for roots, family ties, a passion for the "natural," and for the land, that powerful symbol of connectedness. A fashionable nostalgia is slowly turning into a powerful movement toward older values from a society that may well look better in retrospect than it really was at the time. On top of this, a painful economy is slowing us down. Moving, once a major national pastime, is becoming difficult, or impossible, for all but the rich. Families are forced to live together, sometimes against their will—and home, rather than being a delicious nest, a refuge from the harsh outer world, becomes a trap as unhappy couples, parents and grown children, and families with aging grandparents are thrown together as they never asked to be. We are unprepared and ill-equipped for such forced family closeness, the darker side of hearth and home. And yet, for whatever reasons, we are staying home more.

There is an infinite difference between the home we choose and the one that is chosen for us. Women follow men to the places where they work, and it falls to them to carve out a hollow in the new place and make it work, and men, who choose the places, more often remain apart from the life of the place where they live. In smaller, more traditional communities, women come together through their children's schools and activities and from a desire to create an excellent world for their children to grow up in—a goal continually threatened by economic limitations, community apathy, and a variety of social ills that sift down from the cities, where they generally start, onto our untroubled Main Streets. The constant clash between our expectations of the places where we live and what they actually deliver provides the vitality that keeps our towns and cities alive. When the gap between them becomes too great, we stop trying, hole up in our houses or apartments, and turn our backs on the world. Then the communities crumble and we suffer from a lack of ties to a larger group and either fall back too much on ourselves and our families, trying to exact satisfactions from them they can't provide, or else let certain social nerves starve, to our own detriment.

Since women, in traditional times and places, have been the knitters and weavers of community life, we are the ones who live out this drama of fantasy and failure, the continuous effort to create a lovely and healthy world. This has been a traditional female means of expression, the ability to improve our homes, gardens, and towns for our families and children; yet women may remain immature because of our constant identification with children and what we think children want, which is really what we wanted ourselves as children. If efforts to make larger community changes fail for overwhelming social reasons, we are thrown back into the too small world of our families, which we can destroy with an energy that has no outlet, or else be destroyed ourselves. If women work, we are, like men, inclined to make a home of the office, and having given at the office, we no longer care enough to give at home. Then the energy is used up, but a rift is created in female life, a difficult split that we have been unprepared for, and which we have not yet solved.

The rift is only one more in a series of rifts that have changed the character of the home from all-functioning unit to home-within-community. Until 1830 or so the home was a vast multi-industry which produced its own food and services and educated its children. With the Industrial Revolution, men started going to factories to work, schools were opened to educate the children for a more complex world, and gradually certain products, food or clothes or tools, were produced at a central source and paid for with money. The role of woman, which had been complex and economically essential, was slowly whittled down as one after another of her skills was taken over by mass production. She became more leisured, less needed, more of an adornment than a crucial functionary. To counterbalance her lessening importance, her historic image as depraved sinner (from Eve to Hester Prynne) was changed to holy vessel entrusted with moral goodness—this last to make her feel better about being at home while her husband roved, and to provide her with an occupation, which was going to church. She could, in a limited way, move out into her community and be its beautifier, its keeper of public morality, its guiding light, though with a certain powerlessness like that in her own home—if the ladies' garden club planted the tulips, it was the male mayor who made the decision. But now that her power is increasing—the mayor may well be female—a cruelly tight economy is forcing her to work even if dreams of personal liberation never did. And the tulips may never be planted because of lack of time or lack of money or both, while the woman who used to take care of such things runs to catch the morning train.

If it is true that women who work are becoming more and more like men in their aggression, their ambition, and their desire to make money above all, it is also true that men are taking over more matriarchal functions such as child care and the planting of gardens, and our teetering world may somehow balance out. But community care calls for time and money, and we seem to have less and less of both; and so community care may well come into the hands of those two more leisured groups, the young and the elderly, while the rest of us carry the economic burden.

If we invest the places where we live with assorted hopes and dreams—the excitement and glitter of city life, the tranquillity of a country farm, the affluent image of a house in the suburbs—and if we are less and less able to work to make these places live up to our fantasies, being too busy to plant the tulips, join the school board, help start the opera company, clean the streets—the gap will become greater, the fantasies stronger than ever, the dissatisfaction more painful. There is, besides, a slow erosion of regional differences by mass media culture, but at the same time places themselves become more diversified by the continual migration of groups of people who used to stay put.

In each place we live, there is a many-sided conflict, a little knot of paradoxes—the past and the present, the fantasy and the fact, the place as we see it and as we remember it. There are the very real problems of the community itself, and the way we see them through the veil of our own emotion. In the center of this little logo is our house, our room, our apartment, or whatever we live in, and how we have embodied our fantasies by its decoration, or lack of decoration. No act of self-scrutiny can be complete if we don't see ourselves in relation to these outer shells and understand their influence on us. Even the hermit lives where he does for some reason, and that reason transforms him—if he never leaves his cluttered room or hut, that tiny limited shell cramps him, deadens his brain, or else unleashes a frantic imagination by its very bareness, protects him from fearsome things or terrifies him with its ghosts, which keep him there and forbid him to leave.

I have lived for varying periods in five wildly disparate places since I was a child. Because of the nature of each place, and because of what I was when I lived in them, each changed me—usually against my will, for I fought them all, probably for the same reason we all fight intimacy, the fearful yielding that might hurt. How can we let ourselves love a place too much, when somebody, or something, might make us leave it? And how dare we admit we love some wallflower of a place which may be a joke to others?

I started out in Beverly Hills, California; moved to New York when I was a child; was taken by one husband to Dhahran, Saudi Arabia, and by another to Larchmont, New York. My mother's home for twenty-five years was Dorset, Vermont. Now I live again in New York City, always wondering if, and when, and why, I will leave it, or even if I want to stay; for I'm afraid to sink roots anywhere—as though roots will sap my strength—while at the same time I long for some peaceful permanent place, some soil and structure that are mine. Each of these places has failed to deliver what I expected, sometimes painfully; and each, miraculously, not only survived my leaving but was quite unaffected by it. Each has changed since I first knew it, and all are different, and usually better, in retrospect than they were at the time. I present them not necessarily in the order that I inhabited them, but in the order that they happened to me—that each, finally, made some sort of sense. The reality of all of them, to me, is less what they are than what I made of them, and what they made of me.

My geography is personal and intimate, a grand tour of some places it has taken me most of my life to understand.

NEW YORK

Wonderful Town

We lived in Manhattan, that place of all possibility, of new starts for people who have made mistakes. I was very grudging, in the beginning, about living there, for my father had been left behind in Beverly Hills (a place I longed for and didn't understand) in one or another of the elegant houses we had inhabited during my early life. I had been, I thought, forcibly removed to this gray, grim city with its raw winds and hard sidewalks, where everyone was in a hurry and talked very fast and incomprehensibly.

At seven, I wore my strange California identity like a caul. I was bigger, browner, slower, and more easily bewildered than the other kids where I went to school. My starched white pinafores and canvas patio shoes were all wrong, and so was my big grin. I longed for the pools and lush lawns of California, for the billowing purple vines and hot sun, and the more I longed, the more New York claimed me.

At first we seemed—I must laugh now—to be terribly poor. Our brownstone house was old and shaky, with banisters that swayed in your hand, a bellowing oil burner that made the whole place shudder, a gritty little bricked backyard where my mother tried to grow things in the sour soil. A few yards away was Third Avenue, where the roar of the passing El stopped all conversation and where the winos curled up in doorways. I thought East Sixty-second Street was a slum and wondered why we lived there.

But its ugliness had certain virtues. I felt safe here in a way I didn't in California. Though this was a dangerous place —you could freeze in the snow or be crushed to death by a collapsing El train or chased by a deranged murderer, or else we could starve because we were so poor or be bombed by the Nazis, or any of the other things grown-ups were always mentioning—somehow this house was safe and I knew I could take care of myself. In California I was always worrying about breaking something or making too much noise or making them angry; *I* was the danger, and so there was no safe place. I suppose I felt that here I had some control over my life, or, since the house was, in fact, my mother, that she had control over hers.

Within, our house was very elegant, an embodiment of my mother's fantasy.

She did the house in one of those rare moments when she had enough money to wave her hand, get some help from a decorator, and have it all done at once. Unlike most homes, which are full of debris from the last place, the interior of that house captured and held a full-blown dream, in that case what my mother wanted and wished for herself in 1940.

Clearly she wanted to be a very glamorous creature. The living-room walls were peacock blue, and an enormous ceiling-high mirror surrounded the baroque marble fireplace. The furniture was seal brown and peach satin, and such furniture—two velvet chairs shaped like seashells, for instance, possibly so she could rise from them like Venus. There was a low table made of glass panels, and a magnificent fantasy of a breakfront (which I still have) of glass and gilt and gold and tortoiseshell leaves and curlicues. Ornate Japanese dolls in glass cases stood on the mantel. Everything was elegant, breakable, and slightly unreal.

Her bedroom had blond wood Art Deco furniture and a chaise longue and pale furry carpeting and a dressing table with a flounced organdy skirt. It was a room for a beautiful, naughty lady who expected to entertain guests in that big, satin-quilted bed. And the living room was for a movie star.

Since this was my home, it was all I knew, and I assumed that this was how the world was—this was presumably "normal." I hardly thought about it, in fact, and certainly had no idea what a wealth of information was seeping into my head without my knowing it—information which would eventually help me to understand my mother, myself, and the times I lived in. And of course it took years to be able to look back at that house and read all the messages.

It was important to know, for one thing, that my mother had not done the house entirely alone, but called on a decorator friend for help. Anne Duffy lived around the corner on Sixty-first Street and she had a factory where she made all the glass fantasie furniture, which many of her friends bought for their living rooms. So since half the houses I went to had glass and gold leaf and silver furniture, I thought this was how all the grown-ups did their houses and how the world was supposed to look.

But Anne, who designed such delicate silver filigree and painted such exquisite gold leaf squiggles, was a square, blunt, rather rude woman who never combed her hair and who wore smocks with paint and mustard dribbling down the front. If you wanted to know the truth, Anne would give it to you straight from the shoulder. She gave very elegant parties in her Anne Duffy-decorated brownstone, wearing her spotty smocks and telling everybody how to shape up. Her husband Ed, a prizewinning cartoonist on the Baltimore *Sun*, was fond of going calling in his immaculate pinstriped suit. Together, he and Anne had never once kept quiet so the other could finish—they both unfailingly talked at the same time, as though the other weren't there, and so you looked from one to the other as at a tennis match. They were a devoted but odd couple, Anne with a perpetual cigarette hanging out of her unmade-up face (an oddity during that period of purple lipstick and Max Factor) and Eddie with his bowler and boutonniere.

Whatever Anne was expressing at her factory was in direct opposition to the rest of her life. For another woman, given the same passion for delicate, exquisite, shiny gold and silver trifles, might dress in them or hang them around her neck; for Anne this was, for some reason, verboten—possibly she thought they wouldn't suit her. Like many people, she erected a wall in her head. On one side she lived, and on the other side were her dreams.

In retrospect her dreams seem well suited to the people she knew, who were urban and sophisticated, and to the grim World War II era. Anne's backdrops provided the unreality for which everybody longed, the stage sets for their wit and talent and looks, actual or imagined. Anne must have known this and she found a prize client in my mother. Here was this beautiful lady, newly divorced, pummeled by Hollywood, returned to her New York home with a good-sized settlement for a new life. I suspect Anne took over and even found the house and told her to rent it, and if my mother didn't ask her advice on how to decorate it, I imagine Anne came stamping around the corner and took over. My mother, being the perfect follower, did what Anne said. The result was that drop-dead living room that looked like a stage set; as though Anne, who was very shrewd, knew how my mother had longed all her life to be center stage and how at night she dreamed of being the star in a Broadway show or Queen Elizabeth waving to the multitudes, and how she had expected such excitement of marriage to my father and when he became famous it wasn't the same thing at all. She had learned painfully that a Hollywood wife is usually considered, at best, a nuisance, and she'd come back East to stand on her own movie set.

And how did *she* get this way? Because she was the youngest of five children and her crabby mother didn't pay much attention to her and did their house in deepest Victorian, and when she brought a young man home for some joint-and-pudding Sunday dinner her mother insulted him. So when she grew up she wanted everything to be light, and gay, and beautiful, and she wanted to be in the middle like some Busby Berkeley dancer rising out of an unfolding flower.

And so in a sense she became glamorous, for our homes change us even as we create them. She embraced the image that Anne created for her and wore it as she wore her stylish clothes, to disguise the fact that underneath she was a frightened child whose life had collapsed, possibly in punishment for some wrong she had done, though what she didn't know. And when she made her home at 204 East 62nd Street, it was with bravery and cheer, and the conviction that she was, now, an elegant divorced lady in a lovely house in the most exciting city in the world.

This home could have been intimidating to the puberty-stricken person I was, with my glasses, braces, acne, hostility, and general klutziness. But fortunately my mother wasn't long on housekeeping, and the place was usually just slightly messy and dirty. My friends and I threw tennis balls around the living room, barely missing the Japanese dolls, and pretended we were horses galloping up and down the stairs. It eventually got an air of decayed glamour, which I found comfortable. Extreme cleanliness made me nervous; I was used to the dusty rialto I lived in, a worn and friendly place where, as I grew up, friends loved to come and hated to leave—and where, suitably enough, we all acted out our dramas.

The top floor, two flights up from the living room, was mine. There was a "study" with a fireplace (the only one in the house that worked) and two walls of bookcases where, when I was very young, Nana, my old nurse, slept; and two tiny bedrooms. Mine was on the back of the house, and it looked out onto the branches of a tree of heaven. Beyond, when it was dark, were the lights of the city, a southern skyline dominated by the Chrysler Building. This tiny, white-painted cell contained only a bed, a bureau, and two small closets. By the bed was a prayer rug where I knelt before going to sleep, for Nana was a guilty Catholic, and my mother a Catholic manqué. It was here the croup kettle steamed when I was sick, where the stories were read, where the nightmares came, for I wept for California, the lost land. In the study Nana sat, soaking her sore feet in Epsom salts and listening to Gabriel Heatter on the radio. "Ah, there's good news tonight!" he said. It was here we listened for the air-raid sirens that whined through the night and sent us scuffling down all three flights to the basement, turning out lights on the way and pulling down the blackout shades. There we waited for the bombs that always threatened but never came.

On the bottom floor of the house was the dining room, kitchen, and back porch, all in a row.

There was something very primitive, almost holy, about Mother's kitchen—even if one had a mother, like mine, who was more apt to be in the living room with a martini. Never mind, when she descended she was a very good cook, turning out quiches and soufflés in the forties, before most of the country had heard of them. In her copper chafing dish, she flamed peaches or plums with brandy, and poured them over ice cream. When I was older and gave parties, she made black beans with sour cream and rum for a crowd of insecure fifteen-year-olds. What strange things we ate in my house, how experimental our natures! Imagine cooking with booze!

The previous caveats about food had been strong, and like most other children, I had been brought up on the basic American meals—a broiled lamb chop, a baked potato, split open with a pat of butter in it and maybe a sprinkle of paprika, and a small pile of string beans or carrots sliced in rounds. For dessert, Jell-O or a piece of pie or layer cake. Chicken fricassee with yellow gravy, and rice. (How intense these memories are.) A hamburger made of ground round, and take the fat out of it, as specified by Nana. Beef stew. On Fridays, broiled fish (another gesture to The Lord) which I hated, a boiled potato with a snippet or two of parsley on it. Meat loaf. Fried chicken and corn bread, the greatest treat. Sometimes, oh joy, canned peas instead of fresh ones. Wonder Bread toast for breakfast, with grape jelly and maybe a boiled egg. Hot chocolate at night.

There were, of course, no supermarkets, and everything was bought from the trusty butcher (trusty because of Nana's ruthless surveillance) and Mac's grocery store on the corner, a cluttered, friendly place that supplied not only our food but certain social needs; for I dropped in there every day after school to buy a package of Hydrox cookies, and if we locked ourselves out of the house, which we often did, Louie, the delivery boy, could usually be persuaded to climb through the unlockable living-room window. Mac also had "store cheese," a big, crumbling orange hunk that can't have been as good as I remember; nothing could be. In those innocent days, the bakery was a routine stop, for nobody had been told that sugar wasn't supposed to be good for you, it was considered necessary for energy. Nana stopped by Duvernoy's for doughnuts or a pound cake, where she gossiped with yet another member of her Irish underground. How simple it was then. Did we ever have a salad, other than jellied ginger ale with fruit and boiled dressing? Or potato salad in the summer? Only after my mother went to Europe, and set about changing our ways.

The quiches and soufflés were a kind of parallel action as long as Nana was around, for she regarded them with a good deal of suspicion. They weren't Nutritious. They weren't right for The Child. Lettuce was something that belonged underneath tuna fish. And my Lord, all the wine. My mother and Nana's coexistence was a factor of my life, and worked, of course, because my mother gave in on everything. (Nana was bigger, stronger, less assailed by doubts.) My mother's efforts to cultivate my palate had no effect until Nana was gone—to the hospital, starting a four-year march to her death.

When that happened, I was left, in desperation, to my mother's frightening values—to her optimism, her trust, her carefree ways, her disbelief in the importance of possessions, to her conviction that it was possible to be happy—things that old Nana had disproved daily, by a grunt or a shake of the head, by a sharp comment to the butcher about the weight of the meat, by her sighs as she listened to the evening news on the radio. The world was indeed a place of woe. The bombs fell, people were killed. Hitler threatened the Western world. When you got older your feet hurt, you had to wear a corset, you didn't have enough money. The best you could hope for was a few laughs and a little peace at the end of the day. She sighed at my mother's herby, winy casseroles, muttered and grumbled at this proof of further decay of the old ways. What would happen when she left? I would starve, choke on thyme and rosemary.

The kitchen was as long as the house was wide. If the house were still there and I were put into that kitchen blindfolded, I could cook one of those old-style dinners—a leg of lamb, maybe, with mint jelly and pan-browned potatoes. I could find the old icebox, with its tiny receptacle for two ice trays, and next to it, a small table where the bread box was, and later a remarkable new invention, the Waring Blendor. The stove was next to the old, defunct fireplace at the end, where shelves held pots and pans—mostly Wear-Ever—in which Nana boiled vegetables to a uniform gray, and those white ones that always had a dark circle of wear at the bottom. Over the sink with its spacious counter, a barred window which looked out on the back porch, a later addition which stuck out from the rest of the house. I can feel the water faucet, long and smooth, with its two spigots, and below, the cabinet that held Bon Ami and Ivory soap, with which we washed every dish by hand and dishmop. At the end, the white-painted metal table with its two chairs, where I sat while Nana made hamburgers, or my mother sliced onions for one of her foreign dishes. Two glass-fronted cupboards where the china was kept, black-and-white checkered linoleum on the floor. It was too big, too inefficient, too old-fashioned . . . but it was the way a kitchen was supposed to be.

In the front of the house was the Anne Duffy dining room, sleeker and more "modern" than the living room upstairs. Black linoleum floor, baroque white marble fireplace. An "ivy" theme—ivy wallpaper, ivy-carved chairs, white china with green ivy leaves all around. Here we ate dinner and watched the feet march by on Sixty-second Street, for the bottom floor of brownstones is a few steps below street level, reached via the "arey way," as Nana called it. (It was here that I delivered the message, given me on the phone, that Pearl Harbor had been bombed, and watched in astonishment as a tableful of grown-ups, celebrating my mother's birthday, wept, cried out, rushed to the phone, and mobilized themselves for action.) Behind the kitchen, the chilly back porch with its wicker furniture and audible toilet, enclosed by a wooden stall, its glass-paned wall looking out on the backyard.

The backyard was a dreary little place, defiant of my mother's optimistic efforts at making it bloom. It was mostly mine and the dog's. It backed up against other yards on Sixty-first Street and abutted those round the corner on Third. Above Mac's were tenement buildings whose residents cooled themselves on summer nights on their fire escapes. They looked down at us as we broiled our steak and ate it at the umbrella table, which served to keep the soot off our heads. They were visibly ethnic in their numbers and had a forthrightness of address that astonished me in my world of tact and charm. They argued about money, they called each other names. "Wops," Nana muttered. I made friends, after a fashion, with a girl about my age. Standing in our strongholds, she on her fire escape and I in my yard, we exchanged passionate questions about each other's lives. She had no Nana, she shared a room with two sisters. She went to public school, she ate spaghetti for dinner. She got no allowance. She never went to California. Nana discouraged the friendship. "You shouldn't have anything to do with the likes of her."

The neighborhood was, in fact, receding Wop. The row of elegant residences on our block—each with its Holmes Patrol sticker—was surrounded by Italian tenements on both Third and Second avenues. There was an annual Italian fair up on Second, recently rid of its El train. Fifty-ninth Street, between Third and Second, was all Italian food shops—butchers, pasta and cheese shops, vegetable stands. Farther up our block was a small Italian church where Nana went to mass when she felt too guilty, and my mother went on Christmas and Easter. On Third, the El still cast its shadows on the poor, the halt, and the drunk, who curled up in doorways. Often there was disturbing noise from the Minute Tavern, that bad place across the street on the corner of Third. The drunks rolled out of it late at night, laughing or retching. Was the neighborhood safe for The Child? I should keep off Third, though the drunks were probably harmless. When I was older, my mother told me, "If you ever have any trouble, knee 'em. You—know—where."

At Christmas, there was a block association carol sing.

We went round the block, singing at each house, then somewhere for eggnog. At our house, we trimmed the tree and put our presents under it, presents that seem innocent now. A book. Precious nylons. A new percolator, two new towels from Bloomingdale's, the cheap neighborhood store. Stockings full of Woolworth trivia, carefully chosen—a comb, a pencil, some safety pins, a bottle of nail polish, new barrettes. Such tiny things. An orange in the toe, a few nuts, a homemade brownie. My mother's long nylon, a runny one, bagged down to the marble hearth.

I think now of that house as always being full of people, for my mother "entertained" a great deal—though the word seems wrong for what she did. There was no duty or obligation attached to her dinners, no sorting of silver or agonizing over the table seating. She didn't worry about who would get along with whom or what food would be "right." She was spontaneous and festive, possibly her greatest talent. She could turn a potentially dismal evening with a couple of dateless teenagers into a party. She was, in fact, curiously immune to problems of any kind. If you ignored them they no longer existed, they would fly away like summer clouds. The war would be over, the lights would go on again. In the meantime the thing was not to get "bogged down." If things looked depressing, get together with some friends, cook a nice chicken, serve a good wine. Enjoy it, and leave the dishes till morning. They would get done somehow.

Even now that "somehow" causes old, smoldering angers to burst in my head. Somehow the plates would get scraped, the bills would get paid, the nightmares would stop. Somehow Hitler would be conquered. But how? Who would do these things? Her inertia, her passivity were more frightening to me than Nana's doom-filled prophecies. You kept smiling, you curled your hair. Somebody always drove by to fix your flat tire. Illness, death, disaster? Somehow you'd pick yourself up and survive. This was the person I depended on, this curly-haired person smiling by the roadside, waiting for help. Suppose nobody came? Then what? The climate of her mind, so brave and blind, seemed in my darker moments like a kind of madness. How could she not know the fear that I carried around with me like a disease? Her own fear, which I know now was there, was perfectly sealed over by a seamless surface of rankest optimism, which I longed to break, to wound and make the blood flow. She would hurt as I did, she would feel my pain.

She was strangely oblivious to possessions, which others fasten their fears on, and I was bewildered at the importance other people put on the things they owned. I had one friend whose mother kept her (at the age of fifteen) out of the living room by a velvet rope across the door, and another whose furniture was always covered with transparent plastic. At an apartment on East End, the girl who lived there wept when, during some romping around after a dance, a valuable Chinese vase was broken. At my house I had never once been admonished for breaking anything. Well, maybe a little shake of the head, tsk tsk, over spilled ink, or dog pee in the middle of the living-room rug. But my mother loved no inanimate thing. She admired them, she might be sorry to lose them. She liked to be surrounded by pretty objects, but there was no love for them, certainly not enough to cry over. (Did this extend to me; would she cry if I were lost or broken?) Things were always falling apart. But where was her embarrassment, her housepride when a guest sat in a broken chair and went on the floor? If one of the casseroles burnt, she called it Boeuf Noir. When the ancient pipes burst and flooded the living room, ruining the Anne Duffy furniture and turning the room into a foul, steaming cave, she only said, "Oh, damn," and waded down to the kitchen to make coffee, standing ankle-deep in water. "It'll be fixed somehow."

Well, of course it was. The rug was replaced, the furniture reupholstered. As I got older, and 204 turned into a haven for my friends, I admired her more. My friends had mothers obsessed with neatness and order, mothers who scrubbed broilers, counted laundry, knew how much money they had in the bank. My home, with its carefree mistress, seemed like a dream world. My friends were always welcome, they could come stay for a few days, invite some boyfriend disapproved of at home. Nobody cared, or even noticed, if a bed didn't get made, if a coffee cup got broken, or even a lamp. Many of my friends had keys, which later, when that chapter of my life closed, had to be turned in. How liberating was that missing link, cutting my mother loose from the bondage of possessions—but with what did she replace it?

New York as I knew it then was a safe and accessible city.

I had been quite free from an early age to explore it, for my mother minimized its dangers. I wasn't to go to Harlem, and I should be cautious about the West Side. If there were other restrictions I don't remember them. From about twelve or thirteen, I went with friends to Chinatown on the El, to the Village, to Morningside Heights, the Cloisters, the Empire State Building, Times Square, Staten Island, the museums, the Park, Washington Square. There is an incandescence about those wanderings as I remember them, a glitter that refuses to fade. The place was magic, an unending feast. (Now I superimpose those memories on it.) The most poignant loss is perhaps that euphoric sense of ownership. New York was mine, I owned it. I understood it better than anybody. I knew it was made up of neighborhoods, of warmth, of tiny pockets of beauty, of dauntless vitality. It seemed incredible that there were people who were afraid of it. It seems now that its air was brighter and clearer then, the winters snowier, the autumns cooler and more full of promise. How lucky I was to live in this hub of the universe, when fate might have deposited me in Oshkosh or Bangkok. I am awed, as I look back, at the scope of my own appetite. (Away from my mother, I was brave.)

I—we, my friends and I—had cultural tastes peculiar to the time. We admired Rousseau and Tchelitchew's "Hide and Seek" at the Modern, having finally turned our backs on that stupid armor at the Metropolitan. We discovered Van Gogh and Picasso, Gershwin, Rachmaninoff, Chinese food (shrimps with lobster sauce at Lun Far's), Hemingway, and foreign movies like *Brief Encounter* and *The Bicycle Thief*, which played at dark theaters that served espresso in the lounge. Cultural tastes in the early fifties were anti-American, anticonformist. We longed, like others before us, for the "glamorous twilights of the past," for the lost culture of Europe, though we did not call it nostalgia. We longed to escape the numbing scene of suburban conformity toward which we seemed doomed to march. If it was inevitable that we would end up in Scarsdale, with the kids and the groceries in the back seat of the station wagon, we would fortify ourselves with great doses of beauty and charm, with a well-fed intellect that might prevent our souls from rotting.

Our own country and its culture, as we perceived it, could not even begin to satisfy that longing for a historic past which could be as intense as love, and sometimes became confused with it. We dreamed of traveling to Europe and, once we had done so, cherished its scenes and lights as the best treasures of our minds. We valued New York as a vast depository of diverse ethnic nooks and crannies where one could test Italy one day, China the next, feel the strangeness, the complexity of a history we thought our own country entirely lacked. (It wasn't till the late sixties that I realized, with surprise, that now I found my own country more interesting than all the others.) My own travels back and forth to California, twice a year by train, or to New England or Bermuda or Georgia or wherever else I went didn't "count." I dreamed of some garret in Fiesole, where I could write gazing out on the pink roofs of Florence, or a thatched cottage in the Cotswolds. I dreamed of ruins, tiny crooked streets with dark-clothed women, garlic-scented cafes, men with hooded eyes, guitar music in the night.

I wished that I had been born thirty years earlier, as my parents had. Nostalgia for the twenties abounded in the fifties, though, since things were simpler then, nobody thought of making a buck from it, and it remained a concept rather than a phenomenon. We all learned the Charleston. The center of the civilized world was the Plaza, in whose fountain Scott and Zelda had splashed between trips to—of course—Europe. The glow of innocence was on everything, hopes ran higher. I coveted the freshness of a world that was becoming too explored too fast (by people like me, searching for glamorous twilights). My parents had gone to France on a freighter, they had lived and loved on the Rive Gauche.

Wasn't America, in fact, a dull and sterile place, choked by its own materialism and conformity and lack of imagination—except New York, where it was possible, at least, to taste and smell the past, to half-close one's eyes on Mott Street or Mulberry and breathe the air that was life?

Except for Europe, I believed I would die if I ever had to live anywhere but New York.

During the years I was growing up, I watched my mother and learned how to live alone as a woman in the city—lore that has been, in my life, intermittently useful. Since she was my mother, I tried to extrapolate her messages and make them work for me, changing her truths to my own.

She did not appear to be lonely, though I know now that she was, nor did she take seriously most of the men who marched through her life. (The one she was in love with, Commander Jo, treated her badly, as my father had, as did the one she later married, and I suppose this was what love meant to her.) The others were . . . well, the kind of men available to a middle-aged woman during the war. A bouncy little French wine importer, a lanky albino who took her ice-skating at Rockefeller Center. (When I was younger she had taken me there every Saturday; we wore matching skating dresses with long tight sleeves and twirly skirts.) Others I barely remember. Since she was my mother, my mind could not accept her as a sexual being, even when I read, with breathless guilt, the love letters from my father that still came, and which she kept in her desk. (Recently a childhood friend laughed when I said she had never, in my memory, had a man over for the night, in her big silken bed. "But she did all the time," said my friend. "You mean you didn't know?")

Did she still wait for my father, or did I only imagine it?

With the immense egotism of a child, I couldn't imagine her needing anyone else in her life but me. Was I not, with my friends, enough fun? Who could ask for a better life than the one at 204? My father had remarried, presumably shelving any notions of my parents reuniting, and I considered the idea of a stepfather. I could see Georges, for instance, in his navy blazer and ascot, pouring his special Pouilly-Fuissé at a small dinner for four. He could carve a roast, tell jokes, and keep my mother in a good mood, for sometimes a shadow crossed her face, which puzzled and frightened me. When I went out on dates, they would stay home together, reading the evening papers. If he was handy he could shore up the constantly crumbling 204, with its groans and creaks. He and I could have long talks, of an evening, about the state of the world.

But she was not in love with Georges, she said. So she couldn't marry him.

You had to be in love, she said. That was one of the things life was all about, to find a man you adored so you could follow him to the ends of the earth. Then it didn't matter if you lived in a mansion or a hovel, in New York or darkest Africa. You could endure anything, put up with anything. That was happiness, that was fulfillment. If you had problems, somehow they would work out.

Had she been in love with my father? Yes, madly. But things hadn't worked out, had they? Well, no. The truth was he had been cruel to her. Not that he wasn't a wonderful man, the love of her life without a doubt. It was just that after a while, she couldn't stand his behavior anymore. Maybe Hollywood was to blame. But she had me. That was the other thing; you should have children, as many as possible. She had longed for a houseful, but had been granted only one. Not that I wasn't a perfectly satisfactory child. But would that she could have had six.

Six, to somehow get themselves raised.

But there was a deep contradiction between this dream of female *souffrance*, this kinder-küchen image, and the actuality of our lives during the war. My mother and her female friends, who came to our house almost nightly, seemed remarkably contented considering that the good men were overseas, leaving only 4-F's like Georges and the albino. No doubt they missed their husbands and lovers, but I don't remember them pining with longing. They were too busy both holding down the jobs left by men overseas and doing war work. My mother studied electronics (she sat around, in the evenings, making a radio from a spaghetti of red and blue wires), did technical writing (how to assemble guns), was an air-raid warden, and served in the City Patrol Corps, whose assignment was to keep an eye out for enemy submarines in the East River.

How funny it sounds now, naive, like a child's war game. But it was very serious at the time. The country was together, for the last time, in that profound patriotism. It even sifted down into my world, where little girls at school knitted lumpy khaki scarves for the soldiers, and at home saved bacon grease in cans and rolled the tinfoil from gum wrappers into huge balls. We never questioned this or made fun of it. The war effort was a grand and thrilling enterprise, undertaken nationally. Everyone talked war, followed it, breathed it. In my house four or five newspapers a day (two in the morning, three in the evening) were as sacrosanct as the evening news on the radio. ("There's good news tonight.") Headlines were two inches high. How adored were our leaders, often called, respectfully, Mr. Roosevelt and Mr. Churchill, and how clear and complete an evil was Hitler. It was before ambiguity, the fall of patriotism, multi-interpretation, and psychological interpretation. It was grand and simple, like the movies.

This home-front era oddly mirrored my own concept of males and females and how they fitted into the world. Men—my father and most others, the "good" ones—were absent, adored, romanticized creatures in faraway places. (My father was too old for the war, or too something—at any rate, he remained in Hollywood writing movie scripts.) Someday they would come back, maybe—but you couldn't count on it. In the meantime women ran everything, factories, stores, hospitals, schools, newspapers, besides handling the bread-and-butter matters of everyday life. They were strong, cheerful, and apparently fearless, with no visible guilt. If our mothers were not there when we got home from school, they were at the factory. If dinner was some dreary war casserole made with bacon grease instead of butter, we knew it was because butter had gone to war. Even female vanity was knocked far down the list. Women wore rayon stockings and sleazy dresses uncomplainingly, for everyone knew good fabrics were short and nylon was needed for parachutes.

Of course there was complaining about rationing, shortages of almost everything, and the innumerable inconveniences—travel was difficult and unpredictable, and apartments were so scarce that people read the obituaries in search of vacancies (a practice now returned to favor). There were always people at our house staying for the night or a couple of days, or for a quick dinner before getting back to Grand Central or the Brooklyn Navy Yard. Of course spirits rose or flagged according to the news from Europe or the Pacific. All this brave industry existed against that great day when the lights would go on again, when there would be bluebirds over the white cliffs of Dover, when Our Boys would come home and things would again be "normal."

But I had no concept of this "normal," I had never known it, and in truth I looked ahead to this return of hordes of uniformed men with some misgiving. Since I was too young to have any romantic fantasies about them—I was twelve when the war ended—I only wondered where they would fit in, and I suppose I had some notion that, being wounded, they would spend their time in hospitals or lying around on sofas. I didn't really know what they were for. I had grown up thinking women could manage everything, and assumed that they would continue doing so. But what didn't fit, what never made sense, was the dour commander my mother welcomed, embraced, and waited on as he sat at the table, fussing over his food (which she had cooked in a week's ration of butter), laughing at his doubtful jokes, hanging up his uniform jacket. What was he *for?*

"Stop," I say to the faceless boyfriend, call him Bill. "Don't. Please, *stop.*" Breathing in the dark.

"Oh, come *on.*" More gropes and grapples. "You know you're really a very sensuous girl. Why don't you let go?"

"I just won't, that's all."

"Won't, or can't?"

"What's the difference?"

"*All* the difference. *Won't* is when you decide. *Can't* is when you're inhibited" (one of our favorite words). "Are you afraid of something?"

"Of course not." (Lies, lies.)

"Have you ever?" asks Bill.

"No."

"When will you?"

"Well, not now. Only when I'm really in love."

Oh, Lord, as Nana would say. How many times did I have that conversation? In cars at college, on 204's back porch, in taxis rattling along under the El, while snow sifted down from the tracks above. What did I want? (I knew what *they* wanted.) What didn't I want? That was easy—pregnancy I didn't want, or dreadful diseases, or the things people would think.

My mother and I had, upon occasion, addressed these subjects. Her job, she knew well, was to scare me enough to keep my fearsome lusts under control until I was the safe legal property of some young man. It wasn't, she explained, that there was anything wrong with sex. It was life's glory, as long as you were in love. And *married*.

According to my mother, there were girls who did and girls who didn't. Girls who did ran enormous risks. They might succeed in getting a husband, but there would be a kind of taint on them. And there would be the inevitable seed of distrust in the mind of the most liberal and understanding husband. If she did it before, she could do it again.

Anyway, what would people think?

Surrounding my mother was a multitude of Thinking People, emanating opinion like a collective broadcasting station of public morality. People didn't like liars, cowards, laziness . . . or girls with loose morals. People wouldn't like it if you used four-letter words, didn't bathe, or flunked out of college. Were these things bad or good, right or wrong? Were they selfish, careless, hurtful? Well—it was really just that people wouldn't go for that sort of thing at all.

It was strange that the People chorused in New York, of all places. They were more like the voices of respectability in some small town in New England or the Midwest. Could they have entered my mother's head in Harlem, or Bayside, Queens, where she had grown up? They were no people I knew—certainly not these brave, jolly war women, Ellen, for instance, who, according to my mother, had "the morals of a jackrabbit." My mother must have inherited them all from that sour old biddy, my grandmother, the fun-killer of all time. The idea of the People had been passed down for God knows how many generations like the stick in a relay race.

Like the brownstone, like the magic and promise of New York, the Thinking People took up residence in my head.

What was life all about, anyway?

Ideally it was pleasant and sociable, with a minimum of difficult things. You should work hard (but without killing yourself) and hopefully you would become famous. You would make enough money somehow. If you curled your hair and smiled and were charming, you would find some dear, adorable man who would take care of you. Then you would have your own home and your own darling babies, and people would think you were wonderful.

If by some chance things didn't turn out well, you just made do.

More rage rises at that catchword of my mother's, "It'll do." Half-assed things would do—overcooked eggs, an ill-fitting dress, a half-baked idea. Suppose only three boys and fifteen girls came to the party (which happened more than once)? We made do, that was all. Where was the passion, the perfectionism, that raged in me like lust? She was patient with my obsessions, the pushing of my own mind further than it had ever gone—she smiled politely and agreed. Never did she put me down, make me guilty, or tell me that some course was wrong—for to her there were no wrongs, really, and right was personal contentment. What about the truth, that magnetic pole that pulled all the minute filings into an orderly pattern? She only smiled. Its attraction did not exist in her, nor, she said, did anger.

(But of course it did, and her infrequent bursts of anger over the years, which would have been natural in anybody else, were terrifying coming from her. Many years later, when my small son broke a mirror playing ball in the house, she shouted in tears, "How could you do this? You have destroyed *my house!*")

Her house was a haven, a nest, a living demonstration of moderation, of compromise. It was graceful and elegant; life's coarser, crueler side had no place here. Pain, rage, greed, ambiguity . . . you left them outside the door.

It was also something of a stage set. You felt "on" somehow in that living room. You played scenes.

Me: (I hear myself saying) Personally, I don't think I'm cut out for marriage. I haven't found my identity yet. I'd feel trapped.

Bill: All girls want to get married.

Me: That's a false generalization. I'm very sensitive and creative. I'm planning on at least a year in Rome and possibly Paris.

Bill: Doing what?

Me: Writing a novel.

Bill: Ha, ha. What you really want is a man. You can't kid me.

Me: I don't need a man on a permanent basis. Possibly I'll have occasional affairs.

Bill: How about having an affair right now?

Me: God! Is that all you can think about?

At the parties, which were many and splendid, everybody played scenes. A couple parting forever in the backyard. Another couple falling in love on the back porch. A group in the kitchen arguing about McCarthy. A fat girl crying in the upstairs bathroom, afraid to come out. Close, sweaty dancing in the dining room to "Blue Moon" and "Heartaches" on the Victrola. Self-pity, charm, and rage in the living room. In my mother's room, a little knot of adults with a bottle of Bourbon, talking about how old they felt. Two boys crashing via the living-room window, wherein Louie crept. How grand those evenings were, how unimportant, really, whether they were "real"—for being a child is only a series of tryouts for being an adult.

God knows we tried on enough masks along with our crinolines, our seamed stockings, our four-inch heels, our heavy makeup. God knows we thought we were in love often enough, and it hardly matters—though we discussed it endlessly, breathlessly, far into the night—whether we "really" were. We tried love on, examined its many faces. Probably by today's standards it wasn't "real," because most of us remained virgins. But because as females we had been brought up to cherish our virginity, like a prize, we were able to bestow our love with a dash, a magnificence, a freedom that is now as old-fashioned as an old prom corsage. We could play more and risk less during the years when playing was the only way we knew to learn. We sensed, half-consciously, that in gaining adulthood, we would lose a great deal (how could devotion in a hovel measure up to a 204 party?) and there was power in having one thing that was ours alone to give or withhold, to cause men to fight over, to use as a trump card in the power struggle with those boys who said we could only find ourselves through them. How afraid we were that it was true, and with what fierceness we hung onto the one female condition that was ours alone to control! For once it was gone—which could happen with the speed of light—we would truly belong to men, whose intent I, at least, had reason to doubt, and whose behavior gave me no reason to believe they would put any value on a plucked rose. They *said* they respected my mind, but did they really? They *said* they understood my need to discover my identity, but was it true? And how could you find out, before it was too late?

My mother helped us all negotiate the sexual shoals in her fashion, firing us up about love. My friends thought she was a wonder. She didn't nag, she didn't possess. Their own mothers asked, crossly, what was the big appeal of our house, that they stayed there for days? Of course the location was part of it. But besides that, things were so nice there, so easy and pleasant. And Mrs. Johnson treated kids like human beings, she actually seemed to like them. You could talk to her about almost anything. She was fun. While some mothers might make losing ten pounds, say, an excursion into agony, she went on an *alphabet diet*. Monday apples and artichokes; Tuesday beef, bananas, and beer, and so on. Lobster, lettuce, and liver. Milk, mustard, martinis. She actually did it for the whole twenty-six days. (Quail, quince, quinine.) Never mind that she didn't lose the ten pounds–she liked means as well as ends. She could play. The other mothers were so serious, so dire. At 204 you could pretend life wasn't as real and earnest as they said, as it probably was.

When I was very young, a friend and I congratulated ourselves on living in the very eye of the universe. There could be no luckier place to live than the East Side of Manhattan. (It could have been Hoboken, or some stale flat Kansas plain, or some reeking bayou, or someplace like Detroit.) Better still to be female, for we both knew and liked women better than men. But obligations came with this charmed location, and stronger personal forces were called for. People who lived in other places went to a lot of trouble to come to New York to live and work. They enacted tiny dramas of uprooting from the small town of their birth, coming here to make it on the "fast track." So even surviving here was a triumph, a symbol of expended energy. But if you were *already* here you had to do even better. You couldn't sit in the middle of New York City and ignore the electric compulsion. The energy that had infected Jane X and caused her to leave Main Street and come here was yet to be used up. You had to be the best. If you were not, your failure would be complete.

You had to be tough and ornery, the kind of person who thrives on adversity, who is excited by risk. In quieter, more remote places, you could hole up, close your curtains, and sign off. Not here. The city creeps in, invades every nerve. The sounds of the street never stop, the grit seeps in everywhere. But you could have your little pocket, your little haven, just to run into, to catch your breath and decide how you will next permit its invasion. How you will master it—make the money, have the success, make it yours.

During those years (which ended when the El was torn down in 1955) I felt, for the last time, that the city was mine.

DHAHRAN

Aramco's New Clothes

In Dhahran (the Arabian American Oil Company's main compound in the Saudi Arabian desert) there are, except in rare cases, no grandparents, widows, orphans, or socially maladjusted people. There are no teenage gangs or in-law problems. There are no restaurants, hotels, bars, nightclubs, or department stores. There are no crimes or juries, no package stores, Sunday sabbaths, fireplaces, radiators, or snow, no maids, pediatricians, Jews, haunted houses, or churches, and no dogs, psychiatrists, staircases, train stations, or pine Christmas trees. If these lacks make Dhahran sound like the bare bones of a place, there is, on the other hand, bridge, air conditioning, buffet suppers, oil, oleander and bougainvillaea, Indian houseboys, sandstorms, mail-order catalogues, airplanes, shipments, Siamese cats, guest houses, and wine made of canned blackberries.

There are streets of single-story houses, surrounded by lawns or high walls. The streets are wide and clean, blazing white and empty. Usually there is no one to be seen on them for blocks on end except an occasional Indian houseboy on a bicycle, whistling tunelessly as he rides by. There are a few small squares, which in European towns would contain parks or cafes; in Dhahran they have large buzzing air-conditioning units. At the west end of the town, the widest street, which is divided into two lanes by a strip of grass, runs into the main office building, known as the Kremlin. Clustering on both sides of the Kremlin are a number of small temporary huts, known as "portables," which often appear or disappear overnight as they are needed in another place. They are like wooden crates, clattering with every footfall and full of the cold and buzz of air conditioning.

Farther over, four more portables comprise the canteen, the mail center, the barber-and-beauty shop, and the laundry, and beyond them is a cement-block building curiously titled "Family Issue." In America, it would be called "ABC Supermarket." In this little business center one is struck by the total lack of signs, lights, or displays. Since the oil company owns and runs these facilities, there is no need for advertising or clever merchandising. The goods in each place are laid out with an eye to neatness only, and seem sparse after the clutter of an American drugstore, where space is valuable. Here there is nothing but space.

Back in the other direction are the family houses, which are cool, dark, and buzzing after the silent glare outside. The walls are often green or blue to contrast with the monotony without. There are only three or four designs for the houses, so one always knows where the bathroom is. Furniture rented out by the company is bandy-legged maple, with bouncing foam-rubber pillows in brick, mustard, or spinach, and flat wooden school-desk arms that tilt just enough to let a glass slide off; they are built for people with very short thighs and very long shins. Floors are all of sand-colored linoleum.

The people who live in the houses are married couples,

frequently young and usually with children. The two other kinds of people in Dhahran are the bachelors and the bachelorettes, who live in "barastis," portables of four rooms each which look like the beat-up dormitories of a college with no endowments. Bachelors and husbands, vice-presidents and houseboys, all the males in town wear white ducks, white bucks, white sports shirts, and sunglasses; the houseboys are indistinguishable from their employers except for the color of their faces. This is a kind of democracy that doesn't exist in Cairo or Beirut, where the houseboys wear robes of brocade and golden tarbooshes.

While a good many people in Dhahran find the life there dreary and limited because of its many deficiencies, a good many others find it refreshingly simplified. They find it frees the spirit, rather than cramps it, to make twenty thousand dollars a year and be halfway around the world from their in-laws, to go to Europe annually, to never again shovel a sidewalk or be thrown out of a bar. And gone, too, are the irritations of life in other places, where doctors send enormous bills, where butchers put their fingers on the scales, where desirable women suddenly turn out to have husbands. In Dhahran the chaff simply isn't there, and you always know where you stand. Seldom does anything really new happen, and even emotions seem to be well picked over. One can hardly feel grief or frustration or happiness without being aware that the same things have been felt over and over again, in precisely the same way, in the same house and in all the other houses, for years; it makes one tired before one even begins, and fades the colors of the landscape. The Muslim religion is based on this sameness, the idea that everyone is equal—and low—in the sight of Allah, and it is as though some of this has crept in off the desert and into the camp. Dhahran only came into being in the thirties, but it feels tired and ancient.

The people of Dhahran are divided, like two impotent

political parties, into the ones who like it and the ones who don't. Newcomers are asked repeatedly, for the first six months, how they like Dhahran, and for a conversational gambit, it is a particularly unanswerable question. How do you like bread? How do you like time? One dreads the absolute necessity of taking a stand, one way or the other, because all the planks in the platforms are worn thin with usage. When one finally takes a position, it is based on a large body of old excuses, creaking rationalizations, or ineffectual hatreds, and there one stays, because one must be somewhere. More truth can be found in defining what it is one likes and doesn't like, the camp or the country? American mediocrity or the unique individualism of the desert? Comfort and safety or dirt, heat, flies, and Arabs? The intellectuals of Dhahran put up with the town and cherish the Muslim culture and the barren challenge of the land; the less inspired ones cherish, with equal fervor, the startling efficiency with which the oil company has imported all the comforts and mediocrity of home—the fact that Dhahran is more State-like than the States—and they consider the Arabs repulsive.

In the mornings there is a faint mist over the town and a curious odor of sheep, petroleum, incense, and decay, the musty, meaty smell of the Middle East. There are no traffic laws inside the camp but for some reason nobody drives over fifteen miles an hour—possibly because of the vague fear of reprisal that hangs over the place. One lives more cautiously in a world where the rules aren't written down.

I wrote this just after I left there, in 1958, and know I can never tell better—awkwardness and all—what it was like there then.

Now I've forgotten the things that were familiar, and remember only the odd details—the hot brown of the desert sand, the creamy purples of sunsets outside my front door, and the heavy, strange smells, sheep cooking and sweat and the petroleum odor that was always in the air, like a chronic headache. I remember the strange, heart-stopping quality of a Beduin caravan as it moved across the horizon . . . but I can't remember where the commissary was.

"Do you remember the golf course?" ask Aramco friends, when I ask how the place has changed. "Well, it's all built up around there now. And the road to the Main Gate, that's where PetMin is." Where what is? "The University of Petroleum and Minerals." An entire university has sprung up in my absence. All I remember about the Main Gate is that it had one of those triumphal arches the Saudis are so fond of—green and white, I think—and that was where, it was said, they cut the hands off thieves.

"And the road to Khobar is now a superhighway." Al-Khobar, the fly-specked Arab town on the Gulf where we went shopping. There wasn't much to buy—watches and perfume, cigarettes and ball-point pens, fabric and aluminum kitchenware. There were bins of loose fragrant spices, and some pretty good tailors who could copy something you had, so if you had a dress you liked you could have it done in three colors. And there was the brass and copperware—the big trays that everybody had made into tables, and the coffeepots with that little bead hanging from the lip, and the beautiful inlaid Kuwaiti chests. But these things were like the Siamese cats, which were so plentiful they diminished in value. Now, I'm told, they cost a week's wages . . . and Khobar is a city. Sidewalks, apartment buildings, crowds, people living in the outlying areas, and now Lockheed and Bechtel have big compounds there. And lots of people (not only Saudi people, but Western ones) live in the apartments.

In my day (as I say more and more with the passing years) *nobody* lived in Khobar, and if some people did, you knew they were cross-cultural freaks—a Saudi married to a German woman, for instance, or an American who was crazy enough to want to get away from Aramco and mingle with the ragheads. Or British who were into suffering.

I didn't arrive at this judgment easily. In 1955, when I left for Arabia with my new Aramco husband, there was a feeling of anti-Americanism among certain Americans. If you were of that turn of mind, you deplored your country's materialism and superficial, plastic values. You could preserve your soul only by taking periodic plunges into Old World culture where beauty and tradition still prevailed.

This was the era of David Riesman's *The Lonely Crowd* (which I had been assigned three times at Smith) and *The Man in the Gray Flannel Suit*. Peer pressure was at its height, and Salinger celebrated alienated children frequently in *The New Yorker*. We all wanted to go to France and study existentialism, or to Italy and study Renaissance art, or anywhere to escape the threat of numbing conformity.

In retrospect, I suppose Arabia sounded exotic, though I had been warned more than once that Aramco's homemade, fenced-in town was more American than America. I suggested to my husband that we live in the nearby Arab town where it was "real." I imagined us living in tents of brocade spread with Persian rugs, eating stuffed grape leaves and figs served by naked Nubian slaves. I imagined that Arabic was easy to learn and that before long I would be a familiar figure around the local hareem, where I would mingle with the local women and plumb the secrets of their culture.

Well, it's easy to make fun of such old illusions. But oh, how quickly they went. During our approach through Beirut, Damascus, Baghdad, and then Arabia, which even frightened me from the window of the plane, the speed with which I perceived that impassable gulf between my culture and the local one, between what I had come from and where I was going, was an *éclat*, a vision, an educational experience so total that it made all others seem like wasted time. In a few days I learned about time, space, the rarefied nature of my life, and my own fragility—I who was afraid of nothing. Now I was afraid of everything—those thousands of uninhabited miles, that burning sun, the emaciated limbs of the beggars and their piercing black eyes. Whatever wasn't frightening exasperated me because of my own inability to place or understand it. All my old signposts were gone. I had never experienced such strangeness and never would again.

"Of course now we all live much better than we used to. Everybody added rooms and put in swiming pools." Swimming pools! But of course I left there twenty-three years ago when there was still a faint frontier air about the place. I say faint because it existed mainly in the minds of our husbands, who liked to think of themselves as adventurers—new, enlightened colonials, in the first stage beyond pith helmets. But even back then that spirit was slipping away, and when they talked about the good old days *then*, it was about the period right after World War II when most of them were hired, and they were still in their twenties and hadn't yet had families, and they worked at the Tapline stations in the desert, and even Dhahran was pretty primitive.

I was eleven years younger than Len, my husband, and not old enough to talk about any good old days at all. So I listened to them with envy disguised as tolerant amusement. But in fact I would have loved to have had their adventures, tame though they might seem compared to the *real* good old days of oil exploration in the thirties, when geologists wore thobes and rode on camels. There they were, this group of bright, well-educated, attractive young men, all fluent in Arabic and generally high on the culture of the Middle East, gone out to the land of T. E. Lawrence to make their fortunes. They saw themselves as very romantic, very virile and swashbuckling, very clever and cool about the cultural enigmas that flustered my brain so. They made fun of everything from the blindness of their employer to the bizarre habits of the local sheikhs. They had an enormous amount of fun, in which they tried to include their wives, and we all sat around and laughed politely and tried to imagine what it had been like out on the pipeline that night in June, or that crazy lunch in Rome the year before, or the party in one of the barastis where so-and-so got totally loaded and did this terrific imitation of Banana Nose (King Saud) while wearing only a sheet. It sounded like fun—too much fun, for it made me sad that I would never have such adventures, and that even for them it was over; for at the end of the evening they all got up, each with his wife, and went home to his own little apartment or row house.

Those dull little apartments . . . we lived in a couple of them that I don't remember, then "caretook" other people's houses till we somehow had earned enough points to have our own. It was in the first one I made all my mistakes—made coffee with the wrong water for a woman who came to call (in hat and white gloves), causing her to sputter and spit it across the room; made rubber cannelloni the guests couldn't chew, which popped the toothpicks I'd used to hold them together; and cried when I looked out the window and caused my husband to feel guilty—which of course was part of the purpose of crying. It was there that I complained, sulked, and groped around, trying to understand what I was doing there; it was there that I was forgiven by people who were kinder than I was wise, who loaned the pots and pans, brought the casseroles, asked me if they could pick up anything at the commissary. It was there that I was pregnant, wrote a novel . . . or maybe it was the second apartment, or the third, for they all looked alike, and I have little memory of change or progress.

It took a long time, in Dhahran, to make a home your own. You bought things in the States and sent them out, but you couldn't do that very well until you'd been there and seen what you were going to live in. So you lived through the first contract (which at the time was two years) with the Aramco furniture. Then you spent half of your long vacation in department stores buying all the stuff. Then during the second contract you thought of dozens of things to get next time—though I didn't stay that long. But some people did it, because we caretook a house in which everything was pink and green, right down to the pink teapot. And after you were there for fifteen or twenty years, like my friends, you not only lived in the finest sort of house but you added a room and put in a swimming pool. It was hard to imagine Dhahran as being so grand.

In the sixties, I'm told, the company started hiring a lot more women for part-time work, which must have changed the nature of female life in Dhahran. "When I look back on those days in the late fifties," recalled Bej Tewell, who now lives in Vermont after eighteen years in Arabia, "I can't think what I did all day. I didn't have a job. For years I didn't have any children. I had a houseboy and a gardener . . . what the hell did I do with my time?"

I know what she did, and what I did, and all the rest of us.

We played bridge, a game good enough to breed obsession. Sometimes we went to each other's houses for dinner and two or three tables of bridge, and sometimes the women played in the afternoon. We took turns at each other's houses, and whoever was hostess served tea or coffee and made cookies. Sometimes we had tournaments and sometimes we played duplicate. This was all right unless you hated bridge, or if, like me, you loved it but never got very good at it—which condition eventually leads you to say you hate it.

We went to coffees and teas. Everyone got very dressed up, and the woman giving the coffee often had elaborate silver coffee and tea services, all polished by the houseboy, and trays of homemade coffee cake, cookies, and delicate little sandwiches. Twenty women would gather and nibble and talk about—what did we talk about? The stuff of female life. Cooking, the houseboy, the kids, pregnancy symptoms, or any good gossip that was going around. Sometimes the coffee had booze in it (Cafe Royale) and some of the ladies would get mildly lit by lunchtime.

We went "calling" and other women "called" on us. The doorbell would ring at ten or ten-thirty in the morning and there would be a lady on the doorstep, coming for some of the coffee that in retrospect we seem to have consumed by the gallon. People popped by a lot to make new arrivals feel at home, bringing some dish they'd cooked or information they thought helpful. Everybody was a welcome wagon. After a couple of months I called a halt to this custom, because I wasn't making much progress on the novel I was writing. Writing in Dhahran was hard enough anyway—there were too many strange things in the air, like yeasts, things that kept interfering.

We "entertained"—in my language, we had people for dinner, often and lavishly. The Goanese or Pakistani houseboys were great for serving and cleaning up, and chopping the occasional onion, but their cooking was limited to that eternal, camp-wide dish, the houseboy curry. We not only cooked, but strained to outcook each other. We boned ducks, gelled aspics and puréed liver for pâté, and piled up cream puffs to make croquembouche. We made soufflés and mousses and strudels, stretching the dough thin enough to read the Rome *Daily American* through it. We churned ice cream, simmered stock, and kneaded bread.

Eight of us had a Gourmet Society, which met once a week. The preparation for each meal—which in all cases was done by the wife—took two days, for we featured hand-lettered menus and our most elegant silver and napery, and the gatherings were always black tie. (With all the free time we had, we chose to fill it with ritual.) Afterward we appraised each other's cooking, in a good-natured way.

For some of us there was *lunch*. (Bride to groom, in an old British joke: "I take thee for better and for worse, in sickness and in health, but not for lunch.") In Dhahran a whistle blew at noon to announce the beginning of the lunch hour, and another at one-thirty to announce the end of it. There were no restaurants, and so husbands came home for lunch, occasionally bringing friends. I escaped this, for my husband was one of a handful who worked in Dammam, a nearby Arab town, where they either took lunch in a bag or went to a local eatery known as "Chez Amoeba." Those whose husbands came home had to stop whatever they were doing and produce chef's salad, or grilled cheese sandwiches, or tomato aspic, or whatever.

We made booze, though this was largely a male responsibility. (And why did we make booze? Because the importation of liquor is not allowed in Saudi Arabia, but the Saudi government has traditionally closed its eyes to the thousands of stills in Aramco's towns—reasoning that, without booze, there would be no Americans, and without Americans, the oil would remain in the ground.) Everybody had huge glass crocks (rescued from some facet of petroleum refinery) and a still rigged up from a huge pressure cooker, coils of copper tubing, and other crucial elements obtained from certain hip Manhattan drugstores and smuggled back into the country. The mash was made of sugar, water, and yeast. (When I first arrived, frozen orange juice was also used, then rejected in the name of purity.) The mash sat in a closet for weeks fermenting and festering, then was run through the still three times. (Drinking first-run was considered desperate alcoholism, the sort of thing drillers did, and even second-run was seen as a little tacky. Now I hear everyone makes *fourth*-run.) The resulting 100-proof alcohol was then cut back to 80 or 90 proof, and a clear, vodka-like liquor resulted. You could drink it with tonic and lime, or with bitters to make a pink gin, or with Rose's Lime Juice, very pukka sahib. Or you could boil it up with lemon and orange peels to make a kind of martini, or marinate it in oak chips to make something whiskey-like.

Male responsibility ceased with bottling, and the women usually were in charge of refinements and wine-making (from canned blackberries). At various times in Dhahran I made, or tasted, everything—sherry, cognac, many liqueurs, whiskey, gin (from juniper berries), beer, red and white wine, and even a brave attempt at champagne. Any decent Gourmet Society dinner had at least two or three forms of booze and usually more.

Sometimes we went to the clinic for shots (cholera, typhoid, typhus, yellow fever, and smallpox). Or for stool tests, to get some medicine for whatever worm or amoeba we'd picked up—very likely if you hadn't washed your lettuce in hot water and Tide, as recommended. Or to get our fillings refilled, for Aramco had first-rate dentistry, all free. Or to have a baby. The Dhahran Health Center, where my oldest daughter was born, used to have six beds or so in obstetrics. Now there's a six-story wing, which is strange to contemplate because in my day, *nothing* had six floors. Nothing even had two floors except the president's house, which was the grandest building in town.

We joined or formed groups. A recent college graduate, I was initially puzzled at a kind of life that didn't demand my jumping out of bed at some early hour and rushing off to put something in my head. It made me so uncomfortable that I joined every group I could find, probably all there was at the time, though now there are many more. There was the Singing Group, which met at the house of the directrice, where forty-odd women sang the morning away and then—of course—had coffee. After polishing half a dozen songs we got all dressed up one evening and sang them for our husbands, followed by White Lightning and houseboy curry.

There was the Study Group, a fairly serious enterprise that featured talks by experts or Islamic history, local flora and fauna, and so forth. I remember a Palestinian female doctor who had actually gotten into the tents and rooted out some of the secrets of the reproductive life of those strange, masked Beduin women (they pack their vaginas with salt for contraceptive purposes, and to discourage husbands too horny too soon after childbirth; they put the placenta in a jar and keep it for months, or forever; they wrap up the newborn in swaddling clothes—that's where *that* came from—and keep it that way for months; they wash their hair in camel pee). We all listened to her, going ooooh and aaah. Some was interesting and some dull and I took pages of notes as though I would be responsible for it all on an exam.

There was oil painting, at which I turned out to be amazingly untalented, and some group tennis lessons, where I reached, said the instructor, a plateau—an endless one from which I never moved. There was the novel I was writing and my own reading.

After I had a baby, a year or so after we arrived, the problem of time was remarkably resolved.

"Things changed in the early or mid-sixties," Bej Tewell observed. "A very different lot of people came—people who weren't there to make the best of things but to make a buck, to rip off the company." How on earth did they do that? "Various kinds of private enterprise. The nurses' whorehouse, for instance. That was fairly well known. A nurse I know said she had trouble with Saudis following her around because they assumed that since she wore a white uniform, she must be a whore. Then there was a woman who ran a sort of school for school dropouts, and charged for the service. Then of course there was smuggling—D. [a friend] made a fortune smuggling gold out of India." Quiet, law-abiding D.! "And there were the people who ran their stills twenty-four hours a day and employed a houseboy just to watch them, and made a tidy sum selling booze."

This is not kindly regarded by the company. In his privately printed memoir of Dhahran, *Looking Back over My Shoulder*, ex-Aramcon Larry Barnes tells of "a bright young fellow, who was in a significant management position with lots of good prospects for advancement, [who] was deposited on an outgoing plane on a few hours' notice, leaving his wife behind to pack up. He had discovered that a large market existed for good fourth-run stuff among the hundreds of expatriates in the local economy. He had been in full production . . . for months. But he finally got caught up with.

"When a friend said to his wife that they were sorry they were leaving, she was reported to have [said], 'Don't feel sorry for us. We're going out with a bundle.' Informed estimates run between one hundred thousand and two hundred thousand dollars. Tax free."

If such things went on back in *my* good old days, I didn't know about them. Everybody seemed almost incredibly respectable and loyal to the company. "Oh, everybody wanted to make a buck in the good old days too," said Marcel Grignon, Aramco lawyer and Dhahran resident of twenty years plus. "They were going to go out for a short time, make a buck, go around the world, and then think it over . . . a lot of people thought it over and decided to stay on." Some magic music (to which I was deaf) caught at even the most skeptical —or magic money and irresistible perks. The effect made for an amazingly law-abiding community, docile and faithful. Occasionally something would happen—somebody got drunk at the wrong place or somebody's car was seen in front of the wrong house all night, or somebody spent a few hours in a Saudi jail. But that's all. It was all so well mannered that the occasional divorce was news, a paradigm of fifties complacency. And everybody was so earnest about the company.

"But you're talking about an American business trait as much as anything else," continued Marcel Grignon, "being terribly serious as though the company is the last thing on earth. If you look at an army base anywhere in the U.S. you'd find the same thing, in effect the same atmosphere . . . though not in the sense of having the colonel's wife one step down in the pecking order from the general's wife, because I think Aramco is a little more democratic . . . If I had a dinner party I could invite anybody I pleased, it might be a president or a vice-president or a mechanic, there was no pressure to invite so-and-so. So our social life was based on complete freedom."

Well—okay. Except there was no freedom from the company, because there wasn't anything else, which seemed to bother no one but me. In this strangest of all places I have lived, I felt like a malcontent, a misfit, filling the air around me with cries of discontent. Why couldn't I fit in? I had all physical comforts, kind and interesting friends, a houseboy to free me from the worst chores, occasional travel, all the time in the world. And lucky me, I could write anywhere, I had a portable career—more to be pitied were the women who didn't have that, and had lost their access to work when they left the States. What, exactly, did I want?

It seems now that that whole period *was* a question, or many of them, whose answers are only slightly less elusive now than they were at the time. The particular chemistry of the place came upon me at a bad time, for I've no doubt that now, given the right circumstances, I could live there with equanimity, if not great contentment. But at twenty-two I was too young, too self-centered, and too ignorant of the reasons people have for putting up with anything that is less than perfect. It had simply not occurred to me that people's choices are, more often than not, made from several imperfect alternatives, which they make more desirable by a little self-deception. I didn't yet realize that one of the most useful and admirable of human talents is the ability to make the best out of very little, to scratch contentment out of barren soil; and that those who can do so provide the ballast, the counterweight for those others who chafe, who muddy the waters, who cry out in indignation. I talked a lot, at the time, about reality, and hypocrisy, and what I called intellectuality, which

I thought I understood. I would die, I thought, without personal freedom, and didn't understand that there were people who would die without money and security, having never lacked either, or what circumstances would make these things so important.

I must go back a little to understand the peculiar dilemma that Dhahran produced in me at that time—which, at another time in my life, it might not have, or which, at that same time, another place might have failed to do.

Aramco was born the same year I was, in 1933, with the signing of the Concession Agreement between Standard Oil Company of California and the Kingdom of Saudi Arabia. The Arabian American Oil Company was formed, and the oil geologists arrived and began exploration in the Eastern Province, in the area where Dhahran is now.

Saudi Arabia had only been pulled into a unit a year or so before that. It was a vast, dry, barren peninsula a quarter the size of the United States, inhabited by tribes of Beduin wandering in search of water; political organization was nonexistent until the reign of that mythic king, Ibn Saud (father of subsequent kings Saud, Faisal, and Khalid), who, by conquest and tribal intermarriage, fused the small, scattered, stubborn population of his country into as much of a political unit as it probably will ever have, and then immediately opened the doors to the oil prospectors.

All of history—all of life, all of drama—is a continuing process of opposing forces that meet, clash, and somehow resolve themselves into something that works, more or less, until the next opposing force comes along. In Saudi Arabia's case, it might appear that there was little in this scattered, divided country for Aramco, with its technical values, to clash against. But there was, and is, the culture of Islam, in its fiercest, most conservative form, a religion whose power (it seemed to me) grew and expanded to make up for other earthly lacks. Unlike the other two great monotheistic religions, the Muslims face their God directly, without churches, priests, rabbis, or other intermediaries. It is infinitely more moving to see a Bedu in the desert dropping to his knees to pray toward Mecca than to see your neighbor discreetly bowing his head in the next pew on Sunday morning. Allah is wilder, fiercer, more demanding, more inescapable, more omniscient. In that hard land there is little else, and no place to hide from that stern God.

Islam has many faces and facets in the Arab world, which extends from North Africa through the Middle East, and has pockets in Pakistan, Afghanistan, and Indonesia. But Saudi Arabia is its bastion, because it is the home of Mecca and Medina, the holy cities; and the most important thing a devout Muslim can do in his life is to make the hajj, or pilgrimage, to Mecca where the prophet Mohammed was born. And Saudi Arabia is the home of the Wahabbi sect of the Sunnite, which is the larger, and the orthodox group of Islam. Iran, on the other hand, is Shi'ite, and the two are deadly enemies; and the baffling small wars that are forever breaking out in the Middle East usually have to do with religious or old tribal rivalries that we, with our Western myopia, don't understand. The Sunnis and the Shi'ites disagree over what may appear to be a minute theological point; whether the divine right of descent of the Persian Caliphate—i.e., the historical order of succession of Mohammed's descendants—goes, or does not go, through Ali, son-in-law of Mohammed. But to the Muslims it is important enough to take up arms over. I would also suggest that though it may appear to the world that the Arabs hate the Jews and would go to any lengths to shove Israel into the sea, there is no comparison between their feelings about the Jews, who are, after all, neither here nor there when it comes to Islam, and the important business about Ali's right to the Caliphate. The affairs of our own backyard are, after all, more real and poignant to all of us than the most earthshaking issues that are, after all, somewhat remote.

We are not, any of us, born liberal. The more primitive we are, the more recluse, the more ignorant, the more suspicious we are of those who are different from us, and the process of civilization has been a series of painful lessons in tolerance, many of which are still not very well learned. Most countries have, in their histories, chapters of persecution on racial or religious grounds; it is the most humiliating of levelers.

However, this doesn't for one moment stop us from pretending virtue. As Americans, for instance, we become very indignant about the violation of human rights in less enlightened countries, while temporarily forgetting about our own treatment of American Indians, blacks imported as slaves, and other minorities, which has been less than admirable. Like everyone else, sometimes we have been better and sometimes worse—and possibly it is kinder to judge us chapter by chapter, and forget our irresistible urge to show how much more liberal we are than the next guy—for after all, how else will we look good?

In entering Saudi Arabia, we were going to be much, much better than the British, who have since been thrown out of most of the countries they colonized. Well, possibly the comparison isn't fair—they agreed to be persuaded to be thrown out, it might be said, and besides (hindsight) if you colonize, you ask for it. And we were not colonizing Saudi Arabia; rather an American oil company was making an agreement with that country for mutual profit. From the beginning it was writ that the day would come when the Saudis would control Aramco completely, which process, it was hoped, would take place in a friendly and mutually cooperative atmosphere. The Aramco Americans have always been, and are still, intensely aware of two things—that they are guests in Saudi Arabia, and that *it's the Saudis' oil.*

It's not for me to say, nor does it much matter, whether these two axioms came from our liberal American hearts or whether we were told them firmly by Ibn Saud. But the result has been, as far as I can see, a remarkably sensitive imposition of a Western culture on an older, Eastern one. There has been little intermingling, but no clashing either, or only the slightest jarring. There has been, so far, a workable coexistence, and now the Saudis do control Aramco. It *has* worked, and we have been better—more tactful and sensitive—than the British.

It isn't, probably, that we *are* any better than they are (though, since we threw them out of *our* country, we would like to think so). We learned from their mistakes; without their wounds we would not have had our tact. Besides, the nature of the transaction between us and Saudi Arabia was quite different than that of the British Empire. We came only to get oil out of the ground. We had no mission to change them, govern them, or interfere with their religion or their culture. We didn't long to put them into Mother Hubbards, haul them into church, or convert them to democracy. Whatever they did was fine, and we agreed to respect it, and it is precisely this point that leads to the strange atmosphere of Dhahran as I knew it. As guests in that country, we have reversed the traditional principle of Arab hospitality that the guest can do no wrong. These days the host can do no wrong, but the guests can do plenty.

Back in the old days (not really so good, but old) the Saudi Arabs regarded the newly arrived geologists with some suspicion and great curiosity, even though—or possibly because—they wore Arab clothes and rode about on camels. It seems neither interfered much with the other. After big oil was struck in 1938, and it became apparent that the oil reserves were immense, beyond anybody's wildest hopes, Dhahran rapidly changed from a primitive mining camp to a town that could accommodate the needs of resident Americans, with dining hall, commissary, laundry, air-conditioning plant, clinic, swimming pool, and small houses and dormitories. As World War II increased the demand for oil, a refinery was built at Ras Tanura on the Persian Gulf, as well as a town, then a third one at Abqaiq, and today a fourth at Udhailiyah. Three other oil companies acquired interests in Aramco (Texaco, Exxon, and Mobil, making four "parent companies"). Production rose every year by 10 percent—from 11,000 barrels a day in 1944 to 10,300,000 barrels a day in 1981 (before the cutback). In 1979 Aramco's proven oil reserves were 113.4 billion barrels.

If it all seems unfair and infuriating, considering the current energy crisis, stop and consider that this oil is Saudi Arabia's *only* resource, unless you count its crop of dates, which I am uninclined to do. The country is almost entirely uninhabitable desert. Temperatures in the summer go up to 120 degrees. There are not even very many people. It is not, nor will it ever be, appealing to tourists. There is hardly any rain and little underground water, and nothing—without a lot of help—grows. What few cultural edifices that exist are rapidly being destroyed (except the holy cities, where non-Muslims are not allowed to go) as the Saudis build highways through them and erect more hotels and office buildings. Well, it doesn't console me either, as I pay my Con Ed bills and fill my tank. What it really comes down to is, *it's their oil.*

Arabia, like other strange corners of the world, attracts loners, adventurers, people running away from something, very self-sufficient people, people who want to make a buck, people who . . . but I can't, no matter how I'd like to, categorize the people I knew there, nor can I find anything much in common with them except their lack of commitment to a home in the States. They were of all shapes, sizes, persuasions

. . . though there were, of course, no Jews. There seemed, when I was there, to be a lot of Catholics. Two pockets of the States, Texas and the San Francisco area, were over-represented, because of hirings by the parent companies in those two places. Probably there were more people from small towns, while the native New Yorker would be least likely to choose Dhahran with its sparse cultural life (though I was told more than once that "we have everything New York does," I can't imagine why anybody would expect it to). On the whole the people I knew there seemed to be an extraordinarily attractive, well-educated, interesting group. (What, exactly, did I want?) They had traveled widely and intelligently. They were fun, and the best of them grasped the essential humor of living in this outlandish place and making so much money.

My Aramco husband and his colleagues were Middle East experts, fluent in Arabic, which Aramco had taught them. At that time, for anyone with such training, joining Aramco was almost unavoidable. Its package of perks was hard to resist, as was the combination of financial security, protection from many of life's difficulties, and travel in some of the world's stranger corners. Few of them meant to make it a lifetime career, but many ended up doing so, for Aramco has a suction effect. The longer you stay, the harder it is to leave—partly because the benefits pile up with every passing year (Saudi Social Security alone, if you stick it out, can pay two thousand dollars a month) and partly because Aramco training is singularly hard to transplant.

The Government Relations Department, where my husband worked, was the most specialized of all. Its members were not lawyers, or geologists, or engineers, who might conceivably take their talents elsewhere; they were "Arabists." They were specialists in the minutiae of certain aspects of life in the Eastern Province. They made maps to help the Saudi government define its boundaries and chart its trackless desert.

They translated documents and did research on local history, place-names, and tribal customs, using a phalanx of mangy, grizzled, half-asleep Aramco-hired Bedu as a handy reference library. Others ran interference between the Americans and the more impenetrable aspects of the surrounding culture. Customs was straightforward enough, but many Westerners came to grief over the matter of "personal abuse"—that strange item of local law which favored any Muslim who felt he (his person, his country, or his religion) had been attacked, which he could come to feel with remarkable ease. Such actions were frequently trumped-up, and a thoughtless gesture by an American, such as a friendly slap on the shoulder or other gesture culturally acceptable to Westerners, could turn into a major incident. So the Government Relations people, along with the lawyers, spent a lot of their time keeping Americans out of jail. Other Government Relations people were cultural go-betweens, arbiters of Saudi-American matters. They ran errands, filled bizarre requests, and cooled the easily ruffled feelings of local Saudi officials. One seemed to spend most of his time supplying the local sheikhs with ice. They built things for the Emir, Ibn Jaluwi of the Eastern Province, sometimes unbuilding them later if Jaluwi was not pleased. There was all manner of baksheesh, which was, in fact, part of the job.

These contact points between the two cultures were delicate and volatile, fraught with potential danger, and constantly inflamed by the paranoia of these recluse people, who were inclined to compare themselves unfavorably with the generous and endlessly understanding Americans. It might be easier, in a way, to be colonized; under the British, or the French, or whoever, with their hard rules and standards, their simple, rigid system, everything at least is clear. But what about these Americans, who give in on everything, who smilingly deliver ice in the desert and cheerfully refurbish the guest house after the king's men have burned up the floor with a bonfire and slaughtered sheep in the bathtub? I am ill-equipped to understand what goes on in the mind of a Saudi Arab, but the Saudis are, in fact, human beings and must respond as such; and it seems to me that Aramco was the ever patient and humoring wife, smilingly agreeing to everything, to the unreasonable, tyrannical husband that Saudi Arabia was. (Yes, dear. It's your country.) But even a tyrannical husband knows when he's being conned, and learns to despise obsequiousness—and can turn from friendly tyrant to angry one very quickly. For he knows, in his heart, that his wife knows more than he does about certain things, and has secretly looked to her for strength and guidance; if she is, in the end, a wet rag without beliefs or values of her own, he will be frightened, perhaps frightened into fury.

The particular things Aramco gave in on are a multitude. Saudi Arabia is a theocracy, and the laws of the land come from the Koran and a body of law (Sharia law) that maintain this ancient society as it has been for over a thousand years. The laws extend, in a modified way, to the American compounds, and in practice are more of a nuisance than a hardship. Many pertain to women. Women can't drive cars outside of the camp; until a few years ago they couldn't hold jobs, a right which is constantly threatened. No liquor may be imported into the kingdom, nor (in my day) any dogs, which are considered unclean. No Jews are allowed. No churches on Saudi soil. There is censorship of newspapers, magazines, and now television. Of course these things are modifications of the far greater strictures that govern the Saudis, a society that still recognizes polygamy, that only abolished slavery twenty years ago, that cuts the hands off thieves and stones women for adultery, that has only recently begun to educate its women. Islam (the word means "surrender") at its most orthodox is a tyrannical, puritanical religion.

Aramco never says no to the Saudi government about anything. They might say, "Well, guys, let's talk about this."

And they talk, but what the Saudis want, they get. The closed-eyes policy of the government toward the stills was less a concession than a compromise by avoidance. (The wife enjoys a drink, the husband is a teetotaler. Each evening when they lift a ginger ale together, the wife's has a little gin. He knows, and she knows that he knows, but as long as she's moderate, it will never be mentioned.) Aramcons worship at services in the movie theater, closet Christians that they are. But Larry Barnes says, "A Saudi official in the government once told me that the Americans had lost a lot of respect because Aramco did not insist on the right to build a church for its Christian employees." Did anyone, I wonder, ever say, "We're going to build a church, because our religion is as important to us as yours is to you"? Why should they respect us if we didn't respect ourselves?

I can hear myself arguing, twenty-five years later, and feel the old anger, for Dhahran enraged me as no place has ever done. I can hear my shrill voice going late into the night and see my husband's tired face, hear him again and again trying to explain. It was one of the very few times in my life when I got, like Eliza, "sick of words," sick of excuses, sick of my own inability to understand; worst of all, when I saw, despairingly, that words didn't really provide answers or relief or anything but an unending debate, an infinite argument so precisely balanced that it would never tip; that finally, the truths I wanted so badly were always backed by other, opposite truths, equally convincing even to me—a hopeless Möbius strip where everything turned into something else, right into wrong, bad into good, hopelessly and forever.

The restrictions, Len explained, were not a plot to make me unhappy, but rather a policy of the Saudi Arabian government to protect its people from too harsh an onslaught of Western culture. Take the matter of booze, which had been freely imported for Americans in the good old days but had been prohibited two years before I arrived. (My timing was impeccable.) The incident that had precipitated prohibition was unfortunate and very hush-hush. One of the Saudi princes had gotten drunk and murdered the British consul at Jiddah. Not in cold blood, of course. He'd been a dinner guest at his house and didn't want to leave, or else left and came back. He'd made some direct passes at the consul's wife, and in the fray that followed, had shot the consul. Alcohol was totally alien to the culture of this introverted country, and was likely to be misused. It wasn't anything against us, but *for* them. For their own good.

Well, I understood that. It wasn't the booze business that bothered me, really. There was enough drinking in Dhahran to satisfy the most devout alcoholic. (My father thought it was funny, and offered to send me some old bathtub gin recipes from the twenties.) I missed wine, but after a while I learned to make a drinkable *vin ordinaire*. And eventually I got so used to our local brew that when Len, for my birthday, produced a real martini made from Smirnoff and Noilly Prat (cost of the two bottles—about one hundred dollars) I couldn't tell the difference between the real thing and the old boiled White Lightning with orange peels. Besides, there was something nice about the whole process of the still and its accompanying lore. Even as we talked it was cooking away, the black curtains drawn at the kitchen windows, gin-clear third-run dripping out of the spout.

But how did Len, a Catholic, feel about going to church in the movie theater?

It didn't bother him at all. The British priest from Bahrein Island came over every Friday to say Mass. How come it was okay to do it on Friday, the Muslim holiday? Special dispensation. Hardship conditions. You didn't even have to fast and abstain during Lent—the Church knew it was tough enough to keep the faith out here among the infidels.

Who cared if it was a movie theater? Those who had to have a white church with steeple must be pretty shaky in their faith anyway.

The good Father even came over to christen our daughter. He was all done up in white cassock and surplice, and got drunk in the time-honored fashion. (Not only was Marion to be Catholic, but could, if she liked, choose Saudi citizenship at eighteen. Suppose she was going through some weird stage and chose? "Jesus Christ," said Len.) Father J. flung his surplice up onto a curtain rod, where it hung till next morning, when he came by to pick it up. It was really a very good party, though I was the only non-Catholic in the bunch. Marion's Catholic proxy godparents stood in for more Catholic godparents in the States. Why couldn't I pick the godparents? Because my friends weren't Catholic. And I'd signed up, hadn't I?

How thick the web was, how endless the confusion. I couldn't even define my complaints. What was it, Arabia, or Aramco, or the Catholic Church, or small-town life in general, to which I was unaccustomed?

Most of the women's conversation, I told Len, was boring. They talked about their washing machines, their houseboys, the produce at the commissary, their endless gynecological symptoms. They exchanged recipes and children's clothes. "If you want good conversation, make it," said Len.

My father found this amusing too. "It may be a little startling after the intellectuality of college life," he wrote, "but I imagine in time these subjects will become the meat and potatoes of conversation. Other subjects will be the sauces and salads. But this isn't too bad a balance. Don't forget, people can be bores on intellectual subjects just as quickly as they can on housekeeping problems, and often a great deal quicker." (It was true—now I love to talk about domestic matters, those dependable, universal subjects that can be, strangely enough, intellectual indeed.)

Did it bother nobody but me that there was no charm or beauty, no sense of history, such sterility? No cultural events? Such a sense of isolation, such lack of connection with the rest of the world?

Well, sure it did, but this was unreasonable. What was Aramco supposed to do, provide ruins and quaint little streets? (I scarcely know anymore whether Len gave these answers, or others I talked to, or whether they came out of my own head.) Arabia just didn't have much culture. We'd go out and have a few picnics with the Bedus. If I wanted culture, if I wasn't satisfied with weekly movies, Dramaramco productions, and occasional imported music, so make it myself. Most people in Dhahran came from small towns anyway, and my problem was that I came from New York, which made adjustment harder. And that, by the way, was also why I was so bothered by the absence of Jews, and the anti-Semitic jokes that were told so freely at parties. And what did I care if women couldn't drive outside camp since, for one thing, we didn't have a car and, for another, there wasn't any place to go anyway?

Cutting off hands? Stonings? Beheadings? Slavery?

Well, slavery was on the way out, and Americans were on shaky ground *there*. As for the punishments, they weren't *our* cultural expression. But it was amazing, and more than coincidental, what a low crime rate Saudi Arabia had. Suppose I stole something—would they cut off my hand? Would they stone me if I slept with the man across the street? No—Aramco would protect me.

One last, weary question—wasn't there something strange about the fact that Aramco paid some trained, intelligent person twenty-five thousand dollars a year, plus perks and living allowance, to spend all his time delivering ice to the emir?

I don't remember the answer to that one. Probably there was, but it was the sort of strangeness that was so deeply integrated into Aramco's functioning that a simple answer could scarcely be sorted out. Like the rest, it probably had to do with my innocence. There was ass-kissing everywhere. If a little ice kept the emir in a good mood, why not?

On the way from New York, Len and I had spent most of an evening in Damascus trying to cross a river to get to a restaurant on the other side. It was a very small river, more like a canal, and the restaurant seemed almost close enough to touch. We had seen no other place we wanted to eat and getting to it became an obsession. Finally we took a taxi which went a very long way around across a bridge far downtown. We arrived at the restaurant to find it closed. I sat down and cried, which Len had never seen me do before. He said being in a strange place could be very painful, like being in somebody else's kitchen. You felt like a fool till you learned to make it work for you.

After we'd been there a year or so a woman I knew asked me if I wanted to take over her job. Her husband was being transferred and she could no longer do it. She wrote stories on a free-lance basis for *An-Nida*, an English-language paper in Beirut. About what? Anything, though I should consult with the Aramco PR man. There were certain limitations. She gave a weary sigh. Because this was all very last minute, we never really sat down and talked about it, so I pitched in on my own.

I would write, I told Len, about the culture of Arabia. About the life of the Bedu, about the desert picnics we had attended, squatting on our haunches, eating sheep and rice. About Qatif and Hofuf, the nearby oases. About life in Dhahran in depth. A sociological story about cultural clashes. The expatriate mentality.

Len said to go talk to the PR man.

The PR man, whose name was Vern, slowly shook his head. Some Aramco men delivered their company's edicts with an enigmatic, catlike smile, but this was not Vern's style. He couldn't have been graver; a stance well suited to the occasion, for he was, after all, shooting down my ideas. All of them.

I couldn't, simply couldn't, write anything about the Beduin, period. It wasn't that he didn't think I would treat the subject with respect and sensitivity, but the trouble was that the Beduin were far more sensitive than I, and they were quick to take offense.

Over what? And how, since they couldn't read, and even if they could, *An-Nida* only circulated in Beirut?

Well, if I wrote about their boiled sheep and rice, for instance, they might infer that I didn't like it, even if I did. (I didn't.) Even if I said it was delicious, they would *know* I didn't mean it. Even if I admired their dress, their customs, and their manners, they would know I didn't mean that either.

But suppose I did?

Well, now. Could I, or anyone, give the Beduin unqualified praise? It would sound sugary and made-up. Like everyone else they had faults, and they wouldn't like to be unfairly presented. That would be patronizing.

What I had to understand, he said, was that the Saudis were just poised for criticism. In their secret hearts they felt themselves inferior to us in many ways. But it was absolutely forbidden to even hint at this, much less point it out. Even company literature trod delicately around this point. You never said backward or undeveloped, you said "adjusting to new influences" or "on the threshold of a new era." Best leave the whole subject alone. Stick with informal features about life here in town. And personals, plenty of names, like who's going to Beirut for the 'Id weekend (the Muslim holiday). Write about the Americans and everything would be fine. How about that trachoma research project Aramco was sponsoring? There were a couple of doctors here from Harvard looking for a vaccine. I should go talk to them, there might be a story there.

The Harvard doctors, two pale and weary men buried away in a back wing of the medical building, were very cooperative. They showed me their lab and let me look through their microscopes. I wrote the story very carefully and at their request took it back to them after I'd finished it. The head one, Dr. Whoever, handed it back to me and said, "I'm afraid you can't say most of those things."

"I don't understand."

"Well, it's a little sensitive, this statement that we're looking for a vaccine. After all we might not find one."

"But certainly not for want of trying!"

"Well, Aramco likes results, you know. And at some point we have to go home. Here we sit in this fancy lab, and our colleagues back in Cambridge are practically cleaning out their test tubes with their own toothbrushes."

"But what can I say?" I asked, rather desperately.

"Well," said he, "I suppose you could say that there's a trachoma research program going on here."

Vern, when I stormed into his office, lit another cigarette and said, "Well, it's a problem, the trachoma, the Saudi government finds it a little embarrassing. It's a disease of ignorance, you know. They don't know enough to brush the flies off their eyes."

"In other words I can't write the story at all."

"Well, I guess so. Look, José Iturbi is coming out here to give a concert in two weeks, you can write about that."

I wrote a story saying that Mr. Iturbi's piano technique was flamboyant, and his program selection patronizing, and Vern gave it back and said no dice, it had to be complimentary. After all, if I were Iturbi and had come all the way out here to play, I wouldn't want to be panned. He added that he thought I was sulking. After all, any situation had limits, this wasn't any different than anything else. Certainly I wasn't under the illusion that we had a free press in the States, was I? If it was so free, then why was the coverage of the Middle East in the New York *Times*, for instance, so pro-Israeli?

Inevitably my correspondence job dwindled away for lack of printable copy. In the Wahabbi-dominated Eastern Province, if it isn't in the Koran, it isn't allowed. Part of the blandness of Dhahran comes from the censorship of all incoming media, which allows only the most vapid and innocuous messages to seep through—inevitably giving the Saudis a strange picture of the Western world. Bej Tewell described her job as movie censor in the sixties: "No monarchies being overthrown by revolutionaries, no long kisses, no nudity, gambling, or Frank Sinatra, who supports Zionist causes. And in case you never noticed, a sheriff's badge is a Star of David. In the distance, the badge would be a little blur. But as soon as it got close enough to distinguish, I'd say, 'Cut!' And of course the sheriff goes into the saloon and orders Coca-Cola." The Arab censor, she said, loved *Meet Me in Las Vegas*, not to show to the public—but to buy for himself.

At the time we lived in the pink and green house.

We considered ourselves lucky, for it was a very good house. It was the best type, and it sat up on a little mound, which provided the nearest thing there was to a view of the compound. It was well maintained and surrounded by particularly luxuriant pink oleander, a flower I had disliked since I had been told, as a child in California, that it was poisonous; there was pink hibiscus by the front door, and masses of the inevitable periwinkle.

We had met the owners only once. C. was a big beefy man, an engineer, and his wife a fading beauty much more dressed up than anybody else, with a cloud of pale pinkish hair. ("He married his manicurist," Len said.) She was rather stern. Though she had gone to a great deal of trouble about her house, she was not unreasonable, and she knew accidents happened. But she begged us to care above all else for the Siamese cat. The place could burn down for all she cared as long as nothing happened to Cleo. We promised, I with some misgivings, for I didn't like cats, but Len said they were no trouble at all, and Siamese particularly hated people—it would probably spend the whole time under the bed.

Inside there was pink shag carpeting everywhere, and everything else was pink and green—the wallpaper, the upholstery, and even the tables, which were varnished bright pea green, and the lamps, which were pink porcelain cabbage roses. In the bedroom was a tufted pink silk chaise longue with little satin pillows where Mrs. C. no doubt reclined of a hot afternoon, reading the stack of *Vogues* and *House Beautifuls* which lay on the little carved-dolphin table, sipping tea in the hum of the air-conditioner. All the windows had green cellophane shades which gave an underwater aspect to the living room in the afternoon.

Only the kitchen was unimpressive—not in its basic design, for they were all alike, but the pots and pans and china were a dreary collection, all bent or chipped, and it was clear that Mrs. C. either had no interest in cooking, or else she'd locked up all the good stuff, both of which seemed likely to be true. In fact she'd locked up an entire bedroom, which I might have worried about more if everything else in Dhahran had not been so implausible; as it was, trying to understand it used up most of my store of fretful curiosity. Mrs. C.'s bedroom was no more locked up than anything else.

When I expressed bemusement at Mrs. C.'s weird world and said unkind things about her color scheme, Len pointed out that the house had to be admired for what it signified in terms of time and effort, like San Simeon. Everything had been brought from the States, there wasn't a stick of company furniture in it. She had brought wallpaper back and by some incredible stroke of luck or determination found somebody who knew how to get it on the walls, or else put it there herself. She had measured the floors and ordered the carpeting and managed to get it on the floor. We might have been standing in the living room of a house in Englewood, New Jersey. It wasn't the money, we all had money. It was the commitment, the patience in the face of such enormous odds. Every item had sat on a boat for three months while Mrs. C. waited, terrified that because of some error the curtains would not fit the windows, the pink of the dining room table might clash with the pink of the buffet, the quilted valance might not fit the bedroom window. If even a traverse rod was forgotten, she would have to wait two years to correct it. Put this way the woman's feat did seem heroic. They had been in Arabia ten years, which meant five shopping trips and five periods of suspense. Possibly this trip was for the neglected kitchen, and she would return with pink and green Formica and French ovenware.

The place seemed to have been intended to create a mood, but not one that suited me. It made me feel unreal and terribly sleepy, possibly because of the green tint that everything had, or else because of that Belle Epoque chaise longue. It didn't occur to either of us to change anything. It would have seemed cruel to change what had been put there with so much trouble, and possibly because of that, we both thought we liked it. We still believed that if a person worked terribly hard at something and meant well, the result couldn't be all bad.

I kept dropping off to sleep there during the day, partly, probably, because I had nothing to do—most of the housework and cooking were taken care of by the C.'s Goanese houseboy who came along with the house, as did the Saudi gardener, who seemed to be in the same condition I was—he spent most of his time dozing under the oleanders, or else praying on a small rug he rolled up when he was finished.

Sometimes he came to the door and asked, in Arabic, for

water, one of the three or four words I knew. He was pitifully thin and a little stooped, with a gutra wound around his head and a ragged white garment on. His eyes were weary, his cheeks hollow, and most of his teeth were missing. He could have been twenty or sixty. He held an open can with the label peeled off. I would lead him into the kitchen to the drinking-water tap. I felt sorry for him, having to work out there in the heat, but he showed not the slightest interest in me. You've seen one American woman, you've seen them all, his attitude said. While he filled his can I stared at him covertly. No fine desert Arab this one. He was disreputable, but he was all that was available to me. I stared at his hawk nose, the clouds of black hair sticking out from under the gutra, the patchy beard, the skinny legs. I wondered if he knew how tenderly protected he was, how dutifully guarded his public image. It made him seem very precious, like a rare artifact.

He drank his water and gave an enormous, shuddering sigh. Then he shambled back into the living room, me at his heels, where he stood audibly breathing in the green air; then quite suddenly he sank down on the pink shag rug, limp, as though all his strings had been cut. He closed his eyes and appeared to go to sleep. He was worse off than I was, I had never done that. I had always thought you had to trust somebody to go to sleep in their presence, a theory which no longer seemed to apply. He lay on the floor, propped up against a chair, one bare leg sprawled out, the other bent under him, arm resting on his knee.

Very slowly I reached over and touched the soft wrinkled cotton of his clothes, and then his drooping hand with its dark knotty veins. He shifted suddenly, he must have sensed my alien presence. But I had touched him, felt his human flesh, the closest I would ever get to his people.

Then the Pakistani houseboy appeared, bright-eyed and glossy and impeccable in his white shirt and pants.

"Oh, memsahib," he said reproachfully, and proceeded to jiggle Mohammed till he woke up—carefully, nothing that could be construed as personal abuse—which he did with a start, jumping up and staggering to his feet. There was a small altercation which led nowhere, since the houseboy didn't know any more Arabic than I did, and then he was out the door. "Oh, memsahib, how terrible of him. Are you all right?"

Len took me to a Beduin picnic, an experience limited to the Government Relations people who, through their work, knew the locals.

We arrived at a small group of tents just as the sun was touching the horizon. When it dipped below they would be able to eat—it being Ramadan—and a big pot was cooking over a fire nearby. A little way off the camels stood in silence, their tails flicking, their eyes heavy and shrouded, shifting their weight from one long, knobby leg to another.

We were greeted by four Beduin men in white robes and kaffiyehs. They were very tall and straight, remote, but extremely courteous. Len had told me they were quite well off, and that the host, who seemed to be the tallest one, had three wives. They showed us into the tent and we sat down cross-legged on the rugs which covered the ground, and a servant brought glasses of sweet mint tea. Shortly the contents of the pot, a boiled sheep, was brought in on a platter and set down on the rug in front of us. Now everyone sat on his haunches, which I had practiced at home, but I kept falling over, and Len said I could sit any way I wanted. They were very polite and tossed me the choicest bits, far more than I wanted (which was none at all). I looked around nervously for the eye, which was said to be the ultimate tidbit; if it came my way I would have to risk their wrath if I couldn't bite down on a staring white cornea. I watched Len take tiny bits and chew them forever, and I did the same. After we were finished the remains were sent back to the women, and the servant poured tiny cups of bitter cardamom coffee. It was pleasant, sitting there in the firelight, as though I were a child, listening to the grown-ups talk.

After a while Len told me I'd been invited to go back into the hareem. I went into the other section of the tent, where five women sat with their small children. The women wore black masks with eyeholes in them. They clustered together on one side with their children, keeping their eyes on me, as though watching for a sudden move; and I did want to move toward them, to touch them, as I'd touched Mohammed. I tried to talk to them, but they only looked at each other and shook their heads, and then all of a sudden they began to giggle. It was not the sort of giggling that included me. They were shy, that was all, but I found it painful, another impassable gulf.

Then from outside came the sound of gunfire, which startled me but seemed to enchant the ladies, for they scurried over and opened a flap of the tent to peer out. One of the men was doing a sort of gun-dance in the firelight; he leapt about, he whirled, he fired into the air; he laughed, he chanted, he fired a few more bullets. I thought he'd gone mad, the end had come—he'd start firing into the tent in some excess of woman-hatred. But I had it all wrong, there seemed to be something good about it, for now the hareem women became quite friendly, patting me and pushing me over for a better view, apparently pleased that they could provide such unusual entertainment. They laughed and clapped at each terrifying crash of the rifle, their dark eyes sparkled.

"Yes," I said, "he's simply a scream, I wish Len would do that in our front yard." They laughed at my strange sounds, and I understood that until he started his act, they had been nothing—he gave them courage, freed them to pat me and stroke me and pull at my clothes, which they now began doing rather enthusiastically; and I was just beginning to get a little nervous when the head sheikh came in and shooed them off, indicating that it was time to go home.

Mrs. C.'s cat got sick, a timely punishment from Allah. At first it was a relief, there was no blue malevolent gaze from under the bed. But not only was she alive, she had to be pulled through, according to my neighbor, to whom I applied in a burst of guilt. So every hour I fed her egg and oil by dropper.

"Let it die," said Len, who felt as I did about cats.

"I can't. I promised."

I had to accomplish something.

I watched until she passed the fur ball which had almost killed her, an act of exorcism that didn't make me feel a bit better.

After we had moved on into another house, I went back to see Mrs. C. and to pay her for damage to some small items. When she answered the door I wondered if I were really seeing the woman I had met before. The cloud of pink hair was disheveled and hanging in strings around her face, and a scarf was knotted around her head. She wore a rather smart white linen dress, but her shoes were off and she wore a big dirty green apron. Buckets and bottles of Lysol stood about and the vacuum cleaner stood in the middle of the floor. When she saw me she froze. She was barely polite. She talked of scratches on the furniture and dents I couldn't see and invisible spots and stains. She showed me two broken dishes and a burnt pot, which I paid her for. She pointed to a minuscule ring of rust around the washbasin drain, a chip off one of the porcelain roses.

"But I saved the cat," I kept saying. "The cat almost died, I saved the cat."

She said the houseboy had told her about Mohammed sleeping on the rug.

"Oh, the poor thing, he just collapsed one day when he was getting water."

"He's supposed to use the back door. He's not supposed to come in here. Your husband must have told you that. I must say I was shocked."

I left her with her Lysol, cleaning and cleaning up Mohammed's germs.

Mrs. C.'s purpose was simple–she wanted to seal out Arabia, scrub it out, pretend it wasn't there. There were many people in Dhahran who did the same. But because of some defect or morbid sensitivity, the culture of the country intruded on me and refused to let me alone. Dhahran and its puzzlements became an obsession.

At first, rather than attributing my incessant preoccupation to myself, I wondered what was the matter with everybody else. But it was hard to make it stick. If our friends in Dhahran had been a bunch of red-necked illiterates or pompous bores, I could have been a sensitive soul cast, by a twist of fate, among spiritual peasants, and given up the search for understanding. I could have been a Carol Kennicott. But it simply wasn't so. For the most part I liked the people I met.

I particularly admired these women who could follow their husbands halfway around the world to this curious place and adapt with such grace and good humor. I was impressed with their ability to be moved about the world when their husbands were transferred, to re-camp again in some strange place, to find new friends and dig, as far as possible, into the available culture. I looked in vain for unusual numbers of mopes, crazies, or alcoholics, or even women who simply gave up and went home. There were remarkably few, and who was to say that they would not, in Scarsdale or Pasadena, behave the same way?

In retrospect, it seems that the ones who did best were

the women who had chosen to leave home and had met their future husbands in Dhahran or some odd spot and then returned there as wives. But besides the army brats, or ex-Aramco secretaries or ex-Foreign Service employees, there were many whose strength seemed to come solely from an awesome wifely devotion. They went with their man, that was all, with a sense of duty that was entirely foreign to my experience. At his decision, they had left some American nest where they had spent their lives, said farewell to their families, and gone and made the best of it.

They reminded me, some of them, of my mother, in their ability to fill the hours of the day with busyness, and also in their way of smiling and making some graceful little evasion when I asked them difficult and searing questions. It was a little like Len and his religion—they were going mainly on faith, and there is no discussion about faith. It is simply there. I envied them for having something—it didn't matter what—that I didn't, or so I thought; they had something that sealed off those ragged, wanting edges I had.

But what did I want, anyway?

Part of it was, of course, housewife shock, early stirrings of what Betty Friedan later called "the problem that has no name." Smith had not educated me for faith, but rather to question it. Housework was not enough. An unspoken assumption that my husband was in charge was not only not enough, but was actually offensive after my upbringing in an entirely female household and an education in female schools. It was like a bad joke. It was one thing to admire wifely duty in other women, but the gradual realization that it was supposed to apply to me too was carrying things a little too far.

It wasn't that Len was a tyrant, or that he ever ordered me around. He was in fact reasonable and fairly sympathetic—willing to go along with me on most things, in fact, except the one thing that mattered, which was living in Dhahran. He was, in fact, even willing to leave Dhahran, and eventually we did. But the fact of going there in the first place had never been up for question. It had been part of the deal—marry Len and go to Dhahran—which I, for reasons I did not, at the time, choose to explore, had done. So no matter what he did to help me endure the place, the fact was that every day of my life there was testimony that I had not chosen to be there, but he had.

There is all the difference between choosing a place yourself and having it chosen for you. I felt, possibly wrongly, that I had chosen New York; at some point during my back-and-forth childhood, I had chosen it over California. The deep, almost erotic sense of possession I felt about New York had been a function of my choice. And part of the trouble was realizing too late that I should not have left there while the love was still hot.

Did I want him to quit? Len asked.

Oh . . . well. Guilt foamed up at that one like the Tide in which we washed our lettuce. How could I ever live with that on my head? Anyway, I wanted to try to make the best of it. The damn place would not defeat me. It was such a stupid, artificial place anyway, a phony plastic Levittown. It symbolized everything I had left America to avoid.

The trouble was I felt so alone. I was like the one child who knows the Emperor is naked. Why didn't other people get angry as I did? It would be such fun if everybody kvetched together. And what about Len? Why didn't he ever say, "Oh, I know the place is crazy, but let's laugh at it together and put up with it for a while. Let's share the adventure, then take our money and run. Let's get the best out of it while we're here."

But he didn't—probably he couldn't. He loved his job, and Len and the job and Dhahran were so intertwined as to be virtually indistinguishable. You couldn't attack one without hitting the others. Dhahran was somehow sanctified, you couldn't complain about it the way everybody did constantly about New York, for instance. New York was free game, you loved it and you hated it. But Dhahran, like a sickly child, had to be protected. It became Len's profession and his vulnerability. He became defensive. When I said it was too goddamn hot, he said, "but it's a dry heat." When I said I missed the theater, he said, "but you never went to the theater all that much at home anyway." And we moved further and further apart.

For the real core of the trouble—beyond all the annoyances of censored magazines and movies, of isolation and confinement and boredom—was a profound and incurable fear which had started the day we flew in over the trackless desert and had never really gone away. I could not, like Mrs. C., wash away the Arab culture, paint it over with pink and green. It haunted me. I *was* the thief whose hand was cut off, the woman buried up to her chest and stoned.

Was I any different, really, from those masked Arabian women? They seemed dreadfully like me—dark caricatures of what my life had become. They were some ultimate female form, silent, protected, infantile creatures that they were. If I seemed more evolved than they were, it was deceptive, for they were there first, they were the basic form that pulled and threatened all my culture and education, as though I could be drawn back and turned into one of them if I stayed too long. I was afraid of the power of this place and its violent culture, and I didn't trust Aramco to protect me.

What would happen if there was revolution? War? Mass attack from mad armed Arabs, knives in teeth, eyes glittering? Suppose the Saudi government decided to . . . oh, any number of things. Body-search all females at the airport. Remove the few freedoms we had—booze, cars, worship. Suppose the Mutawah—the public morality committee—made us all pray five times a day . . . oh, anything. Anything was in their power.

I knew Aramco wouldn't protect me. All those nice lawyers could talk their heads off and it wouldn't do any good. (Suppose I was a Jew, and hadn't let on?) It wasn't that I didn't admire Aramco and its achievements. It performed technological miracles. It created whole towns in the desert sands, caused water to run and flowers to bloom. And it did these things with a becoming modesty. "It's nothing," Aramco said. "No big deal. It's just a matter of getting the hang of it." But it was essentially powerless.

It was frightening to have no court, judge, or jury—phenomena I had taken for granted all my life. There was only the local qadi, the Muslim judge, who was not known for his wide understanding. I couldn't, for God's sake, even write an indignant letter to the *Arabian Sun*, the Dhahran paper, a masterpiece of journalistic dissimulation. If I wrote to the New York *Times*, I might get Len fired.

It had been suggested to me more than once that my inability to live comfortably in Dhahran was either immaturity or else the inevitable culture-longing of a displaced New Yorker. It was true that people from small towns did better than I, but I don't think it had much to do with missing the latest movies. I had been willing enough to trade all that, for the time being, for the chance to taste and touch another culture. But probably growing up in New York had damaged my ability to trust any place at all. We are wary, we New Yorkers, guarded, skeptical of authority, reassured by the availability of diverse elements which counterbalance too much strength in one place. We are uninclined to cede our defensive caution to anyone else; we prefer to wear our own armor and take the responsibility for glancing over our own shoulders. At the same time we are addicted to an atmosphere where we can say and do outrageous things, if we want; even if we never do them, we feel that we can, because in our complex, variegated city, outrageousness is part of the cityscape. Old things are forgotten quickly, new things appear so fast we can hardly keep track of them. We trust nothing, ultimately, but our own ability to think fast, move fast, talk faster than the next guy. The idea of shaking off my shell of protection and trusting Aramco to replace it was a joke. Aramco, some big oil company? To me ponderousness was powerlessness. I should trust a monolith? Was I crazy?

The things I feared here were foreign, almost unearthly. I was used to my old dark streets, my familiar suspicious characters, my bad and good neighborhoods. Here my signposts were gone and I couldn't read the replacements. If I were attacked in New York, mugged in a dark doorway, I would, at least, know what was going on (though this might not be much comfort when the knife went in)—I would be attacked because I was white, female, looked as though I had money, and because, possibly, my eyes had deviated from the straight, steady, nasty stare I wore on the street; because the person who attacked me was poor, hopeless, angry as hell, and probably crazy from a life that had dealt him nothing but shit. If I were attacked in Saudi Arabia, I could hardly guess the reasons. But oh, such strange things happened. The American who put a friendly arm around a Saudi co-worker could end up in jail for personal abuse. How could you ever, ever know what you had done wrong, and why was there some solace in knowing?

After two years and a few months we left Dhahran for good, our marriage, though we didn't admit it, already in pieces. Looking back, I know now how frightened I really was. I was afraid to get on a plane, which I had to do, since there was no other possibility. We flew to London and came the rest of the way on the *Liberté*, where I spent five days and four nights asleep, waking only to eat and collect Marion from the ship's nursery. It was the profound sleep of a person who had survived a long period of the most harrowing terror.

In 1956 an anthropologist named Solon Kimball went to Dhahran and wrote up his observations for *Transactions*, a publication of the New York Academy of Sciences, as follows:

"There are certain restrictions placed upon American behavior that are contrary to American habit. These restrictions provoke frequently expressed anxieties that further repressive measures may appear or that certain types of punitive action may be imposed upon individuals, and perhaps on Aramco. This is one of the aspects that contributes to feelings of impermanence and precariousness. The employees look to the high officials of Aramco to provide them protection, although they are also aware that certain breaches of law mean immediate deportation, a fate viewed more favorably than languishing in an Arab jail. It is not that the restrictions are particularly onerous, they are merely expressive of the fact that the American is in a situation where he cannot control all the variables and where he is uncertain of the way the forces operate . . . The paternalistic control of Aramco reaches into every nook and cranny of one's life and gives a security that actually contributes to feelings of impermanence and precariousness. What is given may be withheld or taken away." (From "American Culture in Saudi Arabia," *Transactions*, March 1956.)

The overprotected child is the one who has the most trouble learning to function in the world, and for the first few weeks at home I suffered from timidity, which is not exactly the same as fear. Traffic made me jump, my brain boggled at the lavishness of the supermarket and Bloomingdale's. Charged-up New York talk made me shy, and everything in everyday life seemed incredibly complicated. On the other hand I was grateful for small things, like three kinds of squash at the market, or a bottle of wine, or the sight of many dogs. (But even as I recovered my old New York reflexes, I remained somehow out of sync. The city's beat had changed, or else I had—that old music, that old proud sense of possession, was gone, as surely as was my own childhood.)

I suspect we got out at the right time, before too many more years addled our brains; those who stay in Dhahran for long periods of time develop a strange, childlike trust in Aramco as their savior from all the world's ills. Says Bill Taylor, recently retired head of the medical department, "you get this feeling that Aramco can always save you and get you out of trouble. People act like the only time you should quit is when you have to retire, if you do it before you're deserting the Aramco flag. People keep saying, 'Why are you leaving?' They're all psyched up to stay so if you leave you're undermining their own rationalizations, particularly if you have good reasons." (The Taylors left a few years before official retirement time.) At the same time transferring is hard—Aramco prepares you for nothing much in the States, the work is too specialized, and Aramco waves the carrot with increasing benefits every five years. "The old people will never leave," Bill says. "They pooh-pooh this stuff about Iran. It's up there, not close to us. Happens all the time, look at Beirut, Egypt, Israel, and all that—nothing ever happened to us. You have the feeling that Aramco's going to protect you even if there's a war."

During the 1967 war between Egypt and Israel, there was a little skirmish in Dhahran. A local mob, angry at the United States's strong and immediate support of Israel, threw a few rocks and overturned a few cars, broke into a few houses and smashed things up, while the Saudi police stood around and grinned. The trouble was quieted when the mob was disciplined by Emir Ibn Jaluwi.

But nothing like that had ever happened before, and a group of people, including Larry Barnes, left when the American Consulate said that their government could not be responsible for their safety. "No one has written about it," Larry writes, "mainly because of the excellent discipline of Aramco employees. Perhaps 'brainwashed' would be a better phrase. When Aramco refugees arrived in New York, they were greeted by a small group of reporters. Without exception, no one would give a word of information to any member of the news media. What a well-trained bunch of robots we were. Scared that the company would object if we told the truth, I didn't say anything either and, frankly, I'm ashamed of myself . . . Among some members of management there was a feeling of resentment toward those employees who had been so 'disloyal' as to evacuate. Even some of our friends said they couldn't understand it. They were the ones who lived in the middle of town and didn't see any of the action . . .

"I think we were right in leaving. I did not sufficiently trust Aramco to take all necessary steps for the protection of its employees if such steps were to put the company in conflict with the Saudi Arab government or in any way endanger the (oil) concession.

"I always was willing to sweat for Aramco, but I'll be damned if I would bleed for them."

Saudi Arabia, Aramco's recalcitrant husband, is still acting up, and Aramco continues to endure and protect. Late in the sixties, the Mutawah cut off kids' long hair on street corners, and spray-painted the legs of miniskirted women in Khobar to express its disapproval. Aramco can no longer prevent jailing of its employees. Proclamations come from Riyadh banning Christmas trees, religious gatherings, working women—to remain, be rescinded, reappear in modified form. Saudi Arabia is now theoretically in charge of Aramco, though whether it actually is causes some debate—though nobody doubts the power of Sheikh Yamani, the Minister of Petroleum. Some Saudis "moved up too fast" and did not, in the end, perform well in management. There always was, and must still be, a double standard about work; less is expected of the Saudis than of the Americans.

But if we, or the rest of the world, object to Saudi Arabia and its policies, its image, its apparent greed and irresponsibility, we may ask ourselves from whom did it learn, and who was its model? Did anyone ever tell Saudi Arabia it was wrong? And is there any reason why it should not expect the rest of the world to treat it as Aramco does?

In *Farewell to Arabia*, David Holden, a British newspaperman, describes arriving in Saudi Arabia in 1963:

". . . the old, introverted spirit of Arabia hit me in the face once more, like a wet cloth. The day was Friday, and the gloom was as intense as ever. The airport was empty, save for a couple of surly officials, two or three misguided souls like myself who had chosen that day to disturb their Wahabbist contemplations, and a villainous little man with three days' stubble who misread my health documents and insisted upon stabbing me with a cholera needle that was both painfully blunt and alarmingly tarnished. My hotel was like a tomb and besides water there was nothing to drink but the usual sticky sweet things and a nonalcoholic concoction from Denmark, got up temptingly in green bottles and gold foil to look like lager, and tasting infuriatingly like stale lemonade. The clocks showed . . . three or four different times, and my futile attempts to make a few local telephone calls revealed that Arabian ma'aleesh time was still the only one that really mattered. The women, to judge by their absence from public view, were still in purdah; and the only person from whom I could extract more than a few disgruntled words all day was a Dutch airline official who sunnily informed me that after eighteen months in Dhahran he knew what life imprisonment must be like."

But then there is the other side of it. Lest I forget the clean, well-lighted place that Dhahran was, I am still sent the *Arabian Sun*, the local paper. It is completely, admirably schizophrenic. While OPEC prices threaten the world's economy, while Saudi Arabia buys U.S. planes to use against Israel, this paper depicts a fantasy world. It tells of heat records, local basketball scores, Aramco's latest technological miracles, a little bland history, the latest Saudi to enter management, and the inevitable date recipes. It documents a place where nothing is real, and no bad things happen . . . and where the Emperor is wearing new clothes.

DORSET

A Sacred Place Containing Our Dead

The mountains of southern Vermont are older than the Rockies, the Alps, the Himalayas. Worn down to soft curves, they surround rather than threaten, hover kindly over a landscape sculpted by gentle hands—green valleys, cool and clear lakes, silvery old apple orchards, white boxlike houses with black or green shutters. The houses seem to perch on their flat green plots, and they look as though the first autumn wind would blow them away like origami cubes, bouncing them across the valley floors. But they are rooted by deep cellars in which are the furnaces needed for the rigorous climate, which can frost first in August and not let up till April. In winter the mountains and valleys turn glitter white, etched by the black, stripped trees and muffled by the snow to a silence overwhelming in its completeness.

The towns and counties, sliced up coldly on pre-Revolutionary maps into six-mile squares, bear no particular relation to their topography, but are slung over the tops of mountains or else end, puzzlingly, a few feet from the main road. On the map, the town of Dorset is dropped like a handkerchief over the mountain bearing its name, a peak in the Taconic range in the western, rather southerly part of the state. The geographical center of the town is on some unreachable summit, but its human, magnetic centers have pooled in East Dorset, on Route 7, and in Dorset proper, on Route 30. There is a South Dorset on the map, but its only visible identity is a vegetable stand and an antique shop. A little farther to the north is the old marble quarry, tourist attraction and local swimming hole.

The village of Dorset is just off Route 30, on a small crossway leading to the West Road, Dorset's other artery. On one side of the village green is the Dorset Inn, on the other side Peltier's grocery store and a minuscule bank, branch of the Factory Point Bank in nearby Manchester. Beyond are two rows of white, rambling old houses, the marble Congregational Church, and beyond, around a corner, is the Dorset Playhouse, the functioning summer theater. Across the way is the Dorset Field Club with its nine-hole golf course, said to be the oldest in the country. Out on Route 30 is the library (open daily from two to six), the Barrows House, the post office, a couple of real estate offices, a couple of antique shops, and what used to be Russell Parks's general store, closed since the death of the owner five years ago. Next to the post office is a tiny museum, even smaller than the bank. In it lie Dorset's artifacts—town and genealogical records, pre-Revolutionary diaries, a spinning wheel, an old spice chest still smelling faintly of cloves and pepper, one of Abraham Lincoln's stovepipe hats donated by local great-grandson Lincoln Isham.

The two parallel arteries of Dorset band a valley through which, farther north, the Mettawee flows, but down here, between Dorset and South Dorset, properly belongs to the west branch of the Batten Kill—a barely perceptible stream making its way through an ancient swamp, the remains of what was once a primeval lake. Here rushes grow and mosquitoes breed, an oddity in this land of clear air and rocky soil. Drier parts of the valley have been, at other times, farmland, apple orchards, and sheep meadow, but now, unless they are people's backyards, they threaten to return to wilderness. From within the folds of Dorset Mountain come the source streams of the Mettawee, and as the tiny river flows eastward and then turns northwest, it traces out the area known as the Hollow—which, along with the West Road, comprise the two choice neighborhoods. Rising up to the south are Owl's Head and Green Peak, and on the other side of the valley the weather mountain, Mother Myrick (named after an eighteenth-century widow with many children).

My mother's house is on Route 30 just north of the quarry, a white box on five acres of land. It faces the swamp, and behind the lawn gives way to a field which gently approaches Owl's Head and Green Peak, notched with white gouges into the huge vein of marble and limestone which runs through Dorset Mountain like a layer in a vast cake. When I first went there they were quite visible, but every year they fade a little more into the overgrowth. Behind the house is a marble terrace surrounded by a neat little bed of daisies, iris, hollyhocks, and other odds and ends ("Oh, I don't know what it is, Alice brought it by and put it in"). A couple of steps go up to the kitchen door.

Inside, the house is more capacious than it appears from the outside. The kitchen is large enough for half a dozen people to eat breakfast in, large enough for three or four to cook in at the same time. The living room goes through from front to back, and there are two bedrooms downstairs and four upstairs. It is all inclined to rattle and squeak, and when fully loaded with people it almost trembles, like the lid of a boiling pot. Children crashing down the stairs seem to threaten its very vitals.

As in all good houses the kitchen is its core, its heart.

Here a counter backs up against a sort of booth with table and benches. The seats of the benches lift up to reveal heaps of old books, unread for sixty years and not very good to begin with. Over one bench is a portrait of my mother painted by her long-gone Navy lover, the artist/commander. She sits on a white wrought-iron bench on the terrace of our apartment on Sixty-sixth Street, where we lived for a couple of years before moving to 204. She looks at once serene and suggestive. She wears a blue and white striped summer dress, two-piece, showing a section of "midriff." She holds a trowel and weeding fork. Behind her are green wooden boxes planted with privet and beyond the Manhattan skyline of an earlier age, the buildings lower, pinker, softer.

On the other side of the counter is the working part of the kitchen—the sink under a window looking out on the terrace and the field, an electric stove, a doddering refrigerator. The counters, in brick-colored linoleum to match the floor, are ancient and sticky. The telephone roots to its spot like a suction cup, as does a little thicket of gadgets—toaster, orange-juice squeezer, mixer—that stand on the other end. On the other counter an assortment of canisters and baskets holds flour and sugar, tea and grocery chits, onions, potatoes, coffee. Over the stove hangs a decrepit blue and white well-and-tree platter, visibly glued and misty with grease, and a couple of brown copper pots. Along the wall on both sides of the stove are tiny shelves holding herbs and spices of breathtaking age, most of which smell and taste like pencil sharpenings. (I am unable to explain why I, or my mother or anybody else, never throw them out.) On the windowsill are usually a few green fruits or vegetables, ripening in the sun. Pull chains hang from the overhead lights. In a pantry at the end, by the door to the garage, is the "new" equipment, dishwasher, clothes washer and dryer. None were there when I first went, in the spring of 1957—but since none of us thought of them as necessities, at the time, they were hardly missed.

Within the many cupboards is a bewildering assortment of china and glassware (almost, but not quite, no two alike) for my mother had married a man whose "dot," as he called it, consisted of the contents of three houses in New Jersey, the debris of two marriages and a collecting family. In among remnants of the old ivy china from 204 are Rogers's teapots, parfait glasses, moustache cups, and assorted Victorian bric-a-brac. There is the "magic cup" of thinnest porcelain, ornamented with tiny rings, stars, witches, and crescent moons; and there is the "hunting cup" which holds a pint of coffee. All cupboards are stuffed, but only with what is left of the china; most was given away for lack of space. In the drawers are several sets of flat silver, stashed away in other cupboards are platters, bowls, tureens, tea sets, all the accoutrements of other faded lives and histories. Whether or not any of it is of any value my mother neither knows nor cares. Her love lies elsewhere—in the view from her window, the people around her table. She thinks of tomorrow rather than yesterday.

The living room is warm, enveloping, and "charming." The fireplace is flanked by bookcases, now more than half empty. What remains were the late Rogers's: a history of Columbia University, a fiscal history of New York banks, an old set of Dickens. My mother no longer reads much, but looks at the flickering black and white TV set in the corner. The furniture is squashy and slipcovered, and before the fire is an old cobbler's bench, with its round leather seat, used for a coffee table. Against the opposite wall is an old pine cupboard, and in the corner a Dutch dry sink used as a bar. At night the room is hushed and lamplit, the only sound the occasional whoosh of a passing car on the road and the tick of the old pendulum clock on the mantel.

The bedrooms are all done country-style, with wallpapers in tiny floral patterns, ruffled white curtains, and worn old rugs. My children have named them. Upstairs is the Fancy Room, the High Bedroom (an old four-poster), the Pink

Room (once Rog's office), and the Room Next to the John. Each has its own virtues and drawbacks, discussed by my city children in the car choosing where they will sleep, an unaccustomed luxury. The High Bedroom has charm and a lock on the door (once installed to protect a lady houseguest from an unwanted old professor of economics who tried to pay her midnight visits), a rocking chair, and a rear lookout. The Fancy Room is the biggest, with twin beds and my mother's old Anne Duffy dressing table from 204, kidney-shaped and hung with a white organdy skirt. The recently evolved Pink Room, once Rog's study, is now bereft of huge desk and Friden Calculator—an ear-shattering monster, extinct as the dodo—and has a virginal white bed and storage closets. Downstairs is Grandma's Room and the Little Room, where a large file cabinet is a remaining testimony to Rog's predilection for making a home into an office. Joining all are narrow halls and a straight flight of stairs, and on the walls hang Renoir prints, portraits of Rog's dour Clonmel ancestors, old lithographs of nameless places, framed family crests. Upstairs in the hall is a window seat whose bookcases hold more unlikely literature, two shelves of books in French though nobody, including Rog, reads French. In the bench is a pile of old schoolbooks from New Jersey.

While I was in Arabia, my mother exchanged 204 for this house, her elegant, independent city image for a new one. Now she was a country housewife.

In 1952 she had married a professor of finance at the Columbia Business School, a businessman/teacher. Rog's identity permeated 204 in a way I had never imagined and didn't very much like. Though he was a forceful and amusing man, though he did look wonderful, all six foot three of him in his navy blazer and old school tie pouring Old Fitzgerald for the guests, his "office-ization" of what had been home was painful. Where to put Rog and his Friden Calculator, the size and sound of a truck engine? 204 didn't lend itself at all to home-as-business-deduction. Not the back porch, it was unheated; certainly not the backyard. Not the silky, seductive master bedroom. The tiny second bedroom on the top floor was tried, but Rog and the calculator were simply too big, not to mention file cabinets, ledgers, and reference library; in it he could hardly turn around, or even straighten out his legs. So—terrible day—the living room became an office, the monster desk replaced a pink tufted loveseat in the middle of the room, and the filigree breakfront was filled with file envelopes. My friends and I sat on the back porch, or tramped up two flights to my room. The old free in-and-out spirit of 204 ebbed away, particularly when Rog called in the keys. People no longer wandered in during dinner or at 3 A.M. to sleep. Instead the calculator thundered, recycling the figures of high finance.

Well, Rog made my mother happy, and I was on the brink of departure. It was just another nudge out of the nest, one I might never have left if it had continued to be so inviting. Probably we could not have gone on forever living without men, probably it was unnatural. I suppose what was so deeply astonishing was not the *fact* of men, for indeed I liked them very much, but the way they took over women's lives. I wondered why it was so difficult to marry them, or even love them, without being so invaded, like an occupied country. Len had not taken me over as a personality, but he had done it so completely by taking me to Arabia that I was still incredulous over my own weightlessness. Rog had sidled into his head-of-the-family role somewhat more indirectly by giving up his own apartment and moving into his wife's house. He worked, instead, from within. They gave up the brownstone for a Columbia apartment on Morningside Drive only after I had gone to Arabia, and the changes in my mother were not apparent to me until I came back; for moving gives us a vision we never have if we stay in one place. And they had bought a house in Dorset.

Why Dorset?

"Oh, I don't know," my mother said. "We drove around and looked at places. It reminds me a little of Switzerland."

How evanescent the reasons people have for choosing a place to live. For though the house was to be for weekends and summer vacations, and an eventual retirement home, it was no longer New York that had my mother's heart. She had deposited it in Vermont.

In Dorset my mother and her husband were more of a team, less two inharmonious forces jockeying for position. The house accommodated his and her furniture, linen, china, and kitchenware, tons of it. It was visibly *theirs*. For me, just back from the Middle East with a small baby, it was paradise. It had everything I had missed so badly in the last two years—the fireside, the older generation, the sense of the past, the gentle green countryside. I felt as though by bringing my daughter here I was giving her something infinitely valuable that she would never have had in Dhahran. She was unaware of all this, crawling around on the soft grass in back and trying to eat a daisy, but I told her anyway. She was—I would make sure she was—really an American. By feeding her the fresh local vegetables, the chicken pies made by a nearby farm woman, apples from a Dorset orchard, I was giving her culture and identity.

I watched with amazement my city mother turned country grandmother. Gone were the tailored suits and "smart" hats. Now she wore printed cotton dresses and crisp aprons, and had gotten decidedly hefty. She was up at eight, in the kitchen frying country sausages. She gardened and made pies. She took walks and swam in the quarry, trying to break Rog of his financial fix long enough to go with her. She reveled in the cows that wandered up the base of the mountain late in the afternoon, in the clouds which gathered over Mother Myrick, in the heart-stopping sight of a deer on the road. She reported local gossip and edged into local society as much as she was allowed, for Vermonters are cautious with strangers.

She was kind to me, delighted with her granddaughter. But everything was for Rog. She cooked him nightly the rare beef that he loved, the baked potatoes and strong black coffee, trying to tempt him to eat a few green beans, maybe try a little broiled fish. She was forbearing with his politics and prejudices. She let him drive long after I refused to get into a car with him, for Rog, an old Canadian Air Force ace, denied his fading faculties and loved to break the speed barrier. She accompanied him on his odd shopping trips—Rog was a quantity buyer, and would suddenly be seized with the urge to go out and get "a dozen good wool blankets," a crate of melons, subscriptions for ten new magazines, or a dozen pieces of porch furniture.

Though he was massive and florid, with a mighty head of white hair, he was never well, and she cared for him tenderly throughout his illnesses, some imaginary, some very real. She clucked when he tended his high blood pressure with Old Fitz (served in the new pint-size on-the-rocks glasses), measuring his pressure, and anyone else's who was interested, on his sphygmomanometer (invented, he said, by an uncle) which he often produced in a jolly way to a roomful of guests. "Now you put the cuff on this way, d'you see," and, "Well, now, that's a little high. I'll give you the name of my doctor." She chuckled at his shady couplets, always about lorn women—"Still no dice for Susan Price," or "Who will fiddle with Betty Biddle?" She welcomed Rog's daughter and her family, calling herself Grandma and him Grandpa, a title Rog took with minimal enthusiasm and his usual mordant humor. (When the children were a nuisance, he said, "Why don't you take 'em out and put a couple of plastic bags over their heads?")

The woman who had led the City Patrol Corps squad,

who had left her husband and brought her child to New York, who had created a life alone in the days when it was barely acceptable (and being more concerned than most about acceptability), the doer and the coper, now became the perfect follower. She asked her husband's permission about everything, even times when, I suspect, he was surprised at being asked. Was it all right with him if she bought a dress, took a part-time job, went skiing or horseback riding? Did he mind if she did a little volunteer work at the hospital, had a second drink, took care of a grandchild for the afternoon? Could she have lunch with a woman friend, see a show he was not interested in? The satisfaction she found in being needed seemed to more than make up for the deprivation, for the answer was often no. She took it, at any rate, as need; he would pine without her, feel threatened by other interests or loyalties.

In every marriage, the truth has two faces. Was Rog really such a boss, a bully, so terrible if crossed? Or was he fragile and helpless, unable to bear it if she was half an hour late from lunch? Was she really so loyally adoring, so helpless without a man to merge herself in? Or was she really the strong one, healthier, tougher, of more muscular disposition? Now gone are the tiny hidden moments when his concern about her absence became fear, then anger; or when her own good-natured self-sufficiency threatened to mock her if she found herself again without a husband—for when he threatened to leave her, she believed him.

Near sixty, neither of them wanted to be alone. They would put up with a lot to avoid it. People of midyears bring a lot of baggage into a marriage—two long pasts, fifty years of another life. Children and grandchildren, lost spouses, old habits, a carload of memories. And such is the peculiar nature of marriage—its most dangerous aspect—that the expectations are not much different than they were at twenty, or even fifteen. Both Rog and my mother wanted to be taken care of and each struggled silently to wrest this care from the other. Since Rog's needs were greater, he won—for the most part she took care of him, grateful not to be "one of those women having dinner alone at Schrafft's," giving her philosophical little shrug at life's vicissitudes. She was grateful for what she had. For that was what enraged him most, the unspoken knowledge that she could, and most likely would, survive without him. That was what gave her a generosity he could not muster.

Into this silent struggle for dependency I arrived with my small daughter. My mother's role as grandma was hard on Rog—his symptoms worsened. A baby was fearful competition. I was almost as bad, for though I was now a big girl, published writer, and world traveler, a mother, and "matron" as my mother insisted on calling me, I had come home to Mom leaving my husband behind for ten weeks. Neither Rog nor my mother approved of this—wives shouldn't leave their husbands for so long. We would miss each other too much, it was too hard on our marriage. I was not able to explain the misery I had experienced in Dhahran, nor did I understand it at the time. My complaints sounded whiny and silly—and in fact they probably were, because rooted in the problem of Dhahran was the problem of myself and my marriage, which I was not ready to look full in the face. That I should need to be by myself for a while back in my own land, to reknit my raveled identity, was a little too revolutionary for them.

But I had, in fact, a secret mission, an intense little test to run on my mother. Would this Dorset make up for the betrayal of moving out of 204? Would she make another excellent home? Would the food be as good, the hearth so welcoming? And worse, would she give me all the attention I wanted, listen without boredom to all my stories about the Middle East (which I could tell all night) and anything else I felt like talking about, laugh at my jokes, approve of me whatever I did, pass Test A for Motherhood? Would she demonstrate on my small daughter the love she had shown me as a baby, showing herself to be devoted, unselfish, generous, loyal, and endlessly good-natured?

If Rog and I both called for her at the same time, to which of us would she go? (If Rog and the baby and I called at the same time, to which would she go?)

Before dinner we gather on the marble terrace, bathed in that soft pink light that has such wonderful effects on human skin, where all look more beautiful than they are. The cows roam up the mountain, the leaves of the aspen across the field turn silver in the breeze. My mother and I are drinking martinis, Rog is drinking Old Fitz. The baby has a bottle, and she pulls herself up to her feet to take bits of cheese arranged on a plate. Across the field a dog barks, a crow caws. We look like the most loving group, the very blood that runs in America's better veins. My mother smiles at our *persona*, our collective outer image. She beams at the baby, who is named after her. She has worked, probably, harder than a grandmother whose family has common blood. By sheer optimism and dauntless industry, she has made a family of us. She thinks she has succeeded.

But Rog and I, though we pretend to like each other, have deadlier purposes. We are locked in combat, arsenals at the ready.

I start by telling some interminable story about Arabia (I'm aware that I'm becoming a bore, but I can't stop myself). Rog says something about Middle East politics. I disagree. We argue. My mother tries to mediate. The baby knocks over the cheese, probably to shut me up. I clean it up, and at the same time Rog sends my mother into the house for another Old Fitz. When she comes out I have lost the thread of my story. Rog has won Round One.

Or: Rog complains of mysterious pains in the chest, the belly, the gut. I counter with tales of an intestinal bug I got in Cairo. Perhaps Rog has the same thing, I've heard you can get it here as well. Rog looks frightened. My mother says it's impossible. Rog goes in to lie down. I have won Round Two.

Or: I admire the baby's beauty and cleverness, saying she has my father's eyes and his sense of humor. My mother agrees, tells a Nunnally story. Rog drums on the arm of his chair. I tell another story about my father. Rog makes a deadly wisecrack. The baby suddenly gets up and goes over to him, leaning her head on his knee. Surprised and touched, he puts his big hand on her head. A draw between Rog and me. The baby has won Round Three.

Sometimes it gets heavier. Rog lies in bed, calling for medicine, coffee, Old Fitz, half a cantaloupe with a scoop of ice cream in it. The baby hurts herself and wails, I tend to her, calling to my mother for iodine, cotton, gauze squares, and whatever else I know she doesn't have. She is out of coffee, ice cream, and iodine. She runs back and forth, trying to solace all of us. Rog's voice gets harder: "Come here at once." She gives me a panicky glance and chooses Rog. I am left on the kitchen floor with my weeping child.

Really nobody has won any rounds at all.

Sometimes Rog and I, playing our tacky little games, pretend we are superior to my mother. We are better educated, better informed, faster on the misinformation. We zap each other with American history, which she is inclined to forget. It's our way of having a good clean fight. We (mis)quote Vernon Parrington, and Schlesinger's *The Age of Jackson*. When Rog calls for the encyclopedia I run to get it. My mother wanders around the terrace, snaps off a few dead iris. I like this premarital Rog, the one who turned up at 204 with two bunches of flowers, one for her, one for me, then took us both out to Louise's Italian restaurant around on Fifty-eighth Street. He emerges like this rarely, the wedding vows cleaned him out. My mother makes a point which we both pooh-pooh. Rog tells me I have a good natural liberal conscience, I swell with pride. I have outsmarted my mother.

Sometimes across the terrace or the dinner table, Rog's and my eyes meet in the most naked way—not with hatred, not with fear, but with a terrible knowingness, the look of two people who have each other's number. It only lasts for a second, the light is too bright. We have too much to do to stand such openness.

When Len came a lot of the charge was defused. We fell back into pairs, where we felt more comfortable—Len and Rog talked oil economics or the stock market, my mother and I murmured of food, child care, and local lore, things that I had only recently found dull. Nobody went to bed alone.

But those tiny games never really stopped until Rog died in 1971, for that separation from Len was just a prelude to a permanent one and then I was back in Dorset for longer periods of time, this time with two small daughters. We became less veiled—more cheese dishes clattered to the floor, more little girls howled for attention. I was an anxious, frightened divorced woman clinging to Dorset as a fixture of permanence during one of the worst periods of my life. (I had gone, as my mother said, to the ends of the earth, and it had not worked.) Rog was older and sicker, his needs nakeder and more urgent. I knew they were greater than mine; he was a dying man, and though I was miserable with failure, I knew I would survive; I had years on him if nothing else. Still, it was hard, my own needs were too raw, and now I had two children I felt barely capable of caring for. I felt ripped open by analysis, possessed by my own needs, exacerbated by being around my mother who had, I thought, failed.

I remember one painful night on the terrace when the devil inside made me sit, like Goldilocks, in Rog's favorite chair. He asked me to move; I refused, making a joke of it. My mother, who invariably assumed people are what they seem and better than they are, went along with the joke and suggested an alien chair, where he sat for a while, looking uncomfortable. There was some sort of exchange, while Rog took out his anger at me on my mother, while I half gloated, and half writhed with guilt. Then he got up and went inside to bed, where she took him his dinner on a tray, which she often did.

Afterward, as I sat reading in the High Bedroom, I heard their voices from below—his angry, hers placating. How stupid it was, I thought, to stake out a claim on a chair. Chairs were chairs. It was typical of Rog's infantile behavior. But I knew I had been cruel. I knew how to get him and I had gone for the spot. In a few minutes I heard Rog's voice, the slam of a door, the car motor, the faint crunch of the gravel on the driveway. Then my mother appeared in the doorway of the bedroom.

"Rog has left me," she said, in a fairly calm voice.

Of course, I had known he would, since the moment I sat in his chair. I knew everything that was going to happen and it did.

"We had a fight, and he's packed and gone to Europe. He's going to New York, and has booked passage on the *Queen Mary* tomorrow." She looked frightened.

"But he won't go," I said, with insane prophecy. "He'll drive to Albany and stay at the Henry Hudson. Then in the morning he'll come back on the bus, and you'll have to go to Albany to pick up the car."

"No," she said, looking as though she were about to cry. "He's left for Europe. He packed a suitcase. He took the checkbook. He called the Cunard Line."

"Did he really call them? Did they really answer the phone?"

"He said he's booked an outside cabin." She sighed. "Well." I knew what she was thinking: the Lord giveth, and the Lord taketh away.

In the morning Rog called from the Henry Hudson, came back on the bus, and my mother went to Albany in the afternoon and picked up the car. And that night Rog sat in his own chair on the terrace.

Did all families tremble like this, shaken by things that are never expressed? Things seemed to emerge in Dorset that did not when we were all back in our New York apartments. They were there all the time, but in the city they were diffused somehow, lost in the infectious excitement of the city itself.

It wasn't just a matter of time, though that was part of it. With two small children I was just as busy in Dorset, lugging those plastic bags of diapers to the laundromat in Manchester, amusing two insatiable, endlessly energetic children, and trying, not very successfully, to write. The days were filled with excursions to the Little Water, a tiny stream where the children waded and tried to catch water bugs, or picnics, or trips to some nearby town where an old country store sold penny candy.

It was something else, the suggestions of the place itself. Driving to town, walking across the valley to the West Road or through the orchard next door, I would—I still do—fasten on some quiet old house behind a clump of trees or on the edge of the gentle mountain. A porch, a meticulously cared-for garden, green shutters. Such peace, such age. Such a perfect fit into the curve of the land. Silvery old apple trees. A glimpse into a tidy kitchen. Clothes flapping on a line. I was jittery then, in the early sixties, a little crazy, up and down emotionally. I cried easily. Such an old house, a metaphor for the safety I didn't have, made me ache with envy. The tears would well up. Of course I assumed that the family who lived in the house was more perfect than mine, more at peace. I imagined them sitting down at the table at sunset, saying grace. Passing the stew and the biscuits, the homemade applesauce. Never mind that the children I saw were so fat and pasty-faced, the women so dour. If there was one of those tiny graveyards behind the house with its cluster of family graves, my envy became awe. It was a sacred place as well, their home. They had buried their ancestors on their land.

Home, according to Reynolds Price, is a religious place containing our dead.

At the time I hadn't the slightest idea where my dead were buried, though I now know some of them are in a town in Georgia, where my father came from and where many members of his family are buried. My mother's are misplaced. "I think we left them at the crematorium," said she of her dead parents. And her older sister, my Aunt Margaret? "The boys" (her sons) "did something or other with her." (Now I know that she has been sprinkled in the garden of my cousin's ex-wife.) Rog has similarly been lost. She was never concerned with such things and was surprised at my morbid fancies. The thing is to look ahead and find happiness.

But in Dorset the past drags me back. There I am conscious of being a waif. My parents moved, rather than stayed; instead of digging in and sinking roots, they left in search of freedom, love, money, adventure, or a creative atmosphere. There's been too much leaving in my family, in fact, too many bursts of liberation. Parents too strict, the old life too claustrophobic? You leave home. Marriage gone sour? Turn it in for another. Job too dull, doesn't pay enough? Quit, get a better one. The muscle of adjustment is virtue, hope the fuel of life. We have no ghosts, we have left them behind and forgotten where.

I believed the people in the old house to be larger, stronger, more immortal than I. They were part of a family in a way I was not, and death was not a departure to the unknown, but a return to an ultimate home. They reverberated more, yet somehow the sound of their errors was cushioned more. They were not, as I was, so entirely accountable to myself, my own sole inhabitant.

In Dorset, I find solace in brushing against other people's ghosts since I don't have any of my own. It gives me pleasure, and provides my children (waifs like myself) with a sense of the past, a symbol, if not the actuality, of permanence. Surely, I think, every time I drive up Route 22, this time the place will transform us. The fallacious logic (we look like a family, therefore we are one) will work. The clear air, the pines, the soft pink light will smooth our differences, that clear, icy water will drown our city ills. The house will unify us. That it never does is twice as painful as in the city, where I expect things to be difficult and complicated, live my life on nerve ends, and drink trouble with my morning coffee. In Dorset our troubles seem a vilification of the very landscape, of a history I imagine to be more tranquil, more trouble-free than mine.

Once or twice in my life, when things hadn't worked out, I thought of going to live there. I would grow vegetables, send the children to the local school, maybe learn to sew. Then one day in the car my mother pointed out a man by the side of the road and said, "That's the local bachelor." And there the fantasy ended.

For the first twenty years I went to Dorset, I never thought much about Dorset itself. I went, like many others, looking for ghosts, for the past, for purity, for the evocation of a previous age when things seem to have been simpler, less infested with greed and technology than they are now. I longed for homely symbols of our early history—Grandma's kitchen with its fresh, homemade food, natural fabrics, country life, and handicrafts—as though as a nation adulthood has proved too plastic, too mass-produced, too cold and unreal and dangerous.

I skimmed the surface of the locale without ever associating myself with it in any way. A product of an acquisitive society, I only wanted to take things—a view of the cows, the local produce, the sight of family graves—like tokens of a place I visited but could not possess, without giving anything back. Dorset was my metaphor for home, but I knew absolutely nothing of its reality.

I have watched it change over the years, but to me change was mainly in the form of small annoyances. The farm in the Hollow where you used to be able to get a big basket of fresh vegetables for a dollar or two no longer functions. The chicken place in Manchester where you used to be able to get those melting homemade chicken pies is no longer there. There are too many madras jackets and Izod T-shirts at the Field Club—and too many people in them. You can't get a tennis court, and the quarry is too crowded with people who leave beer cans around. Parks's store is closed which is too bad because there used to be all those quaint old characters there on Sunday morning saying "Ay-uh."

It never occurred to me that I, and people like me, were making profound changes in the place simply by being there, that we were affecting the very nature of the place at the same time that we were complaining about a loss of innocence and imperiled integrity. The Izod T-shirts were mine, and it is my economy that has driven out the farmer in the Hollow.

Almost in penance, I set about understanding the real place that underlies the one in my mind, to find some real connection with a place whose surface I have hardly dented.

Dorset's history is proud.

In the beginning, Vermont was always somebody else's battleground. In the seventeenth century, part of the French and Indian War was fought there, and in the eighteenth century the area, then known as the New Hampshire grants, was continually bickered over by the governor of New Hampshire, the governor of New York, and the British Crown. The most oppressive of these was New York, which has always been something of a bad guy to Vermonters—a feeling that still lingers. (Oddly to our ears, New York, up there, means New York State—New York City is so remote, and so insane, that it barely merits discussion.)

It had been bad enough to be a nameless annex of New Hampshire, but it was worse when George III delivered the ownership of the townships over to the governor of New York, remapping them and requiring the owners to buy their own land over again. This indignity was responsible for the rise of the local hero, Ethan Allen and his Green Mountain Boys ("twelve or fifteen of the most blackguard fellows he can get, double armed," according to Zephine Humphrey in her charming book *The Story of Dorset*), whose cause was to protect the local people from unscrupulous outsiders.

It was at Dorset that Vermont's identity was truly forged. On the eve of revolution, the problem of the New Hampshire grantees was not so much whether to fight the British—which they were quite prepared to do, even though they were not one of the original colonies—but under whose banner to fight. At a series of meetings in Dorset, at the Cephas Kent Tavern on the West Road, a series of decisions was made to promote Vermont's revolution within a revolution, its desire to set its own destiny.

First, application was made to the Continental Congress in Philadelphia to form the New Hampshire grants into a separate district, with discouraging results. Then in January of 1777 Vermont's Declaration of Independence was drawn up, with its resolve to fight the British, along with a strong statement against the "disengenuous conduct" of New York State toward the New Hampshire grants, and the "several illegal, unjustifiable and unreasonable Measure[s] they have taken to Deprive by fraud, violence and oppression those inhabitants of their property and in particular their Landed interest." Though the state constitution was actually adopted at Windsor, and the bastardized French name Vermont chosen, "It was in Dorset that the idea of Vermont was born, and everyone knows that the idea is the dynamic reality and the fact its shadow . . . although we make no public claim, we know in our hearts that Vermont is particularly ours, that Dorset, the child, is father of this man."

Dorset was settled in 1768 by intrepid pioneers "who could have stayed" (writes Miss Humphrey) "in the older colonies where their lives would have been easier. They craved a fuller freedom, a more perfect independence; perhaps they even craved the utmost exercise of brain and muscle, the sternest proof of stoutheartedness." In that hard life of clearing wilderness, building log cabins, grinding corn, and keeping wolves, bear, and moose at bay, the Vermont qualities were born: industry, deliberateness, caution, gravity, ruthless honesty (it saves time), brevity (likewise)—these are the virtues this rocky land gave its people.

These early settlers and their sons fought in the Revolution—giving the Republic, as Miss Humphrey points out, more than they got, for Vermont "was not on good terms with her neighbors or with the Continental Congress. She had been badly treated on every hand. Small wonder and no manner of blame would it have been if she had refused to concern herself about the general cause of American independence. But she was generous." Up until 1791 (during which time Vermont with difficulty held on to her status as an independent republic) New York, New Hampshire, and even Massachusetts continued to juggle boundaries and make trouble. "We were harassed, distracted, and thrown utterly on our own resources. The situation bred in us an uncompromising spirit which had a good deal of the daredevil in it. Since we must work out our own salvation, we would!"

By the time of the Revolution the Green Mountain Boys were being paid by the Continental Congress for their services and a regiment had been formed in the New Hampshire grants, with Bennington's Seth Warner as commander. At the Battle of Bennington, they joined with Brigadier General John Stark's battalions to defeat Burgoyne's Hessians–though Ethan Allen (who had previously captured Ticonderoga) was by then himself captured by the British in an attempted surprise attack on Montreal.

When he was released, in 1778, he and his brother Ira again applied to the Continental Congress for admission to the Union and were again turned down; at which time they negotiated to turn Vermont to the British cause, and failed. This rather feeble Tory gesture had less to do with strong pro-British feeling than a sort of desperate "somebody has to take us in" feeling. Eventually an invitation to join the Union came from, of all places, churlish New York, and in 1791 Vermont ratified the new United States Constitution.

The early settlers were hardworking and devout, if a little rough at the edges. A traveler described them in 1789 as "nasty–poor–low-lived–indelicate–and miserable cooks. All sadly parsimonious–many profane." Besides, there was "no cheese–no beef–no butter . . . the maple cyder is horrible stuff" and the women "dress coarse, & mean, & nasty, & ragged . . . are these women of ye same species with our fine Ladies? tough are they, brawney their limbs" yet "kind & obliging & good-natured." A 1797 church roster lists most of the old pre-Revolutionary names: Farwell, Barrows, Kent, Curtis, Holley, Sykes, Hanks, Underhill, Dunton, Morris (people stay in Dorset, and those "who have tried to leave our valley only . . . find themselves irresistibly lured back to it") along with some others; Marsh, Stannard, Martindale, Collins, Manly, Sherman, Bloomer, Armstrong, Morse, Fuller. The population was then 1,100, only 548 less than it was in the 1980 census, a rate of growth that seems, to those who live there, just about right.

In the early nineteenth century marble quarrying, Dorset's glamorous industry, brought a period of local prosperity.

Out of the quarries came headstones, hearthstones, lintels, and the lions which stand in front of the New York Public Library, plus Harvard Medical School and other public buildings (the Supreme Court and Arlington War Memorial come from the same vein, but mined over in Danby, on the other side of the mountain). Besides the eight Dorset quarries, there were mills for sawing the marble, marble shops, and shops for finishing and lettering. There were sawmills and gristmills, asheries and tanneries, blacksmith shops, coopers and cabinetmakers and potters. There were factories for cheese, hats, woolens, latches and wrenches of East Dorset iron ore, wooden bowls, and stockings. There were five taverns, one the present Dorset Inn, and several stores—one of which, the Williams store on Route 30, is still there and functioning as though the last one hundred and fifty years never happened. There were the cornfields and apple orchards, sheep and turkeys and chickens and sugar maples that made up what was once a prosperous agricultural economy.

There were occasional artists, but they sprang, says Miss Humphrey, from unlikely soil, amid an unappreciative audience. "Shall we people of Dorset never learn to recognize and honor the prophets in our midst?" she mourns. In spite of this not uncommon problem, artists have always come to Dorset, the most famous being Reginald Marsh, who didn't paint the area, but came to rest his urban eyes.

By the middle of the nineteenth century, descendants of the old pre-Revolutionary families were settled in ancestral homes along the West Road along with a few newcomers, such as the Gilberts and the Wests, and another group in the Hollow. A tight society evolved. Not only did they all know each other intimately, but "the whole neighborhood was related by blood or intermarriage." Life must have been pleasant in a way that it can only be in a society that is stable to the point of petrification. The adults are secure, the young gasp for breath and long to break away—building up the very energy that makes for later success. Miss Humphrey puzzles, "In spite of the fact that we" (a collective Dorset voice) "were all very busy and had never even heard of laborsaving devices, we seem to have had more leisure for sheer sociability than we have now" (written in 1924). There were picnics and day trips, sugaring offs, church gatherings, dances and suppers and charades.

Where did all this time come from? Because nobody was trying to do anything else, or go anywhere else, or think about much else than life in Dorset. Nobody spent time apartment hunting or taking the cat to the vet or going to court for more child support or waiting for Bloomingdale's to deliver a chair. For as quickly as we find a way to save time, we find another complication to fill it. It's the diffuse nature of our lives that wears us down—the overload of choices, our ambivalence, the number of places we inhabit, the decisions which rain on us at a rate unknown to those nineteenth-century Vermonters, whose lives were structured and simple.

By the end of the century the fluctuating marble industry was in decline and was over by 1913 except for the grand finale of the New York Public Library—which commission was fraudulent. Carleton Howe, Dorset resident since the twenties, says, "When bidding, the people in New York wanted to know what kind of marble they were getting, so they took core samples of the marble. With great sleight of hand they" (the local marble barons) "got good cores from another quarry they didn't have control of and substituted them and they got the contract for the library on the basis of swapped cores. Spaff" (Spafford West, head baron) "disappeared, nobody knew where he went but they put a gravestone up there for him." The second-rate marble was used for the library—and it came out of the swimming hole on Route 30.

Though "the throb and roar of the quarry permeated our whole weekday life, seeming the very pulsebeat of our existence," marble didn't change Dorset's character, though it temporarily swelled its population. But in the late 1800s the first summer visitors began coming, which apparently innocent development transformed the very nature of the town. In 1891, Miss Humphrey tells us, the top price for board was nine dollars a week, with some cottages going for one hundred dollars a season. (Now a house in Dorset rents for at least eight hundred dollars a month in the summer and ski seasons.)

Miss Humphrey is nervously gracious about the summer people, like a hostess with a great many noisy, unpredictable guests. "So far, we have been singularly fortunate in the character of the people who have come to sojourn with us. They are largely professional or artistic folk, clergymen, physicians, teachers, writers, painters, musicians, widely intelligent and glad to give us of their best. Moreover, their tastes are simple, inclining them rather to adopt our quiet ways than introducing urban elaborations of custom and dress . . . we look to them with confidence though with a certain anxiety, as the fated arbiters of our immediate destiny and hope they realize what a power to make or mar lies in their hands.

". . . More and more they seem disposed to equip their houses for winter use, and already several families of them have stayed through the whole year with us . . . That is the best thing that can happen to us. Dorset and Vermont and the United States would be gainers if more city people came and did likewise." But "We cannot help fearing the effects . . . of a career of conformity to alien standards, or a prolonged functioning as a mere vacation ground" on a town that is "dignified, self-reliant, serene, a little crotchety, very lovable."

Miss Humphrey was right. Dorset has been entirely taken over by the guests.

In America it all depends on which wave of immigration

you arrived on. We all came from somewhere else, or our forebears did. But if your forebears were here before the Revolution, or before the Civil War, you are closer to being a member of the only aristocracy we have.

On the West Road, Honey West Mitchell now lives in the house built in the 1830s by her great-grandfather and consecutively inhabited by her grandparents, her parents, herself and her four children and eleven grandchildren. She and her sister were born there, as well as her father and grandmother. "In those days we all lived together, everybody looked after everybody else. The house was enlarged so Grandfather wouldn't have to move half a mile away."

By the fire in her living room, I feel all of their presences. I ask her if I may wander around, partly to see the house and partly to try and absorb the past which lies so heavily in the air. Because of the cost of fuel, most of the rooms are shut off and unheated, and we walk through the cold upper halls. It is the sort of house where a child has both a summer and a winter bedroom. Everything looks "done" and walls have been charmingly stenciled by Honey herself. The fireplace features a wood stove and there are handmade hooked rugs on the floor.

Honey sits knitting in a deep window seat looking out over her garden, darkening though it is only four-thirty of a November afternoon. She grew up in Dorset and tells me what a perfect place it was in the twenties. "There were dances at the Field Club with loads of boys, the stag line was three deep. Nobody really seemed to have jobs, they just played all summer." What she takes for granted is to me a link to immortality. If anything was ever home this is, the fire, the old books, the window seat and the dusk. She is cordial as I leave, but she has told me she likes being alone. Of course she isn't alone at all. The place is filled with her predecessors, old Spaff West the marble baron who switched cores and put the quarry on the map, all the Wests who married Sykeses, who married Gilberts and Kents.

The Gilberts have lived on the West Road since before the Civil War, and in Vermont for two hundred years. If you spend any time in Dorset you can't miss them—there is a Gilbert Brook, a Gilbert hardware store, and the Congregational Church choir is made up almost entirely of tuneful Gilberts. "I don't know if I can help you," said Ethel Gilbert when I asked her what she could tell me about Dorset. "I've only been here since 1915." If the family is not as pre-Revolutionary as the Stannards, say, or the Barrows, it can probably be said that they are one of the oldest, most continually marrying, intermarrying, and procreating family in the village, along with being one of the most visible, for the Gilberts have long been associated with community contribution. The name dominates village history. One Charles Gilbert was a clergyman in Dorset for forty years; his grandson Rufus and his wife Ethel built the Dorset Playhouse and started the Dorset Players, which still operates successfully. In the early days "the church and the Players were the two central themes of the town." They did Shaw and Noël Coward and an original play called *Green Mountain Grit*. "I'd memorize my lines with the play book propped up over the sink while I washed the dishes. At night we used to hear the youngsters tramping by, singing the songs from the play—'We trust in the gods of the hills, they watch over us.'"

The Gilberts stopped producing apples three or four years ago, leaving just one operating orchard over in East Dorset. How do you stop producing apples? You just stop spraying—the trees are old anyway. It seemed sad—I always liked their apples better than the East Dorset ones, particularly the ones I had seen lying on the silky grass of their orchard while my kids picked them and put them in baskets.

"We had sheep too," Ethel Gilbert told me, "we kept them across the road in the meadow where the cornfield is now. You know this was originally a farm town, and now the farmland is completely gone. But we still let Junior Nichols use that land for his dairy, and Rufus has never charged for it because he says anyone who uses the land is putting back in as much as he takes out."

Ethel Gilbert comes from an educated family, one of seven children of a peripatetic Methodist minister who "moved so often, I lived in many places in Vermont and New York State. So I did want to stay in one place. I love every inch of this place because it's my real home," she says. She and Rufus met at Burr & Burton, the local high school, and they had been married for sixty-five years when Rufus died last year.

Their two-family house is a kind of compound where most Dorset Gilberts live—in the other half live other elderly relatives. The big farm kitchen where we sit is battered, well used, redolent with the lives that have been lived here. We drink coffee at an oilcloth-covered table. The Gilberts have raised four sons, all of whom flew planes during World War II, and one of whom, Sykes, was killed in action. "I took *The Daily Worker* all during the war," she says, surprisingly. "It was the only paper I could depend on for accurate news, and I was keeping track of Tim in Africa, Bill in England, Sykes in France, and Charlie bombing Japan." It was delivered in a plain wrapper. "I brought up four boys with the theory that war settled nothing, it was time there was no war."

The rest of the house shows its one hundred and fifty years. The beams are low, the bathrooms sparse, the stairway tiny and steep. The rooms are cluttered with the debris of several lifetimes—pictures, paintings by one son or another, books, bits of sculpture, sets of antlers, mobiles, mementoes. Gilberts are in the very walls of this place; they could only be exorcised, if some owner wanted to do so, by burning it down

—and possibly not even then. It is the sort of house that makes me feel immensely privileged to be in, it is so very personal and private, truly the inner fold of the family that lives in it. I might have walked into a family album.

It's hard to believe that Ethel, who seems so indigenous, was once a transplant—though unlike many later ones, was anxious (and motivated by her marriage) to adopt Dorset ways. Though longtime Dorseters describe the village's social change in terms of the breakdown of one homogeneous group into several (often abrasive) factions (post World War II transplant Marcian Skinner calls it "one of the most sociologically complex towns I have ever been near"), it sounds as though there were, back in 1915, the haves and have-nots, as there are anywhere. "During apple-picking when Rufus's birthday came, I would always have a birthday cake and coffee and invite all the workers out on the lawn in the middle of the afternoon. But we never invited them for dinner because Rufus said they would be uncomfortable and I'm sure they would have." (Said Rufus, "You mustn't make too much of that.") Ethel was surprised that "they always called us by our first names. The woman who came to get the laundry to take it home and do it for me, I was always Ethel. The first time she said it I was startled, I had never been called by my first name by anyone but my intimate friends and family, and I said, 'Rufus, is that what they do?' and he said, 'That means you've been accepted.' So then I felt comfortable."

But part of the difficulty over the years between the natives and the transplants has been that "the new arrivals have hurt native pride because they employed them. The Vermonters have been their maids, their caretakers, but there was no mixing socially. Now it's more meshed—but not really. But there are people who have come to appreciate the Vermont qualities, even though they're unsophisticated."

She speaks carefully—this is painful ground. Now she's a Vermonter, somebody could employ her. The price of acculturation is that it makes you vulnerable to the new wave of rich immigrants. This is what hurts most. Vermonters are poor, and the transplants—retired executives from Westchester or Long Island—are glaringly rich. There are very, very few ways to earn a living in Vermont, particularly now that the farmland is so diminished. This is the seat of pain. Jack, a Gilbert grandson now living in the compound, was waiting on tables one night at the Toll Gate Lodge, an elegant restaurant in Manchester. "This loud-voiced man came in and said, 'What would these towns have been if we people hadn't come and brought the money?' And Jack said, 'They were very self-supporting and happy.' It made him furious. And he said, 'I'm the third generation of Gilberts who own the farm.' Oh, I don't mean to sound snobbish, but you see what it did, it changed the whole town." On the other hand, "It isn't that I don't enjoy many of the people here now, and as the boys grew up I was glad of the influx of intellectuals and writers and artists. I did need this. But we were never really close."

Marcian Skinner of the Hollow manages to be liked and accepted by both groups.

Not only is it because she and her husband have lived here thirty years or so, but because Marcian never hires any of the local people. "Of course as soon as you hire 'em then you're getting into this business of boss and employee. I mean you aren't going to consort with your maid socially. I do all my own work so I can go into anybody's kitchen because they all know that I clean my own house unless I'm sick or something like that, a reasonable excuse. We cut our own wood, grow our own garden . . . there's nobody in Dorset who wishes to clean house for anybody. We've frozen out everybody of that sort. Over on Peace Street" (the local shantytown) "there's a last little clutch of people that work out. But they're so busy you can't possibly get them, they're the most sought-after people in town—isn't it ridiculous?" Who hires them? "The summer people—the ones who are coming now. They belong to Ekwanok [a golf club in Manchester] instead of the [Dorset] Field Club, they live in the Hollow or on the West Road and they play golf or tennis and they're always having cocktail parties. They wear those little white skirts. You can tell 'em from the others like you can tell robins from blue jays." The other groups? "People like the Gilberts, the more affluent, intellectually strong natives. They had good farms, were part of the town government, came from excellent stock, excellent. They aren't too sophisticated, but they can match the wits of any outlanders that come here, believe me. They have this dignity, and this pride, and they don't intermingle. They're really neat. And they're all interrelated. I proved it. I invited one member from each family for Thanksgiving dinner and told each one to bring a relative or spouse. Everybody in town came."

Marcian, who resembles a girls' school gym teacher of the very best sort, went and stirred her applesauce, made from her own apples. "Then there are the other—poorer natives. You know how things separate, does it everywhere, does it here too. They're nice people, but they don't have quite the wits about 'em. They just didn't make it. And then there are the old-time summer people that have been here for so long, and they're quite different from the new ones. And there's another group of us, I assume where we fit, and we came along after the war. We grew up in Farmington, Connecticut, but the war changed it to suburbia, a bedroom of Hartford, a whole kinda life I didn't like. So we headed for Vermont and bought property in Dorset. In those days it was what we remembered Connecticut to have been in our childhood. Between 1959 and 1979, it changed so here, now you can't tell much difference between Farmington and Dorset. In fact my brother who lives in a little town in north Connecticut says, 'Marcian, you're much more suburban than we are. All those signs, everybody's name on their houses, you aren't simple at all and we are.' We just got the road signs last spring. I said to Polly Barrows, 'You ought to have some road signs, it's terribly hard to write for the paper' [*The Bennington Banner*]. 'But Marcian, don't,' she said. 'We'll be suburban.' I guess we are suburban. A lot of these road names are dead wrong, people didn't even know that the selectmen just kinda picked them, named after people who only recently arrived instead of oldies.

"It's a nifty place to live, though. When we first came we lived on a farm like a commune for four years, but our children were small and it was too hard. There are two times to come to Vermont—one when you're young with no children, or else when you've made your boodle and you're retiring."

The dread of "suburbanization" is in the heart of every true Dorseter, particularly the older residents. "It has been apparent for some time, certainly since the First World War, and with increasing acceleration since the Second," wrote Bill Gilbert in a series of articles in *The Bennington Banner* in 1971, "that two communities were developing in this small corner of the world. One community, the original, was fighting desperately for its very life, and the other, the new, or transplanted, or suburban, growing faster and faster as the sixties went by and the seventies procured the condition my friends, neighbors, and fellow natives refer to as 'the invasion.'

"Two communities exist in Dorset, and they are basically antagonistic. Our life here, as it must be in many other New England communities, is a constant and wearying attempt to make two separate life-styles . . . that have almost nothing in common, work side by side. We know that the work ethic has almost nothing in common with the retirement ethic. We know that twentieth-century suburban life produces outlooks that are quite different from the outlooks of nineteenth-century country life that we 'native Vermonters' consider our most precious heritage . . . the transplant destroys two things when he chooses Dorset for his address—he destroys the economy of a New England community and he destroys the very thing he came here to enjoy . . . native Vermonters can no longer count on controlling their own town or lives . . . what the community is and what it will become can no longer be determined by the selectmen or the elected representatives of the town or the town's long-standing resident population. The character of the town and its dynamics are now in the hands of fiercely competitive real estate dealers, primarily suburbanite."

The retiring corporation executive is a typical transplant. Taking advantage of the law (changed in 1977) that required him to rebuy, after selling his primary home, within a year or else pay capital gains, he sells his paid-up Scarsdale home for $200,000 or so and goes to Dorset, or some place like it. He and his wife fall in love with a charming old farmhouse assessed at $40,000 but having much more than that in his pocket he would rather invest it in a house than give it to the IRS, as the real estate agent well knows. Up go the prices—and the taxes are based on what was paid for the house. "So the guy up the hill who paid $150,000 for his house paid a lot of property tax," explains Marcian, "and he looked at the Skinners who were paying $112 or some silly little thing, so they all got together with a list and said this isn't fair, look at the land they've got, all these old farmers, Gilberts and Edgertons had lovely land and teensy bills. They got pretty excited about that, the outlanders, pretty soon elected solicitors who were outsiders too and said this is terrible, we're being robbed, we'll have it reappraised. So in sixty-one they reappraised the town.

"I was mad as a wet hen. I didn't mind if we'd done something new to our house or if it was a 10% for inflation straight through the town, but to say my land was worth more because so-and-so paid $125,000 . . . They said, 'But Marcian, the person there paid $60,000, and that makes your house more valuable.' And I said 'It's only the roof over my head, and until I sell—it's like buying General Motors in 1932—when I sell, be my guest. But until then it's no more than my house. The same old piece of ground, the same old roof, the same old sides. Don't penalize me because I was smart and got here first.' But they went ahead and did it."

Sid Meachem, Manchester attorney and longtime resident of Dorset, told me, "We have an influx of people who seem to have a great deal of cash or leverage, which is using a fairly high income or cash flow to borrow heavily against, not based on any accumulated assets—borrow as much as you can, put as little down. We have so much that prices have been driven up so it's virtually impossible for our young people to stay here. The [local] economy is a house of cards." And will it collapse? "There was a slight recession four or five years ago and there were a hell of a lot of chalets for sale in a hurry." Though the second-home market remains stable, the primary residence market is caught in the nationwide crunch.

The result of all this is that a Westchester, or Connecticut, or Long Island economy is imposed on the frail one in Dorset, forcing prices up to artificial heights and virtually starving out the old residents. Farming in Dorset has just about ceased, as it has in most of southern Vermont and many other parts of New England. The young people leave because there are no jobs (Dorset has only one industry, the Adams woodworking factory). The few who stay "find the suburbanization confusing," wrote Bill Gilbert. "They do not have the extra money necessary to join the ski and club world, which is a business feeding on suburbia, a sort of mutual leeching of one member by the other for the supposed advantage of both . . . the ones who find employment in the ski and service industries . . . are not able to live the hopped-up life-style, nor do they particularly want to." They are, furthermore, baffled by the hippie movement, the sixties rebellion of suburban youth against suburban values—those values that are supposed to be so terrific. Why should those "supposedly better-educated and certainly better-off young people want to throw out their life and return to the primitive? . . . if the local boy or girl follows along, there is nowhere for their life to lead but backward . . . they get out."

Perhaps the most destructive of all is "the shadow community of skiers. They are rarely seen. Their cars race up the roads Friday nights in winter . . . [and] speed to the mountains Saturday mornings. They jam all available restaurants and bars Saturday nights. On Sunday afternoons they careen southward, passing on curves and hills and risking the lives of man and beast . . .

"Skiers have virtually only one connection with the town life—they pay either rent or taxes. Their children do not go to school here, the adults do not go to town organizations. Their excess money, which they seem so eager to leave behind for wildly overpriced ski equipment and prohibitively priced ski-area facilities, goes primarily to New York or other metropolitan banks. The services they buy are basically outside-owned, and only rarely locally owned.

"They use the area, temporarily dominate its local life with the frenzy of their desperate attempt to get a three-day vacation from their suburban or city life, and produce an equal frenzy of money hunger in their preferred stores or services. As a recent survey has shown, and as many people of both long and short residency have known for a long time, the ski industry is a 'negative' influence as far as the local economy is concerned. Its primary effect is draining . . . its residual effect on construction and services does not compensate for its divisive effect on the life of the town."

All this contrasts with a nineteenth-century life-style "of mutual respect, majority rule, and the devout belief that the accumulation of more of the world's goods than you and your family could use must be based on immoral principles, and probably a certain amount of illegality. If you wanted to make money you went somewhere else." (Bill Gilbert, *The Bennington Banner.*)

"The sociological problems are just immense," Sid Meachem observed. "We've substituted a whole new set of values for the values that did exist. It's getting more and more difficult to find a handyman, someone to cart away the trash. Why the hell should they work for you for three or four dollars an hour when they can get twenty dollars caddying, enjoy themselves and to hell with everything else? Country club life has become too important." Besides, some of its unpleasant values have filtered down. "Recently some friends of mine were asked to leave the golf course because they were Jewish. These values have been superimposed."

It is an "occupied society," a place whose function is to service another way of life.

The rural fantasy brings us all to Vermont—retirees, transplants, summer people, hippies on their communes. The sixties live on there in such pockets as Goddard College in Plainfield, where my daughter was graduated. She describes a Vermont mystique: disdain of possessions, vegetarianism, the dream of living off the land, pursued by those young who feel they were born ten years too late. But it's just as hard to live off the land now as it was three hundred years ago. If the older migrants come with more money and fewer illusions, they share the same dream of the past.

But if transplants and summer people really want the rural dream, why do they keep suburbanizing the place at such a rate, putting up road signs and giving cocktail parties? (New Hampshire has hardly any road signs at all, probably to discourage strangers who end up, bewildered, in somebody's vegetable garden.) It's the illusion they want, without any of the inconvenience. The real Vermont might actually scare them. Carleton Howe, who did live off the land for fifteen years, told me that though the Hollow, where his farm was, is pretty suburbanized (there are a few cows and sheep left there) people never go past the end into the woods because "city people are fearful of isolation—you know, bears, Indians, and all that." Anyway, Dorset transplants are elderly and not about to go clambering over rocks or fording streams. It's often the last stop before the nursing home, and they want it to be comfortable.

One might wonder why these old people come when there's no doctor in Dorset and the nearest hospital is thirty miles away—particularly since Vermont is an expensive place to die. "The rich ones establish their residence in Florida, which has no inheritance tax," said Marcian Skinner, "so they have to evacuate by the end of October to make sure they have their six months there. I call 'em parasitic, they don't help our community at all other than the fact that they pay their taxes." The pivotal point seems to be whether—or how much—outlanders contribute to the community, and the summer people are more often guilty of noncommitment—or rather overcommitment. Marcian: "I've been soliciting for Ethan Allen Community College" (a miniature college in Manchester) "and I'm very interested in it. One family said, 'Well, you'll have to remember we have our place in Naples, we have our dairy ranch in Wisconsin, and you know, Marcian, I'm still loyal to New York City, and after all we only spend three months here—in fact we pay more of the taxes because we're here and so we pay for your snowplowing.' Boy—I restrained my tongue but it was difficult."

The second-home people (or third- or fourth-) are inclined to use the community without giving anything back to it, though of course this isn't true of all of them. "Look at all the things I do," my mother said indignantly, when I called her a transplant. "I write for the paper" (*Manchester Journal*) "and organize the church rummage sale and do jury duty."

She was right, and the cop-outs are being supported by people like her and a few others.

But no matter how Westchester-like Dorset has become, there is one crucial difference. In Larchmont or Scarsdale everything is for the kids, but in Dorset they are regarded, if not with outright loathing, with coolness. Since the mean age here is around sixty-five, this is understandable if a little surprising—aren't elderly people supposed to dote on small children? Well, apparently not *en masse*—fond though they may be of their own. Recently the Dorset Field Club again voted down the recurrent proposal to put in a swimming pool. Why? Partly because it would raise the dues (a "porch" membership is now one hundred dollars) but also because members are afraid it would attract too many kids. The mothers would come and dump them with the lifeguard and go off and play tennis and there would be pandemonium. (In Westchester hearts flutter at the thought of denying the kids anything.)

Dorset is also un-Westchester-like in that the town is largely made up of old ladies—the men are mostly dead, whereas in Westchester they are alive and can be seen palely loitering at the train station mornings and evenings. Dorset parties consist of elderly transplant widows; the infrequent widower is swamped with invitations. My mother told me there are only a couple around and their phones never stop ringing. There was a third, but he married my mother's neighbor, after carrying on with her in plain sight. "Frank's car is often in Edith's driveway for the night, and can you imagine, nobody says a word about it." Men are too precious; life is too short. And the transplants—some of whom are unconventional artists and writers—have brought their own values.

There are strange contrasts in Dorset, constant reminders of wildly disparate cultures living next to each other. Everyone goes to the Congregational Church on Sunday, but in the upper quarry (a strenuous climb from the main quarry on

Route 30) another group—or sometimes even the same group—swims in the nude and smokes dope. Homosexuality is tolerated but breaking the game laws is not. Everybody hunts (bear and deer) but vegetarianism abounds in Vermont (Goddard College has sought-after "veggie" dorms). Ethel Gilbert hung Van Gogh's "Sunflowers" in her kitchen. "It's always been like this," Bill Gilbert told me. "In the nineteenth century the farmers read Emerson." In scrutinizing the local factions it would seem that there is no conflict between the agrarian and the intellectual life—they go very well together and always have. Carleton Howe combined farming with an intense intellectual life of reading and travel to obscure corners of the earth. Intellectual life in Dorset isn't dead, he says, but it isn't as lively as it used to be. The trouble—as usual—comes from "all those retired IBM executives wandering around, they don't read, they don't know how to fill their time except to stare at football on the tube. In the old days people read maybe not more, but better. If they can use their hands—garden or something—they're okay. If not they're in trouble." The strong, self-sufficient native or long-term transplant has little or no tolerance for those who haven't learned that most difficult of life's lessons, how to fill the hours of the day—the corporation men without their corporation, the machine that told them what to think.

Dorset's obsession (and every community has one) with the past and the land was reflected in a recent court case, a sort of triumph of the old agrarian, family-centered values. Junior Nichols, the last functioning farmer in Dorset, informally inherited his two hundred and seventy-five acres twenty years ago from his mother who picked him over several siblings as the one best suited to running the failing family farm. "You can keep it if you promise to take care of me in my old age," she told him. None of the other children objected—the farm was losing money anyway—and they had other lives and interests and were glad to get out of paying the taxes. For twenty years Junior and his wife ran the farm and turned it into a successful enterprise, and took care of his old mother besides, only taking, it is said, a single one-week vacation the entire time.

In the meantime the value of the land increased to what it is now, three thousand to ten thousand dollars an acre. When the old mother died a few years ago, the other children, seeing that the old farm was now worth something, sued Junior for part of the land. The court awarded the farm to Junior, which was softened somewhat when Junior, having no children of his own, promised to leave the land, on his death, to his nieces and nephews. But this didn't satisfy his brothers and sisters, who are now appealing the case.

The news of a large piece of land escaping subdivision gives the same satisfaction as the story of the developer who threatened to put condominiums on our mountainside where the cows used to roam. "They won't even be visible from your house," he told my mother. They would be tastefully hidden in shrubbery. But he didn't count on Dorset's steeliness—an impractical songwriter, he thought this was the place to make a fast buck. "I wouldn't loan him a nickel," said Carleton Howe, who was on the board of the bank where this hapless young man attempted to get financing. He still owns the mountainside, but from our terrace it remains as pure as ever, ungouged by an approach road or other signs of human habitation.

But these little tales of resistance are scarce. Like it or not the future is here. Surveyors' ribbons fleck the forests (which are growing back rapidly, another effect of the new economy; after two hundred years the clearing of the land has stopped), developers are always on the horizon, and the Field Club has been taken over by people in little white skirts. It can't be all bad—after all some of the transplants have been there for a long time now; they must have acculturated. For every loss, something new is formed. What's good about the change, and is there any way to come to Dorset and live there happily without it taking twenty years to be accepted?

There is, and Jay Hathaway, the young proprietor of Peltier's store, has done it.

Up to about five years ago there were two stores in town —four if you counted Williams's, that fragment of the nineteenth century which sells harnesses and ten-year-old cans of beans, and a dreary place opposite the quarry called the Quarry Shop. The two main stores were Peltier's grocery store on the village green, and Russell Parks's store on Route 30, where all those old characters hung around saying "Ay-uh." Parks's was where you went to get the New York *Times* every day, especially Sunday, and you could also get breakfast there or pick up magazines or maple syrup or gum or aspirin, or Russell's snowscapes which hung on the wall, and there was a gas pump outside. Katie Parks, German by origin, was always friendly, but Russell, a Vermonter to the bone, wasn't exactly given to effusion—it took around ten years of buying papers before I could detect the faintest recognition in his eyes, and then I wasn't sure if I was imagining it or not. (But never mind, that's what gives Dorset its integrity.) Five years ago Russell died of a stroke, and Katie closed the store down. It was the end of a crucial landmark—the place where, according to Bill Gilbert, the "Dorset consciousness was most clearly expressed."

At the other store, Perry Peltier was getting so old that it took him around twenty minutes to shuffle to the back, lift the cover by a pulley from the ceiling, and cut you off a piece of the local cheese—and he wouldn't let anybody else do it, either. The store functioned all right—possibly because it was the only grocery store in town—but Perry was ready for retirement. A new proprietor was needed, and Jay Hathaway, the young manager of the short-lived Quarry Shop, was suggested for the job. Jay, a bright young underachiever from Connecticut, and his wife Terry got their foot in the door and their personae in the public eye when Katie Parks gave Jay a treasure—the master list of Dorset newspaper subscribers. "They had to come to us on Sunday," Jay says. "Nothing else was open."

The suggestion to buy Peltier's was rather like being tapped for Skull & Bones. After some persuasion Perry agreed to sell. Oddly enough Jay and Terry seemed to be able to afford the twenty thousand dollars down payment. "We'd saved some money, how I didn't know. All of a sudden we had twenty thousand dollars, if we liquidated everything—shoes, socks, everything." But something went wrong. There had been an accounting error—they owed the feds ten thousand dollars. "They told us this just before Christmas and we were moving on the thirtieth to our new home. Now we were fourteen thousand dollars short to buy Peltier's." Jay went to Ed Le Fevre, prominent citizen and owner of an all-marble house on the West Road, and told him he was in trouble. A committee was formed and fourteen backers found, each contributing a thousand dollars so Jay could buy Peltier's. "It's fantastic, the kindness," Jay said, "fifteen years to pay it all back and almost all of these people will be gone by then. They had faith in us. It's pretty wonderful—even my best friends wouldn't come up with that kind of money. Every January we pay them their interest and send them a card about how things are going. We have a deep commitment to them. It could only happen in Dorset."

Peltier's has changed—but subtly, carefully, almost invisibly—which is the only way change is tolerated here. Perry hadn't changed anything in thirty years so Jay moved cautiously. "He had an old Coke case in the front of the store and I moved it out, people hated me for it. Then I put a new walk-in freezer in the back framed in the same dirty grungy wood as the rest of the store. It fitted right in." It was true, I'd never even noticed it and probably wouldn't have liked it if I had. "There will be subtle contemporary merchandising programs, but I'm not going to put down tile floors or fancy things. Why should I? Peltier's is the most exciting thing in the world. How could anything be more exciting than owning Peltier's? It's an institution, the only store in Dorset except Williams's. It's the best store in the state. We're sophisticated. We're expensive, too. What do you think the highest price in the store is?" Steak at $7.99 a pound? "No—crystallized violet petals for $28 a pound. And we have candied ginger and rock candy now." And croissants and egg rolls and Dorset, Vermont T-shirts, and a wine and cheese annex, and hot chili sold by the cup, and Boston and New York newspapers, for Peltier's is now open on Sundays. But basically it's the same dirty, grungy old place it always was.

What really lights up the old place is the Hathaways' enthusiasm. Jay cares—every carton of milk and bottle of Clorox is part of his identity. It drives him crazy when somebody asks if something is fresh. "There are some people who test you on things, it's as though you're the enemy for some reason. Most stores are sloppy and not very well run, but Peltier's is *damn* well run and it's very clean. I don't like it treated like another store, it's not another store. Number one it's a business. Are you going to test the president of IBM, 'Now look, there's a scratch on that machine'? Then don't do it to me. As a customer I'll give you every courtesy but start kicking and pushing me and I'm not going to do it anymore. There's one person a month that does it, it hurts for a week. I'm very sensitive, if somebody doesn't like me it bothers me."

Jay and Terry don't see, or are unbothered by, or don't choose to mention the natives-versus-transplant struggle; though the cries of elderly natives are getting fainter as some new "consciousness" begins to emerge, some third Dorset still undefined but certainly there. Jay doesn't see the social distinctions that so bother some of the older residents; he finds it a refreshing contrast to the stratifications of suburban Litchfield, Connecticut, where he grew up. "Here we all seem to be in the same basket, you're no better than me, I'm no better than you. It's kind of a family area, the butcher, the farmer, everybody's the same, especially the younger ones who are moving here to establish their families. You can come up here and be a grocer and nobody thinks it's strange. A lot of us came up here saying, 'Who cares what we're supposed to be? We can be what we want here.'" Wait—what young people? "They're starting to come—now I order Pampers," though the nearest pediatrician is forty-five minutes away in Rutland. (The town clerk told me there was a small but definite influx of divorced women with children, fifteen or twenty of them, mostly in East Dorset.)

Jay is unconcerned with Vermontization. When he was told recently that in a few years he'd be a real Vermonter, he said, "I don't care what I'll be. I'm here doing a job, living the way I want to live. I'm not struggling to be a Vermonter! Who cares—I like what I'm doing and I'm happy with my life." The Hathaways have taken and passed the cleaning-lady test. Terry employs one (the Hathaways have three small children), but when the cleaning lady comes into Peltier's, she is Terry's customer and Terry serves her.

During that hard summer of 1962, how badly I wanted my mother to speak honestly to me, and how difficult it was for her to do so. Marriage had clamped her jaw, buried the raw things in her head under a layer of obedience.

That year I had, like many of the newly divorced, an affair with an unsuitable person. Bill, as I'll call him, had—to put it as gently as I can—a good many problems. He drank too much. He was subject to great mood swings. He had a wife and several children. He was a minister, and even that docile-sounding fact was fraught with difficulty because he was considering dropping the Cloth. He was given to long, tormented diatribes about God, sex, good and evil, booze, and the Way, which could go on half the night. I think in retrospect he was crazy, but I was going through one of those tiresome periods, common also to teenagers, when I thought craziness was interesting. I was also very unhappy, very lonely, under a lot of stress, and in the first passionate stages of psychoanalysis, when each session brought more mind-splitting revelations about how badly my parents had treated me and how completely they had rejected me.

Bill and I fed on each other's madness like the two lost souls we were. He would phone at 3 A.M. (drunk) to tell me what Jesus really thought about sexual intercourse. In bars he would explain the nature of evil to the waiter. My two small daughters loved him, mainly because children (whom he considered holy vessels) drove him to manic glee and he would spend an hour playing frenzied games with them, tossing them into the air and catching them, crawling around on the floor and telling them ridiculous jokes, while I tried to stay awake —for during that period I kept trying to shut out life's difficulties by falling asleep, anywhere at any time. Then we would go forth and after a martini or two I was able to debate morality and madness, lust and the afterlife.

After some weeks of this murky existence it occurred to me to take Bill and the children to Dorset for a few days. With the enthusiasm of the utterly confused, I really thought this was a good idea. My mother and Rog could not fail to like Bill, who had a certain pungent charm. They of all people could hardly object to his drinking. We would sit by the fire and debate religion, which Rog would enjoy, and my mother would make her Viennese plum cake. So I arranged it all and phoned her. It sounded all right with her, she said, she'd just check with Rog. At that point, I was beyond even seeing the possiblity that this might be a simple bit of consideration between husband and wife. Rage clawed at my breast, unspoken words coursed through me like fire. Probably it was progress that I knew I was angry, even if I couldn't shout: Ask Rog?

Isn't it your house? Do you ask his permission to breathe? *What are you, anyway?* A couple of days later she called to say that Rog objected, Bill couldn't come. I sat there staring into the phone, feeling sweat break out from head to foot.

"Why not?"

"Because he's a married man with children."

"So what?" I was feeling very strange—dizzy and almost light-headed.

"Well, Rog doesn't want that sort of thing going on in this house."

Let me draw back a bit and look at what I was at that time. I was twenty-nine, thin and tense, with long straight hair down my back. I smoked too much. I was trying to master painfully ill-fitting contact lenses, so I had a perpetual squint. As the past lunged into view and my present life joggled around and I tried to fit its disparate pieces together—my children (whom I loved with an intensity overconnected to my childhood), my stopped work, the crazed Bill (who was, at the time, important), and the necessity of paying the bills—I was in rougher waters than I had ever been in my rather protected life. That first cry of adulthood—that nothing was working out the way it was supposed to—went through me like earthquakes. I was slowly understanding that there was really no help. With marriage I had lost the right to make claims of my parents. Divorce was indeed my problem.

I was, besides, Freud's archetypal female hysteric, the woman whose right hand was paralyzed from repressed fantasies of masturbation, whose foot ached from an unconscious desire to kick her mother in the ass. My body converted stress into a host of physical symptoms. I had aches and pains, tingles and twinges, numbness, and strange feelings. My head felt as though it was blowing up, my nose felt as though it was sinking inward to my brain, my stomach curdled, and my chest felt as though there was a large hole through it from front to back through which a cold wind blew. My shoulders melted and my legs floated around, my feet grew and my hands shrunk. All this took a lot out of me while I picked away at—or tried to avoid picking at—whatever had caused it in the beginning. I suppose I was as close to crazy as I had ever been or ever would be. And I wanted to go home to Mom, and I wasn't invited.

I slammed down the phone and went off to tell Bill, who was at that time staying in a seedy hotel near Grand Central. Going up in the death-green elevator, I had never felt so sordid, so full of rank self-hatred, besides numb of limb and nagged by an idea that my insides were starting to ferment. Bill, in shirt sleeves with bags under his eyes, opened the door to let me in the room.

"Half a mo, doll," said he. "I'm stuck on the phone."

He went back to talk to his wife, a woman seemingly saintlike in her ability to forgive, and to explain to her the exact moment of the birth of the human soul. Sitting there on the side of the bed, he made faces at me of the most excruciating boredom.

"When it *quickens*, Pam," he said. "Not before. Before that it's a fucking *protoplasm*," giving a mock yawn in my direction.

All of a sudden, before I knew what was happening, the room spun around once, very quickly, and I passed out.

I know this now, but only knew then that seeing Bill sitting on the bed was the last clear memory of that strange day —a series of patchy images fading in and out like an old movie—that ended in the hospital. I was on the bed, I was in a taxi, I was in the office of Dr. S., my analyst; Bill's face, ghastly pale, floated in and out of my field of vision. Finally, that night, I was alone in a large ward, the only available bed, in between a young Spanish-speaking girl who was in for an abortion and a body so motionless I was sure it must be dead—as indeed it was, a day or so later, when it was quietly removed.

I watched all this as though underwater, more tranquil than I had been in years. I would have been happy to just lie there all day, smiling at the ceiling, except for my guilt-ridden visitors; Len, who told me none of this would have happened if I hadn't left him; Dr. S., who said he wouldn't charge for the visit; Bill, who said God knows what; and finally my mother, who had come to New York and was staying at my apartment with the children until I recovered from what was really a collapse of function, a sharp signal from my body that I had pushed myself too far.

My mother came in wearing one of her Dorset cotton dresses, looking very serious. She sat in the chair, her back ramrod-straight, her hands folded in her lap. "I'm afraid I have something to do with this." With what? "Your being here. I've talked to Dr. S." Well—could be. Maybe. Through the rosy haze certain familiar little jabs were beginning to return. I asked about the children, and she looked uncomfortable.

"I suppose Rog didn't want you to leave Dorset."

"Well, I told him it wouldn't be for long. Do you think you'll be out in a day or so?"

"How should I know?" I asked. "Go back to Rog. What the hell do I care?"

"But what will I do with the girls?"

"Take them out and put a couple of plastic bags over their heads."

She was, forever, beyond me. Mercifully she left, and I went back to the slow task of recovery, like tracing a path through a deep woods. What do I want from her, I wondered, and if she can't give it, why do I keep trying? Back in my half-furnished apartment, fighting for survival, I would think of Dorset—the meadow of tangled silky grass and wild flowers, the white wooden fence, the chill shadow of the dark blue mountain as the sun dropped behind it; the firelight on the brass fender, voices and clatter from the kitchen, the deep velvety night; another lost home.

LARCHMONT

Glass Walls

We went to the suburbs, as many do, because a great many things suddenly became impossible.

It happened suddenly, just when everything was supposed to be fine (for I had started again, with another husband, and another child). We lived in an apartment high in a white brick building on Seventy-first Street, with a very long, narrow terrace abloom with roses and petunias. There were three children and three bedrooms. The school was all right, our lives were all right. But the city, it appeared, was not. There was a burglar who entered apartments by climbing, like a fly, up building walls and onto people's terraces. Chain locks began appearing on the stores along Third. You rang, they peered at you, then opened the chain. Why? A rash of robberies. It was a high-crime period. Anxiety crept into our lives like the first tiny trickle of sand preceding an avalanche, and I suppose we thought we could escape it.

I think back on the person I was then with a certain

bemusement. I went to the hairdresser every week. Sometimes I had manicures. I wore Pucci dresses. We gave rather ridiculous parties, chartering a bus to drive people back and forth between two apartments. I spent more time cultivating the terrace garden than I did with my children. I worked, but in strange ways, ways that would now be unacceptable. Jack and I sat on the terrace, drinking white wine under the willow, while a young Columbia student typed up the manuscript of my new novel, occasionally asking me, through the window, to translate some illegibility. We had a nurse for the baby.

Of course we did have a lot of kids for our premises. My daughters Marion and Paula lived in a very small room and the new baby slept in the study. Another pregnancy threw our fragile arrangements off. We equivocated—our marital custom, our distinctive style of operating. At the time we thought it was fun, playing with alternatives. It was like the party with the bus going back and forth. Should we go or stay? If we left, where should we go? New Jersey or Westchester? Westchester or Long Island?

Most people, asked why they chose a certain suburb, reply, "We moved for the schools." They mean more than that—they dreamed of shady streets, kids walking to the neighborhood school, fathers going to work, mothers in the kitchen. An unfragmented community. Jack and I, with our urban neuroses, were no more immune to this spell than anyone else. I didn't understand until we lived in Larchmont what *moving for the schools* really meant.

A private school child, I could hardly believe that there were good schools that didn't cost staggering amounts of money. That free education is taken for granted by most people in our democracy had not occurred to me. In my experience you got what you paid for. Having long thought of schools as commodities—you looked them over and chose one—it took me a while to understand that a public school *is* its community, a metaphor of its locale and a reflection of its values. If I heard, as I did, that Scarsdale and Larchmont and Chappaqua had the best schools, it meant that the adults in these places had strong educational values and the money to implement them. If Yonkers and Eastchester did not, there were ways in which those communities were found wanting. When we learned that friends in Teaneck and Englewood sent their kids to private schools, we eliminated New Jersey. Bronxville was out because it had a tradition of anti-Semitism. (Long Island was out because of the traffic.)

I would no more have moved into a town where there was busing than thrown my kids into the river, and I didn't care who was being bused where. Not my kids, not my community. Mine would be whole, a place of integrity. If it happened to be lily-white, so be it. If it was half black, that would have been all right too as long as not a single one of those black kids was angry, desperate, or culturally deprived, or disturbed my life in any way. Wasn't life tough enough?

But what about reality? we wondered as we drove up and down the Bronx River Parkway, the New England Thruway, the Cross Westchester Expressway. The suburbs were an anachronism, a bee preserved in amber. The Larchmont Yacht Club didn't admit Jews, and Jack said he would never join it. I didn't believe it was true, it was impossible in 1967. The ACLU would have gotten them. The Anti-Defamation League would have gotten them. They would have lost their license. Ah, but it never would be admitted, said Jack. Other reasons would be given for rejecting the application of a Jewish family. Since nobody had ever rejected me on such grounds, said he, I didn't really know (Jack had an Italian name, and had once beaten up somebody who called him a Wop). I saw everything through rose-colored glasses. I was just like my mother. How far-reaching were the implications of *moving for the schools!* Our very characters were on trial, and I had thought we were just buying a house. None of this came up in the city, which was probably where we belonged anyway.

Social issues aside, there were few people less fitted for suburban life than we were. For one thing, neither of us was the least handy. Jack could hang pictures, but only if I stood by with tools, tape measure, and advice. He could prune roses, and he said he could make veal scallopini, though he never did. He could make very good martinis, with the tiniest drop of Pernod, and he was good at placing furniture in a room. But that was about all. Like me, he was used to calling the super. I knew how to cook, and could operate certain household appliances. I could paint furniture, and had learned how to take care of babies. After that I was as helpless as he was.

It became obvious, during our travels with real estate ladies, that we lacked a vast sea of lore about houses, and were too embarrassed about our ignorance to ask. Neither of us knew oil from steam from natural gas, nor were we sure that hot water actually came from a hot water heater (and if it did, how did more hot water replace it?). And what was a storm window? At first I had an idea that *some* of your house's windows were storm windows, but certainly not—probably not—all; and that somehow it was all designed so that storms only blew at the storm windows, which functioned rather like lightning rods, while the more fragile ones were in protected places. What was an outlet, what had we to do with gutters? Jack thought, but wasn't sure, that he knew what crabgrass was; I had an idea that termites crossed your lawn in a line, like driver ants, and could chew your foundation to dust overnight. We didn't understand mortgage rates (for we also knew pitifully little about money in general, and looked upon the ebb and flow of our checking account as determined by acts of God) and I wondered why the word mortgage incorporated the word for death.

I was slowly beginning to understand—at thirty-five, for the first time in my life—the nature of ownership. I had lived in houses before, and so had Jack, here and there, on and off. But they were always other people's houses. In Dhahran, if something broke, you picked up the phone and called Maintenance, and three depressed Saudis would arrive and fix, more or less, whatever was wrong. 204, the brownstone, was my mother's problem, and she never worried much about it. But this was our dough, our guts. It had to be maintained or it would lose its value. It was our investment in the future, our stake in the American dream.

It appeared, in fact, that everything you owned had to somehow be taken care of. Cares did not cease with the signing of a check. Everything, from a pair of blue jeans to a furnace, from the lilacs in the dooryard to a box of frozen string beans, from a car to a child, demanded attention to keep it working. The more things you owned, the more your life would be measured out not only in cleaning and repairing, but in an ever-increasing demand for attention to trivia. My precious, educated brain would slowly—already had, in fact—become a storehouse for tedious and boring information. I far preferred vacuuming the rug to reading those dreadful, ill-expressed directions which purported to—but which really didn't—tell me what was inside the fucking machine and why it didn't work. There were those who had pride in their shiny Hoovers or KitchenAids, whose eyes lit up over the joys of dismantling, searching, and solving. I blessed them and only wished one of them lived in my house.

A lot has been written in the last twenty years about the essentially frustrating nature of women's work, the work that doesn't stay done. Far more painful to me was the anticipation-of-disaster mentality that settled on our heads like a storm cloud. The purpose of ownership lore was to stave off many horrors—half of which I had never heard of—that lay in wait. If you let garbage go down the drain it would stop up and you had to either fix it yourself (which you didn't know how to do) or get a plumber who wouldn't come till Thursday and would cost a fortune. In the meantime the sink would be unusable, dishes would pile up, roaches would come, etc. If you didn't *immediately* remove the hollandaise from your Pucci it would remain forever and you might as well throw it out. If you didn't get a child's temperature down he might get brain damage. If you didn't have the car checked it would die in the middle of the parkway. If you didn't have the stonework around the garage fixed *now* it would cave in and the only stonemason in the area was seventy-five and frantically busy, and when he dropped dead nobody else could do it. If you didn't spray the trees . . . have the pipes fixed . . . close the freezer door . . . clean the flues . . . have the bathroom tiles fixed . . . make your husband have an annual physical . . . watch the roast and sew the seam, disaster threatened. There was one rule: everything had to be done *now* and preferably ten minutes ago. Planning was everything, life was a jungle of threats which could only be avoided by interminably adding to your mental library of tiresome minutiae. That was what mortgage meant: my brain would be mortgaged, turned over, *killed*, for the doubtful satisfactions of ownership. When the day came that I got it back—if I ever did—would it work anymore?

The closer we got to house-buying, the more frightened we got. We thought it was something we were supposed to do. It would fix everything. It would make us a family, which, we deeply felt, we were not. We lacked common blood, even though, with our Italian name and apparent fecundity, we appeared to be Larchmont naturals. A house seemed to have magic properties. But sometimes, secretly, I dreamed of some cool stone cave in the side of a hill, where we all wore sheets, or nothing, slept on the ground, bathed in a stream, and ate from a common bowl. But how bored we would get, how naked would be our differences! Ownership was a distraction, a way to deflect energy from those primitive forces that moved us, that we pretended were not there.

It was easier to talk about property taxes than about love or fear; it was easier to rage at the plumber than at each other. Ownership itself was a lightning rod—perhaps that was its purpose. It must have one, other than the rather theoretical satisfaction of knowing you owned the lawn you were walking on. (If you didn't feed it, seed it, kill its fungi, and balance its pH, it would die—and what more terrible *mort* than a brown lawn?)

As we trudged through the houses of Westchester, we covered our fears by romantic homeowner fantasies, fueled by the real estate ladies. Life would be a perpetual dinner party. "You can put your lovely china in that corner cupboard. Look at the dining room, perfect for entertaining. Of course, a powder room is essential. See the wonderful double driveway—lots of room for extra cars." We filled each house with ghostly guests, waltzing through the night. They laughed and talked, parked their cars, hung up their coats, ate from the lovely china. Jack was the genial lord of the manor, I was the charming hostess. Fires crackled. The children were asleep or briefly present in matching bathrobes, while a shadowy nanny lurked behind.

The search came down to two houses, between which we seesawed back and forth.

The house we liked was in Hastings-on-Hudson, but the town we wanted was Larchmont. (We could not, it seemed, have everything we wanted.) At the time our differences were vaguer, more ill-defined. Jack was—sort of—for Hastings, I was sort of for Larchmont. The available house, an old Victorian, made me nervous, but the Larchmont schools were better. In fact neither place was right, but I was not—as the saying goes—getting any less pregnant, and our lease in New York was running out. Since, as always, we equivocated instead of planning, we were faced with crisis action. On a gray, rainy day early in 1968, we bought the house in Larchmont.

I remember the scene with pain. We had come that day for one more look. We sat in the small living room, drearily furnished, with the owner, a retired admiral, and the real estate agent. Rain trailed down the (storm?) windows, the room was damp and chilly. The house was full of squeaks and murmurs—not the ghosts of waltzing couples, but of a family of six and their twenty-five years of sour diapers, pot roasts, and rosaries. The children were grown and the parents anxious to sell, having already bought their retirement home in Connecticut. The admiral looked cross, his wife, when I met her, was thin and exhausted-looking. The place looked rundown, she no longer had the strength to care. That gray depressed face had clutched my heart like a cold hand. The past and the future lapped over each other.

The real estate agent had brought a binder form. This was going to be it—they were tired of our incessant, indecisive visits. The admiral wanted to get it over with. We were like deer caught in a headlight, paralyzed. I kept thinking obsessively of the other house, the one in Hastings. It was new, bright and clean, designed for easy family living. (This was a rabbit warren of thirteen rooms, built seventy years before.) It was a split-level, with a family room in the basement. (This had three floors and two flights of stairs.) It was cheaper, it had a lower mortgage. I could have walked into that well-equipped kitchen and cooked dinner. *This* kitchen almost called for roller skates, and it lacked appliances. BUT: this old place had seven bedrooms, and the Larchmont schools.

We were moving—whether we knew it or not—for the kids.

I watched, hypnotized, as Jack signed the binder and pulled out his checkbook. I had not forgotten that he had gracefully given in on this house, giving up fantasies of rooftop aeries and flowering decks in Hastings, because he thought I wanted this (if I did). He had told me more than once that it was important to him to live in surroundings that were, if not beautiful, at least bright and attractive. (In Hastings light poured in through the picture window, outside was a wood and a tiny stream.) Now, in the gloom, he wrote out a check. He was doing it for me. I was the one, after all, who wanted the schools—*his* kids were still babies, or unborn. A debt, another *mort*. Now I owed him something. No wonder we feared decisions.

As we left I looked at the admiral's gray-faced wife. She was sitting on a rocker on the porch, a rocker that, as it turned out, came with the house. (Though the house was in her name, he did the negotiating.) Would I, in time, rock on the porch? Outside it looked better. The sky was clearing, and there were banks of azaleas by the house, of fiery pink and purple. (I had been told by one real estate lady that sales rose remarkably during azalea time.) The apple tree leaned charmingly if precipitously—shortly we would pay a shocking fifty dollars to have it wired up, our first expenditure. In the bed by the side of the house were irises and peonies. The trees on Prospect Avenue, our new street, were tall and shady. They met at the top, forming a cathedral ceiling. Jack's car was parked underneath, at the curb.

"Congratulations," called the admiral's wife, as we drove away.

Larchmont, the ultimate suburb. I kept trying to recall what it symbolized, from many old jokes. Dullness. Squareness. Resistance to change. It is a punch-line name—". . . and so did my aunt from Larchmont." Scarsdale is slightly different, in fact and myth. It is richer, pushier, more competitive. Aunts don't go there, big shots do. They have the biggest and the best in Scarsdale, the shiniest, the greenest and best-trimmed. Larchmont, as one woman said, is a little frumpy, like that dowdy aunt. A little down-at-the-heels, definitely old-fashioned. In fact that was why she liked it. (Jack hated that story, and said he wished we'd moved to Scarsdale.)

Larchmont Village lies twenty miles northeast of Manhattan, just past New Rochelle, just before Mamaroneck, on the Boston Post Road. Our part of town—called, elegantly, the Manor—lies between the Boston Post Road and Long Island Sound. The Manor is bisected by Prospect Avenue, which starts at the imposing Manor House and ends at the water. Since this is, by most people's lights, going from nowhere to nowhere, there is almost no traffic. It is said that underneath Prospect lies a tunnel that was once part of the Underground Railroad, and that there are hideaways for slaves in the Manor House's basement.

The Manor itself is a peninsula whose five-mile littoral winds and bends into small points and inlets, one of which forms a beach for the village residents. This waterside park is meticulously kept, bright with flowers, and on Sundays, full of strollers with dogs. It is Larchmont's showplace, and justifiably so, for probably there is nothing else like it so close to New York. It sparkles with a slightly unreal, preserved beauty, like some Fragonard picnic spot. The little paths curve carefully, and on one small point is a wooden gazebo looking down over the rockbound Sound. When I first saw it, from the real estate lady's car, I thought surely I would walk there almost every day, sit on the rocks with a book, and possibly sketch the sailboats in the harbor, but I never did. It was partly because I never had time, but also because the place seems so discovered, so predictable. Somebody else has always gotten there first. I am too aware that I am walking on a million dollars' worth of real estate.

In 1661 the parcel of land that is now Larchmont and Mamaroneck was bought by John Richbell from the Siwanoy Indians (for a bunch of kettles, skirts, stockings, hatchets, ammunition, and firearms), who then cannily turned around and sold it to somebody else. The land was eventually determined to be Richbell's. A form of government was set up that remained the same until 1934, when a council form was established.

Larchmont's history is, characteristically, uneventful. In the teens and twenties the village was a resort where families came to summer in the unheated Victorian houses, putting their imported Irish "girls" up on the third floor. Famous people came to Larchmont in those gaslight and horse-and-buggy days—Mary Pickford and Douglas Fairbanks, Anna Pavlova, Flo Ziegfeld, Laurette Taylor, Theodore Roosevelt, and Woodrow Wilson. From 1910 to 1950 the village grew rapidly and the "second village" on Palmer Avenue evolved. By the sixties the mile-square village was "finished"; there was no more room to build. And in the seventies, following a nationwide trend, the population dropped back slightly to the current 6,308—a census count fought (and lost) by the village and county, who feel, like all good Americans, that there is something immoral, even shameful, about lack of growth, beyond the loss of representation in the state legislature. The result of this is a remarkably intact town which stubbornly resists change, clings to old values, and watches its real estate climb in value. There is no house in Larchmont, I'm told, for less than $130,000.

In 1968, $130,000 would have bought a mansion on the water, and a small but perfectly respectable house (the kind real estate people like to call "starter" houses) could be obtained for $40,000. Ours was $62,500—thirteen rooms and a quarter of an acre of land. A one-car garage. A wide, wraparound porch. A leaning apple tree. A stained-glass window. Four fireplaces. A thousand hopes.

It has often been observed that people grow deeply attached to their homes, sometimes to the point of irrationality. They will remain in the face of danger, financial ruin, and extreme inconvenience. Take Mr. Truman, who lived on the side of Mount St. Helens, the volcano. He refused to leave his home when warned, and perished in fire and lava. Or old Helen Berkowitz of City Island, slain in her home because she refused, against all good advice, to leave the declining neighborhood where she had lived for thirty years. Look at Alan Alda, Hollywood's darling, who insists on living at home in New Jersey, or H. L. Mencken, who lived in the same house in Baltimore for fifty years. Beyond the rather well-documented tide of shifting, migratory Americans (who move, according to Vance Packard, fourteen times per lifetime) is a growing group of stubborn souls who sink roots and won't pull them up. Psychosociologists, or whatever they are, characterize these "stay-put Americans" as conservative, skeptical, prudent, and thoughtful, indifferent to the excesses of materialism. ". . . These unmobiles seem more than usually satisfied with life's small things. They derive pleasure in its dailiness, in its small bits of friendly exchange, in welcome sights and familiar faces." (Robert Kanigel in *Human Behavior*, May 1979.)

We would never move from Prospect Avenue, I thought. It was the kind of house and town you stayed in. I was inordinately tired of moving—I had already lived in about seventeen places. In half my life I was already well beyond the national average. It was true that I hadn't thought of them all as homes, the series of apartments in Dhahran, or the string of houses in Beverly Hills when I was very young; a home being, presumably, a place where you meant to stay, or at least wanted to stay, if the situation was out of your control. Moving had usually been the decision of whoever had been in charge—my parents, Aramco, or the person to whom I was married, who was paying the bills.

There had been one apartment in New York that I had chosen myself, and paid for myself, or mostly. It had been, intensely, *mine*—the first place I had lived where I didn't consider someone else's opinion about how it should look, or what room to sleep in, or whether it should have a rug. I'm not sure why, but I never did very much to it. I liked its bareness, its clean-slate look, which to me at the time meant "keeping my options open." Or else it meant I didn't intend to stay, for I wasn't sure if a home counted if it didn't have a man in it, if it was all right for me to be satisfied to live alone with my children—even though the place that really *was* my home, the brownstone, had only my mother and me.

It was people like me, who had moved seventeen times, who really had the obsession; who would go anywhere, pay anything, do anything for an old brown house with fireplaces, and little dormer rooms on the top floor, and a window seat in the front room looking out over the garden. I would peel off the wallpaper with my own hands, if necessary, tote the logs, pull the weeds, even learn to read the directions for the vacuum cleaner. Only let me stay there.

The actual move was a marvel of no planning. It took twenty hours, because we had emptied no closets, sorted nothing, and made no decisions about anything, such as the trees on the terrace, which we ended up bringing to Larchmont. Possibly we didn't really want to leave. The movers were visibly stunned—other people, it seemed, at least removed the ashtrays from the coffee table. One of them spent half an hour wrapping each of Justin's marbles in small bits of newspaper. At three the following morning the move was accomplished. I lay half asleep on the window seat in our new house, watching Jack write out that enormous check. And I had never been so happy.

Happiness comes at those occasional, almost accidental moments when our fantasies match life as it is happening; when, for a moment, the gap between what we want and what we have closes. I woke up that morning on the window seat, stiff and uncomfortable after too little sleep on too large an abdomen. Before me was a sea of boxes and crates. Driving up in front of the house—*our* house—was a station wagon full of painters, for another masterly bit of shortsightedness was bringing the painters the day after we arrived. But it didn't matter, for I felt, at that moment, that I had never wanted to be anywhere as much as I wanted to be where I was.

My God, how we worked, those first days and weeks in the house—all of us, Jack, me, the children, the painters removing seven layers of old wallpaper, and a series of Caribbean nannies. I think—I want to think—that the others were as happy as I was. The days were full of accomplishment; a room put in order, a table delivered, pictures hung. I spent a lot of time deciding where to put things; where would the scissors go, the nails, the silver, the sheets? The place mats and tablecloths, the mop and broom, the brass lamps? Which would be Jack's side of the closet, which mine? Which side of the bed?

The house was full of oddities. A laundry chute (on which Jack put a padlock, for fear that Justin, then two, might fall in). Ashpits . . . I had never heard of an ashpit. At the bottom of each fireplace on the first floor was a sort of little flue that you pushed, and the ashes dropped down to some nether place, where, eventually, they had to be cleaned out. A larder—a big, cold storage closet off the kitchen with plenty of shelves, where you could keep a half-eaten turkey carcass, for instance, or a big pot of soup, or bread, or all those large things that didn't fit into the frig (a relic that dated back to about 1945). A butler's pantry. I hadn't seen one of those since my palmy youth in Hollywood—the little room off the kitchen where Harold or Essex arranged flowers or rolled butterballs with a pair of paddles (an activity I considered normal). Ours was between the kitchen and the dining room, and was really more of a bar. (We were always going to make a pass-through, so Jack could stand behind the bar and make drinks, but never did.) It probably dated from the renovation of the kitchen which I guessed dated from the early fifties, and it had a small stainless-steel sink, with a very high, curved faucet, to accommodate flower vases. Between the back door and the kitchen was a tiny area called a mud room—a place to leave your snowy, muddy boots before going on inside the house.

It was August and stifling hot, but it didn't matter. At night we picnicked wherever we could, on whatever could be scraped up, and nobody complained. We were on a grand adventure. We marveled over our house and its wonders, the genius of ashpits and mud rooms, the cleverness of a laundry chute. Imagine the mind that could think up a larder.

(A woman I know, also a Manhattan child, went to visit her new in-laws in their old farmhouse in Michigan. She described it to me one evening after she and her husband came back. "There are these beautiful things on the floor," she said, "antique wrought-iron grilles. You can look right through them—imagine looking through the floor! And sometimes this lovely warm wind rushes through them, maybe from outside somehow. I'd stand on them and feel the warm air rushing up my legs—like a subway grating but inside." Her husband listened to this, his face a study. "*Registers,*" he said. "She's talking about *registers.*")

We had no registers, but we had old-fashioned radiators that knocked in the morning when the heat was coming up, just as we'd had at 204.

We were, in fact, so enchanted with life's small things that we remained mercifully blind, at first, to all the inconveniences, and the dawning realization that we were living in a dream world was slow to come. Jack's and my concept of the good life included servants—a nanny, of course, for Justin and the new baby, someone to clean, and possibly a cook. Naturally we needed a gardener, and Jack would have liked a "man"—not exactly a butler, but somebody who turned up a few times a week to repair things, clean the basement, mix drinks for parties, and flick a chamois over his Datsun 240 Z. Then, when the boys were older, a sort of wonderful house manager, a warmhearted Mrs. Danvers or a more diversified Mary Poppins who kept everything under control—possibly a French-speaking one who would teach the children a second language.

It's tempting, as an ex-wife, to blame Jack for his unreality, his tenacious refusal to deal with things as they were. But the truth is that one of the things that had attracted me to him in the beginning was his style—his elegant helplessness, his romance, his touch of Gatsby. He was meant to lead a very grand life, and his unbearable disappointment was that this turned out not to be possible. He grew up on Gramercy Park and spent his summers going back and forth to Europe in outside cabins on ocean liners. When he first went to Yale, he lived in a suite of rooms cleaned daily by a chambermaid, and ate in a palatial dining room, set with fine silver and linen and served by waiters. But war and family disruption changed everything. Back at Yale after his stint in the service, tin trays replaced the Spode and the fine old blue blood was muddied by GI Bill students. In his own life, the money disappeared, which was harder on him than it would have been on somebody who grew up polishing his own shoes. To his credit he did what he had to do, and became a professional success. But his head was full of a luxurious life, of long-gone times, and when he married he tried to re-create them—and I, with my half-repressed yearnings for my Hollywood childhood with its butterballs and finger bowls, gardeners and Cadillacs, joined him in a fantasy world that I knew, in my bones, was impossible.

There was a certain irony in our choice of the Prospect house, which was built in the days when every middle-class family had a couple of Irish girls stashed away up in those dormer rooms (where my daughters now lived), who came down the back stairs on chill mornings and put on the porridge. In the beginning the only appliance was an ancient washing machine in the basement. There was no dryer, no dishwasher, no freezer, and only that decrepit refrigerator with holes in the front, left by the admiral and his wife at the last minute, in case we wanted an extra one for cans of soda. But there was not to be a first one. Not long after we moved in, we found ourselves broke; the new dream kitchen was not to be, nor was the little hallway closet ever to become a darling dark bar with funny posters on the wall. We couldn't afford a second car. We could not, for some months, even afford carpeting; and every shout and footfall rattled and echoed through the entire house and our very bones, until we said, one day, to hell with it—and went to Macy's and bought wall-to-wall carpeting throughout (pale golden beige, guaranteed to show every spot).

Into this rattling, unequipped house, loved only by those who adored ashpits, came a series of unhappy maids and nannies. Three cleaning ladies left after one look around, because, they said, the place was simply too big. Sheila from Trinidad, whom everybody loved, patiently hung our enormous wash on lines in the basement until the authorities discovered her illegal status and sent her home. Others came and went like summer storms. As Jonathan's birth approached the need for a nanny became acute.

We found one through an agency and I remember well coming home from the hospital, which was in Manhattan, with Jack, the brand-new baby, and a crackling-white nanny wearing a great deal of makeup, smiling in anticipation of being a sleep-in in a gracious Westchester home. She told us, as nannies do, about the other lovely places where she had worked, the generous employers who had showered her with TV sets, many days off, and stocks and bonds, the high standards she was accustomed to keeping, etc. She inquired about the other children and beamed when we told her the size of the house.

Her wide smile lasted until we got inside and dropped off rapidly, never to return. It was before the carpeting, and my daughters' feet crashed up and down the two flights of stairs, along with shouts of joy at the sight of their new brother. I had done my best with the nursery, but its floor was still bare; there were no curtains, and it remained, and always would, a large, barren room. She recoiled at the dismal basement and the tired old washing machine, until I hastily promised a diaper service; and I don't think she approved of me either, for I wandered around the house in an old paint-spattered smock, whatever skirt or pants I could fit into, and no makeup. In the three days she lasted, there were a couple of disasters, I can't remember what, to enforce her quite valid belief that she was not in a well-run home; on the third day she tripped over the kitchen trash can, claimed that she was the victim of a plot, and left.

It's almost too easy to make fun of the people who move into other people's homes to do their domestic work. They are, of necessity, oddballs—full of eccentricities, curious snobbism, and the strange values born of rootlessness and isolation. We had one who closed herself in the nursery with the baby, stuffed the cracks with (clean) diapers, and played Wagner loudly on a transistor radio; and one who refused even the washing machine and endlessly washed, washed, washed baby clothes in the tiny sink in the nursery and hung them all over the room. There was one who insisted on photographing us, producing many orange pictures, who was addicted to grated carrots. There was wonderful Mandy, who told us stories of how she got married on a raft in the middle of the Amazon River, to the tinkle of native bells and the scent of jasmine, with piranhas snapping about; and who, because she was so wonderful, left for another job. We begged her to stay, but Mandy was a star, and stars are booked solid. There was a thin, lovely, angry girl who left after two days because, she said, she was having a breakdown . . . and finally there was Verona.

We plucked her straight off a plane from Barbados when Jonathan was a year or so old, and brought her home. She was small and plump, and dressed rather like Queen Elizabeth—in a neat tailor-made and a hat with a single flower growing straight up out of its middle. We took her into the kitchen, waiting for the gasp, the recoil, or the curled lip we had seen so often, and Verona said nothing. When I offered her a cup of tea, she said, "I don't mind." She said that a lot. "I don't pay no mind," she said. How we needed her serenity! She would rock Jonathan until he was quiet, talk to Justin and calm him down—for our sons were active and nervous, tense as high wires. When she sat down with them, one on each side, they became peaceful—and so, for a moment, did we.

Once the girls were in school and Verona there to watch the boys, plus a cleaning woman who had agreed to stay, I tried to work.

In the study on the second floor, I found it terribly hard to concentrate. Should we have the desk refinished first, or replace the curtains? Should we do neither, and do something about the kitchen? Did those lamps really belong where they were, or would they look better in the front room? I would get up and putter, move things around on the mantel, change a couple of pictures, and sit down again. The room was mostly furnished in things from Jack's old bachelor apartment—his desk, his green rug, his queen-size sleep sofa. The place was alive with questions. Whom had he slept there with? Did he wish he was back there again, all the roads still open? How had that spot gotten on the rug? Who had spilled the glass of wine or dropped the take-out Chinese food?

The house was on a rather small lot, and the windows of the house next door were close enough to look into. *Their* bedroom opposite was much more furnished than ours, more finished-looking. Their kitchen, viewed from ours, was newer and more attractive. The woman (whom I had never met) sat there and drank coffee in the morning, talking on the phone or making lists. She seemed to be more leisured than I—her children, like most of the children in the neighborhood, were in high school. I watched her covertly, afraid she would see me spying on her. We had smiled in our front yards occasionally, but she made no moves toward further acquaintanceship, nor did I.

Prospect Avenue was lovely, shaded by magnificent old trees, and alarmingly quiet. I would watch Verona walking down toward the beach, Jonathan in his carriage and Justin riding on top or walking next to her—three tiny figures moving silently through the flaming, golden arbor of fall. Watching my children leave, I would feel a sense of loss so deep it seemed to have no end, it drenched every part of my consciousness. Why? Why, when I had sent them off so I could work without interruption, did I count the minutes until they returned?

It seemed, sometimes, to be love that had invaded me and prevented me from working, a love for my children, my house, for a life I was trying to make that remained just beyond my grasp. Sometimes it seemed to be sheer frustration, the housewife's haunted mind. The dinner menu, the checkup for the car, the dry cleaning, the fuel bills crowded all else out; the abstractions in which I worked were frail ghosts which flew away in the face of the lists which inhabited my head. The house invaded me, swallowed my energy and attention. How did other women write in their homes? Right down the street Phyllis McGinley, the local scribe, had written Pulitzer Prize poetry; farther on, by the water, Jean Kerr wrote her satire and comedy—hiding, she said, in her car.

Sometimes it seemed to be a terrible loneliness. Such enormous houses, such empty streets. Occasionally a woman would come out of one of the houses, get in her car, and drive off. Sometimes a couple of older kids went by on their bikes. The trees moved in the wind, sent down small golden showers of leaves. (Sweaters, I thought. The kids need sweaters. The girls need shoes.) A car door slammed, another motor. A car crept slowly up the street, past the Manor House, toward the Post Road.

Where in God's name were the people?

Manhattan streets teemed with people, all kinds. The halt, the lame, the chic, the beautiful, the mad. The streets of Dhahran were empty, but that, I thought, was because of the heat. But where were the people of Larchmont? Where did they hide?

Where were the neighborhood children we had thought came with the deed? Where were the other mothers, and why weren't they out walking with their babies, gathering in little groups to talk, or sitting on somebody's lawn? Where were the ball games in the street, the shouts and squeals? Would any small boy come to our front door and say, "Can Justin come out and play?" On weekends, couples in tweeds walked quietly to the street with their dogs.

Did all this even exist, or had I gotten it from Andy Hardy movies?

At the very least, I had expected the sort of back-and-forth we had in Dhahran. If I spoke scornfully of those women who had nothing better to do in the morning than get all dressed up and ring my doorbell, it was because I had no experience with this sort of kindness. Women brought casseroles if you were sick, offered to pick up something at the commissary. We were all very close in a way I took entirely for granted.

But Larchmont was more like New York in the soundproof glass walls that divided us up—the glass wall between me and the woman in the kitchen next door, between the houses and the town, even between the towns themselves—for one of the surprises was that New Rochelle ran indistinguishably into Larchmont, Larchmont ran into Scarsdale, Scarsdale into Mamaroneck in one undifferentiated suburban mass. I had really thought (another funny fantasy) that in between the towns were stretches of country. But there were only tiny signs.

Why was there no central gathering place—some sort of village square where women would dip their buckets in the well and stay to gossip? Some riverbank where we all beat our laundry on the rocks? Why couldn't I hear the tribal cries?

They were probably there, but as I came to discover, they were subtle and complex, for the tribe was subdivided. There were the people who went to the Catholic church, those who went to the Episcopal church down on the square, and others who went to the Temple. There were the pure-blooded Yacht Club and Shore Club people. There were tennis people, sailing people, and beach people. There were people who just knew each other for one reason or another, the least of which, probably, was that they lived in Larchmont. Networks of interest were superimposed over the invisible boundaries of the town just as they were in the city. Simply living in Larchmont—or other Larchmonts—did not make much of a common bond, it seemed. What were the passions, if any, that bound the town together?

After leaving Arabia, Len and I lived for a period in a Columbia apartment on Morningside Heights. Every afternoon a group of mothers and small children gathered in a certain area on Morningside Drive—not down in Morningside Park, which was considered unsafe, but on a certain part of the sidewalk, on a particular string of benches, opposite St. Luke's Hospital. There our children played and we talked, occasionally pausing to fish something out of a baby's mouth or break up a fight. The women were wives of young Columbia professors or interns or residents at the hospital, and we were all poor. Our talk ranged from politics to literature to where to buy baby clothes at discount or what to do with that old pound of hamburger. We consoled Mary when her husband was in the hospital with a coronary and Audrey during her divorce. Our lives were all more or less difficult and we needed each other.

Perhaps Jack and I were too rich for this sort of herding instinct. It might have existed in a poorer area, where couples and children were younger, where struggle was in the air—for on Prospect Avenue struggle, if it existed, was invisible. Somehow we had the wrong amount of money. We were beyond the humbler pleasures of casserole exchange and back-and-forth baby-sitting, of husbands mowing lawns at dusk and wives gossiping over the back fence. Not only could we not afford the accoutrements of the high life, but we couldn't even find the money to put a new roof on our house—even though, when it rained, we all ran around with pots and bowls to put under the leaks. There was something drastically wrong with either our concept of how we wanted to live or else our arithmetic, and probably both; for we had both assumed, without thinking about it twice, that living in the suburbs was going to be a bargain—for why else would anybody move out of town?

If Larchmont cost as much or more than Manhattan, if the streets were hushed and silent and the women hidden in their houses, if the husbands struggled back and forth daily by train or car on crowded parkways, why did anybody live here at all? If there was no village water hole—if you couldn't even tell where the village stopped and the next one started—if you just had your same old friends in the city, who were less and less willing to drive or take the train twenty miles for dinner, if you had to join the anti-Semitic Yacht Club or go to mass on Sunday to be part of a group, what were we doing here, anyway?

There was supposed to be a certain feral satisfaction in living on land that you owned yourself. An occasional Prospect husband could be seen mowing his lawn, and there were two or three spectacular gardens that gave evidence of love lavished and time spent. But for the most part a truckful of gardeners whisked in and out, keeping the yards generally tidy. There was—and this came closer to the bone—something called "equity." If you gave up everything for your house—clothes, vacations, good restaurants, trips to Europe, private schools, the theater, all costly pleasures—you would be compensated, someday, by selling your house at a profit, though you had to immediately buy another one to avoid half your profit disappearing to the IRS.

It had been explained to us often enough (by people speaking slowly in one-syllable words, as though to small children) that rent money was poured down the drain and a house was an investment for the future. You always had a house, and houses never went down in value. Besides, you could deduct this and that from your income tax all along the way—a tricky argument that, for it sounds as though somehow you didn't have to pay for this and that, when in fact you do.

So thousands of dollars of this and that, from paint to fuel to roof repair to gardeners' bills, went, as far as I could see, down the drain exactly as rent money did. And those monthly deductibles, the taxes and the interest, were gone forever. In the slow-dawning reality that began to break through that first year or two, I read an instructive case history in some low-level primer of family finance. Two clones with identical incomes each have, say, twenty thousand dollars in the bank. One buys a house, using his twenty thousand dollars for the down payment; the other rents an apartment and invests his twenty thousand dollars at the going rate. Their tastes and priorities are identical and their living places computer-fitted to their incomes. How do they come out twenty-five years later? Exactly the same, almost to the dollar.

The slow realization that we were in over our heads moved upon us like a shadow. Not that this was anything new

—we had been in over our heads in the city, too, which was one reason we had moved. But we had really believed that we were doing a prudent and sensible thing by buying this house. It was to be our symbol of adulthood, proof that we were at last able to take our responsibilities seriously. But whatever gods we were trying to appease had played a cruel joke on us. Instead of the rent money pouring down the drain, now it was Jack and I who were being drained of our energy and our hope, even the belief that we could better our lives. We suffered from some vast ineptitude, some distortion of vision whose consequences were just beginning to emerge like a message in invisible ink that had been there all the time.

At night, after everyone was in bed, I sometimes sat in the kitchen, that paradigm of our failure. It was a big, square room with a long, pea-green Formica counter down the middle, flanked by a line of stools where the children sat to eat. Periodically one of the stools broke down and whoever was on it would drop out of sight with a small shriek. Later I would repair the stool and in a few weeks or months another one would break. It was an exercise in futility—the whole kitchen should have been redone, but we had run out of money. I would go on repairing stools forever, and they would continue to crack under the weight of steadily growing children until I was old and sere.

The wallpaper had one of those cheery kitchen designs with cute coffeepots and funny little spoons, once red and white, but now the tan of spilled coffee and the orange of old face powder. I had patched up the holes in the refrigerator door with white plastic tape, but the wooden block that kept it from rocking back and forth was forever being kicked out of place.

I burned with the desire for a new kitchen as I had never, I thought, burned for anything in my life. Sitting at the Formica counter with a cup of coffee or a glass of wine, I would imagine that glorious room—the neat, shiny cooking area, the copper cookware hanging from the ceiling. The butcher block counter, the matching glassware, and Italian pottery, which I had already chosen at Bloomingdale's. Over on this side, a big oak table with sturdy peasant chairs that never broke down. Right over there a little Scandinavian stove, brick-red, or blue and white porcelain, to cook a steak or else to just warm our spirits. Here we would sit and eat every night, all seven of us . . . for one of the things that was wrong was that Jack got home too late for the children to wait, and he and I had dinner alone in the baronial dining room. It further divided our family.

I prayed to my kitchen-god, my elf of the cinders. Was it really so much to ask, this simple American dream? I would never want a yacht, or a mink coat, or fabulous jewels. I never even thought about a Porsche or a Ferrari, and hardly ever a swimming pool . . . couldn't I have a kitchen? Hadn't I worked hard, striven for admirable goals? Wasn't a kitchen a good and generous thing to want, proof of my nurturing spirit?

One night as I sat there dreaming through half-closed, self-pitying eyes, trying to decide where to put the wall oven with the rotating spit and hanging bunches of onions overhead, the lights switched on in my neighbor's well-equipped kitchen (not as good as my imaginary one, but a lot better than the one I had) and the husband of the house, to whom I had nodded a few times in the front yard, came in, followed in a moment by the wife. He looked tired and tense, she, in her bathrobe, a little distraught. He opened a cupboard, took out a bottle of vodka, slammed the cupboard door. He was thin, balding, a little paunchy; he was tieless and his button-down shirt was half out of his gray pants. She—as the saying goes—must have been pretty once, but now she was puffy-eyed and her long hair was tied back in a messy ponytail. She seemed to be doing the talking—gesturing, pointing, crossing and recrossing her arms.

A fight! He poured too much vodka into a glass, stalked to the refrigerator (brown double-door Amana) for ice, which came magically out of a little niche in the front. She took cigarettes out of the bathrobe pocket, lit one, handed it to him, and lit one for herself. He took his ungratefully. She went to the cupboard and grabbed a bottle of whiskey . . . (Could they see me? I crunched down to be mostly behind the bush in front of the window.) *She* slammed the cupboard, filled her glass.

They talk, though I can't hear them. She cries. He looks guilty. She starts looking around for what turns out to be a box of Kleenex. Now he talks, slamming the counter occasionally. She blows her nose, gets mad. She is scornful. She laughs—the wrong kind of laugh, for his face contorts. He walks over to her and slaps her in the face.

No, I thought, no. It's not happening. As I watched, the woman staggered back, both hands to her face. When she slowly dropped them, her face was more surprised than anything else. Stunned. She was beyond pain, beyond anger. She was too astonished to cry. He looked like shit, self-hatred in a Brooks Brothers shirt. Anger struggled with repentance (here lay the struggles of Prospect). I could almost see his thoughts in a comic-book cloud over his head. I'm a bastard. I'm a prick. I've lost my mind. As she stared at him as though he had sprouted another head, he dared to meet her eye. He was sorry. His face crumpled. How could he? He hated himself. He begged forgiveness. He reached for her . . . but she was gone, so quickly I wondered if she had ever been there. Grabbing the glass of vodka, he followed, turning out the light as he left.

The bedroom upstairs remained dark.

There is a progression of spirit following a move to a new place that resembles a marriage, the birth of a child, a love affair, or a new job. A romantic honeymoon period is followed by a slump into depression as reality punctures the early fantasies, which is then resolved, hopefully, by a more realistic acceptance of goods and bads and a fresh injection of productive energy.

The house ran fairly well. The girls adjusted to life in a suburban public school, if not seamlessly, satisfactorily. The boys' lives fell into a routine. I managed to do some work—if not my best, at least nothing to be ashamed of. Now I spent a lot of time driving children around in my nine-passenger station wagon, which I had bought with a book advance and felt immensely proud of. I drove to the supermarket. I drove back and forth to the middle school and the high school as part of a car pool. I drove to the shopping center in Eastchester. I drove to the beach and the dry cleaner and the car wash and Macy's. I found that there were other children, and mothers to go with them. If we never gathered at the village well, we phoned each other and met for cups of coffee.

I treasured these fragile connections to the town and even tried to use them to replace my old ties to the city, as though one would weaken the other, and possibly it was true. I avoided going into New York, and began thinking of it as a bad place. Certainly I never drove there. In time I heard myself joining a sort of chorus, which came up at every local gathering, about the woes of the city and how lucky we all were to have escaped. It was filthy, difficult to live in, and downright dangerous. Apartment rents in any decent part of town were astronomical, the public schools lousy, the private schools unaffordable. We collected mugging stories, burglary stories, and ugliness stories—one little boy had asked his mother why the subways all smelled of pee. Central Park was a dust bowl, Broadway was going down the drain, and God knows you couldn't park anywhere . . . why go into town at all? Westchester—like Dhahran—had everything New York did, good restaurants, first-run movies, shops, local theater, with grass, trees, and sports facilities thrown in. Not to mention equity. Not to mention the schools, which were so much more connected to the real world than snotty Trinity or Brearley, those overpriced, overrated bastions of unreality.

The connection between the schools and equity was profound, and explained, in part, one of the primary female obsessions of Larchmont—the continuous intense relationship between mothers and teachers. One of the time-fillers for those mothers who didn't work (fewer than I had thought) was going up to the school and raising hell. There was too much homework. There wasn't enough homework. The math was too new or too old. Johnny couldn't read, or he was so brilliant he was being held back by the slow pace of the morons in the class. His curriculum wasn't creative enough, or it was so creative he didn't know who discovered America. There weren't enough after-school activities or else there were so many the kid didn't have time to eat dinner. The theory was—and I have no reason to doubt its truth—that if you yelled loud enough you usually got what you wanted. You kept pounding on higher and higher desks till you got to the top; you wrote fulminating letters to the paper. For if the schools went down, down went your equity. Everybody knew that schools in New Rochelle and Mount Vernon were no good (b-l-a-c-k). Let's keep Larchmont what it is, okay?

But how did you know what you wanted? I had no experience, as I grew up, with parental involvement in school. At elitist Brearley, where I went for four years, there were girls who were humiliated by perpetually interfering mothers. Mine, fortunately, kept her hands out of a part of my life that I regarded as entirely my business. What did she know? She'd paid her bill and she expected them to educate me.

Questioning this Larchmont freebie would have seemed ungrateful. I had an immense admiration for the work that teachers did. They conducted the activities of twenty-five six- or ten-year-olds like Bernstein conducting his orchestra. How did they do it? I could hardly manage four children. If they were doing anything wrong, how could I blame them, or how could I even tell? For all I knew Justin's kindergarten teacher was conducting a black mass every day between nine and twelve. Would he ever tell me? Never—because how would he know it was not normal? "Nothing," my children said when I asked them what they had done at school, or what they had learned. Or I would hear some curious story about Billy and a box of Milk Duds. But in fact most of my children's teachers seemed to be immensely sensitive and competent people, certainly as good as the private school teachers I had known, and often better.

So we had indeed moved for the kids. Excitement and diversity, those city intangibles, had been sacrificed for those elements better suited to the young. Jack and I had known this on some level but since neither of our families had thought in such terms we didn't really understand it. We had both grown up living where the adults wanted to live. Though in most ways our fathers had little in common, they were both successful men who demanded comfort and convenience in their domestic lives. I couldn't imagine either of them putting up for a moment with the conditions of commuter travel that many Larchmont husbands endured daily—inching through the Bruckner Interchange in an interminable traffic jam, sitting in the Bronx in a sweltering, hellish, stalled Conrail car, where men have been known to bang their heads against the window, refuse to buy tickets, or even try to jump off into the gravel. Those weary breadwinners who arrived home every night gray-faced after such daily exasperation had to be a different kind of man; their families must have a different tilt. Father no longer knew best. Mother no longer automatically agreed with him. Both had discovered in therapy the damage that such strictures had done to them in their own childhoods, both smarted from the wounds of parental insensitivity and misplaced authority. They were willing to put up with a lot (which our parents were not) to do better by their own children.

As I learned where to look, the children appeared.

If they were not on Prospect, they were on the beach, on the village streets, sweeping around corners on ten-speed bikes, or in Flint Park on Sundays, flying kites, tossing Frisbees, picnicking on hamburgers and Diet Pepsi, and in the winter sledding down the hill. They overflowed passing cars, restaurant tables, and supermarket carts; they spilled out of the schools and the streets at certain hours of the day, they swam in the pool and skated at the skating rink, played tennis and football and baseball. They were, in fact, not only Larchmont's primary inhabitants, but its major product ("Our sole industry is our children").

Typically they were pale or red-haired and suntanned, sprinkled with freckles, straight-legged and blue-eyed, with snaggle-toothed smiles in various stages of orthodontia. Of course there was every other kind of kid, with black hair and curly hair and knock-knees and mournful faces, swaybacked and moonfaced and flat-footed kids, kids with assorted noses and ears and some with big black heavy-lashed eyes. There was even an occasional ethnic face, black or Oriental or Indian. I knew, as I had known since kindergarten, which ones led and which ones followed, which ones moved ahead confidently and which ones ached because they felt different, which ones found everything easy and which ones had to struggle for every small success. There were still, as there always had been, the ins and the outs, the ones with tranquil souls and the walking wounded, and somehow, as always, they found each other.

They began to appear around our house and, with the clear vision of children, ask killing questions. Why did we have so little furniture? Did we go to church, temple, mass?

Why did some of us have different last names? That they even asked these questions was a sign of the times—I doubt they are asked anymore—and to Larchmont's imperviousness to change. They were not meant critically, for the curiosity of children is pure.

They were interested to see that though we lacked furniture, we lived in a sea of expensive toys, Jack's way of handling some guilt of his own. The roof leaked, hunks of the ceiling fell into the downstairs toilet, the stools cracked under our weight, but the front room was a child's dream. Dozens of large red cardboard bricks tumbled down the stairs and into the dining room like an avalanche; scattered on the new rug was an infinite number of small plastic pieces that probably went with something, if anybody only knew what. Verona and I were always trying to stem the flow which eddied around us like a river. Every night Jack brought home more. Trucks. Airplanes. Ventriloquist's dummies. Costumes. Tricycles, sleds, pogo sticks, scooters, roller skates. Marbles, GI Joe dolls, games, tents, stuffed animals, guns. Records and coloring books and paintboxes. Our taste was catholic and infinite.

At Christmas the toy buying escalated into a kind of frenzy. Jack stayed up till three in the morning putting toys together. The entire front room was filled with a sea of boxes and parcels, huge stuffed animals and functioning machines. It took hours to open them and afterward the children appeared glutted, their eyes glazed. Nobody knew who had given what to whom, nobody knew what they had gotten. To a certain extent nobody even cared. The orgy over, the participants got up and left.

On holidays we act out our love, in ways that are sometimes graceless—but in Larchmont, always for the kids. At Christmas, not only did garlands wind the banisters and candles glow on the mantels, but a funny Santa decorated the front door. On Halloween not only did pumpkin faces glow in windows, but people turned entire rooms into intricate fun houses for trick-or-treaters, places of horror where water-filled rubber gloves hung from the ceiling, skeletons glowed, and witches (on tape) screamed. Mother, father, and children dressed as ghosts and goblins.

Once I took Justin to a birthday party for a classmate in an apartment in the village. The place was so strange it took me a few minutes to understand what I was seeing. It was alive with animals–birds in cages, iguanas in a glass aquarium, loose kittens, and a large dog. Two entire walls in the child's room were covered from floor to ceiling with Habitrails, alive with gerbils and hamsters, like a giant anthill. Through their loops and chutes and plastic boxes, dozens of rodents scurried around in their monstrous home. The parents showed all this off with great pride. There was very little furniture, and what there was was covered with Mexican throws.

I remembered the apartment of the girl whose mother barricaded her living room with velvet rope. I remembered the silent living rooms of the houses in California, and the "front room" of Nana's Irish family in Chicago, dark and musty and unused, waiting for some important family event that never occurred, while the family sat in the kitchen. I remembered a room where all the furniture was covered with sheets of plastic. How they spoke, all these rooms, but how often they communicated things their owners never intended. They had almost evolved themselves, spelling out their messages as though on a Ouija board. Neither Jack nor I had ever intended to have a front room furnished largely with red cardboard bricks and metal fire engines, but something in us had caused it to happen.

After we had lived in Larchment for about five years, and I was working on a movie script, I went to Nashville for a couple of days with the producer on some business regarding our project—specifically, to make ourselves so irresistible to a certain well-known director that he couldn't refuse to work on our script. Hale, the producer, was an old and dear friend, and as everyone knew, gay—gay in the old-fashioned sense of the word as well as the current one. He was, besides, as rich and richer than producers are supposed to be, and since he happened to get along well with women, was a delightful traveling companion. It was hard to hide the fact that I went off on this little journey with great pleasure, as a break in a life that had become humdrum and difficult.

We arrived back at night, having, we thought, hooked the director, and went directly to Larchmont in Hale's car-plus-driver. I thought, as we drove up in front of the house, that I sensed a dark chill, the smell of *mort;* but nevertheless I asked Hale in for a drink, and he accepted, after a slight pause —probably he sensed it too.

We went up on the porch and I opened the door. Inside the tidal wave of toys was deeper, vaster than I had ever seen it. There was hardly an empty place on the floor, and on every surface were more blocks, tanks, crayons, little T-shirts, and small plastic objects, plus sticky glasses, cups, half-eaten cookies, and all the other impedimenta of children that mothers are always sweeping out of sight. It was as though a great wound had opened, disgorging its contents. On the piano was the encrusted tin of a TV dinner. The red cardboard blocks flowed everywhere, and they seemed to have multiplied—now there were hundreds.

Little cries announced the presence of the children, and Justin came in from the living room, followed by Jack carrying Jonathan. It was hard to explain any of this scene in the horror of the moment, one of the questions being why, at this hour, the children were not in bed; but Jack's face was dark with accusation. I had left him. I had left the children. I had gone off with another man. Without me he was helpless, he couldn't pick up the toys. Hale didn't stay long—stuttering something about the driver, he fled. He had, after all, arranged his life to avoid family confrontations. The only ones in this little tableau who looked pleased were the children, glad to see Mommy. I took them up to bed and undressed them slowly, reading them a long story, while Jack stayed below amid the chaos.

In the morning Verona and I picked up all the toys and put them away.

Very slowly, almost without our realizing it, the house had ceased being a haven and become a trap. Not for the children, who liked living there, and who, in their various ways, carved out lives for themselves in the town; but for Jack and me, who were edging apart. His vast discontent—of far greater scope and depth than I ever suspected—drove me to endless, doomed attempts to make him happy. The more depressed he got, the harder I tried. I thought I could drive away his demons by sweat and determined cheer. I thought if I could keep the house from crumbling into dust, if I could make *it* work, our marriage would work too.

I scraped all the old wallpaper off the kitchen walls and painted them, but he said he didn't really like the color. After he had gone to bed, as I sat crying in the kitchen, my troubled neighbors, whom I had half-forgotten about, appeared in their own kitchen. Their difficulties had escalated, and so had the sound, for it was summer and the windows were slightly open. If they saw me they didn't care, so angry were they.

You don't understand me, he said. You never have. You never will because you don't try. Hah—said she—if anybody understands you, I do! I know everything you hate me knowing. I know your fears and your tiny cruelties. I know that you resent your own son because he's more successful than you. I know you've always tried to buy his love and now it's not working. I know how you feel about me . . .

His voice is thick. You know nothing because you're stupid. You can't understand a man and what makes him tick. If you were a real woman you'd know such things by instinct. You have *problems*, Marilyn. Do you know that? Real, serious problems. You can't keep running away from them.

My God, cries Marilyn, reaching for the gin. I'm the only stability this family has had for years! If I have problems I'm willing to face them. If you're so together why won't you go to the marriage counselor with me? Three appointments I've made and three times you've made excuses at the last minute . . .

He lights a cigarette and puffs furiously. I don't like the guy, that's why. I can tell he's a fraud. You picked him because you heard he was a big women's libber. Lib, ha! Look who's liberated, slugging gin all day!

She smiles. You're threatened, aren't you? Scared shitless. Poor Stu. Why don't you call your mother? She always has wonderful advice. (Marilyn, I whispered, take it easy. You're going to get your neck broken.)

Stu advances on her. Leave my mother out of this, he says, sort of flexing an arm, but ending in a grab at his glass.

But Marilyn goads him on. Going to slap me, Stu? Hit a woman? Terrific. That proves what a big man you are. Go on, do it. I dare you.

She doesn't believe he'll do it, the sap. But he does. As I watch hypnotized, he slaps her in the face. Once. Twice. Enough, Marilyn? he asks. His face is a Halloween mask, a mad fixed grin, holes instead of eyes. How about one more time? And one more time he slaps her. This time it's hard enough to send her staggering. She starts screaming, which makes Stu nervous. He darts a look around just as I duck behind the counter. Can he see the top of my head? I crouch on the floor, my heart pounding. Should I call the police? Abruptly the screaming stops. There is a deathly silence, and when I cautiously lift my head high enough to see, the lights in the kitchen are off and they are gone.

Sometimes, as in all good American homes, our mothers came to visit. They came one at a time, each, in her fashion, casting approval and disapproval, running her finger ever so delicately along our already exposed nerve ends.

Jack's mother swept in, tall, slender, still beautiful, in elegant black suit and rakish hat, bearing an armload of pastry boxes from her favorite bakery near Gramercy Park. Croissants, brioches, doughnuts, Black Forest cake. I say she swept—she partly swept, and partly hovered, an ambiguity only she could master. She stood in the doorway. "Well," she said. "Well. I suppose you didn't think I was really coming." After a while I gave up trying to think up answers to such statements, or even to understand what she meant by them.

With the babies she was marvelous. She sat down with a small grandson on her lap, jangled an armload of silver bracelets, and went through a jargon loved by and only intelligible to someone under three. She crooned, fussed, fed bits of chocolate cake, sang songs, and talked nonsense. She brought expensive gifts, which she could ill afford—handmade Italian puppets from Schwarz, Swedish wooden trucks, an imported paint set. She made the puppets dance and rolled the trucks down the street. She liked babies so much she could forget about us, forget to come to dinner. With older children she was more qualified, though of course in this case the older children of the house did not share her blood. "Well," she would say, as Marion and Paula came in. "I see you cut your hair."

"I didn't," Paula would say. "I just combed it differently."

"Don't contradict me." Then, teasingly, "I know you cut

it. You can't fool me." She approved of one daughter and disapproved of the other—just as, years before, she had so divided her own children, and would later her grandchildren. Divide and conquer, I suppose the theory was. It mystified the children, but then she was, in many ways, mysterious, of a highly refined and elegant complexity that was hard to grasp until you understood that she was, beneath it all, very frightened.

She was ambivalent about me, as I was about her. I would say that with all the forces there were to set us against each other, in spite of them all we liked each other. I liked her for her guts and her orneriness, her determination to go down, if she must go down, fighting. She had had a difficult life, partly because she was so given to being unpleasant.

She would come into the kitchen in the morning as we sat on our rickety stools. "Well," she would say, "well. Jack never ate in the kitchen in his life until he was married." I would choke down the urge to brain her with a frying pan. Better to think of a fast answer.

"No wonder he can't cook." She never granted me permission to call her by her first name, and the only person who had the nerve to do it anyway was my mother, which infuriated her. "So nice to see you, Marguerite," my mother would say cheerfully, while Marguerite froze with anger at such impertinence.

Before her stay was over she managed to become deeply insulted—by me, Jack, the children, or her daughter and her husband, if they happened to be there. She knew she wasn't wanted. She had known it all along. She didn't have to come, she was perfectly fine by herself. In fact it was an enormous effort to come all the way out here. She had almost decided not to come and probably she shouldn't have. Then she would dress in her black suit, her black coat, and her smart black hat and call a cab. What happened next depended on the degree of Jack's guilt. She wanted us all to beg her to stay, to make her feel loved. Sometimes we did. Sometimes we let her go to the train, sometimes Jack drove her home. If she left we all ended up feeling slightly sick, stale, even bereaved. For in some curious way we needed her.

She carped because her son was forced to live in such dreadful circumstances, in this tumbledown old house, after he had been raised in real style. Well, *almost* real style, but *real* style was the way *she* had been raised. The family always had French cooks. Buildings in Boston were named after her uncle. She had been closely chaperoned until she graduated from art school. She had once had auburn hair to her waist, she had won ribbons in horse shows. Things were always done in a certain way. It was hard for her to understand why we did some of the things we did—having Verona sit at the dinner table with us, for instance. It wasn't because Verona was black. It was that she must have been uncomfortable there; she would be happier in the kitchen. I was less concerned about whether she was happy than that she should feed Jonathan in his highchair. With Verona happiness wasn't really an issue. She didn't see it as her inalienable right, as the rest of us did, to our grief. God, the things we argued about. Debate was a way of life in Jack's family. Quibbling was as natural as breathing. It was so utterly different from my own family that I found it stimulating at first, until I found that most of the arguments went in circles. Jack's mother was a difficult and puzzling woman. I swung back and forth about her, but she helped me understand some of Jack's deep mysteries.

My mother, on the other hand, came on a tide of cheer. Rogers died in 1971, after a long illness, and though she tried to appear suitably downcast, she was something of a merry widow. She had a little money, she was enjoying herself. Unlike Marguerite, she was specific about her visits. "I will arrive tomorrow at four," she would say, "and I will leave early Wednesday for Dorset." She was always on the run between

New York and Vermont, stopping here and there on the way to visit friends. She wore one of the Sybil Connelly suits she had bought in Dublin the winter Rog was teaching at Trinity College, and *her* rakish hat, red with a feather. Indeed she had a life.

Unlike Marguerite, she was cool about babies, which I had learned many years before. She didn't scoop them fondly to her breast. She held them, if she had to, at arm's length, saying, "I hope he's waterproofed." It wasn't that she disapproved of them. She admired them enormously in theory—she had, after all, wanted six of her own, and had even tried to persuade Rog to adopt a Vietnamese war orphan—an idea that lasted about ten minutes. "You're out of your mind, dear," he said sensibly. She loved her grandsons for a while, then began asking where Verona was. I once heard that people's reactions to children at various ages has to do with their own happiness at those ages. Marguerite's fondness for her grandchildren slowly abated, and my mother's grew. She liked more finished products. It made sense; she once told me that when she was little, her mother wasn't interested in her. As Verona arrived and bore off the boys, I remembered my own childhood, of being presented to my parents for an hour or so in the evening, bathed, combed, and bathrobed.

My mother bore no gifts except her unflagging optimism. Whereas Marguerite's sharp brown eyes could detect every rip, stain, and flaw in the house and in our lives, my mother saw only the good things we had almost ceased to notice—the space, the quiet street, the children's progress in school, Jack's and my professional success, wonderful steadfast Verona. The azaleas and the peonies. The clean air and the beach only three blocks away. How pleasant it was to sit on the porch with a gin and tonic. She liked to skim our surface—breeze in, check up on everybody, exchange some news or gossip about relatives or old friends, and leave. "I'm off," she'd say at eight in the morning, hat on, suitcase packed, car at the ready—

whereas Marguerite would sigh, linger on, talk about leaving, have another cup of coffee, search for justifications about whatever she decided to do. Each made me nervous, but my own mother, of course, more so—because she was my mother, because each time she left she was rejecting me, fleeing from me, choosing some more interesting place to go, some other, more lovable people.

There were two games to play with her; either to go along with her cheerful blindness, which I could no longer bear to do, or to try to pull her down into the swamps of reality, which made her unhappy, but which I couldn't help. I could no longer deny that life was difficult and painful, its smooth surfaces the cruelest of deceptions. Her denial of this patently obvious fact enraged me with an old, tired anger that went back to my beginnings. I told her about everything that was wrong, and the impossibility of finding solutions. The house was a mistake, a crumbling antique that needed tens of thousands of dollars of repairs to make it minimally habitable. Jack felt like a trapped animal, grinding back and forth in traffic, arriving exhausted at a home that afforded him little satisfaction. I lived a life of frustration trying to run the goddamn place, take care of four kids, write, and come out human at the end of the day. Move back to the city? Not a chance—the tuitions would kill us. Go back to the analysts? The bills would kill us. There were some school problems, and no wonder. Probably every last one of us needed a shrink. At this she threw up her hands. "Oh, God. How about guts? How about muscle? How about coping? You're too conscientious. You can't solve it all. Let a few things slide."

It would work out somehow. It'll do. Slide! Everything was sliding! I was obsessed with dragging her into what I saw as the rotting dregs of my life. Look, Mom. This is what it's like. See? Put your hands in it, for a change. I wallow in it, why can't you just dip in a little and see what it's like? Why has everything always been so easy for you, and so hard for me? Are you numb, are you blind? What's the matter with you? Feel the slime, smell the *mort*. How sad and old was my trickery, and how self-defeating, for though I wanted her to stay, I often succeeded in driving her away. "I'm off," she'd say, hat on, feather aslant. Off to some pleasanter place, to people who didn't complain so much.

Once while she was there, the police came to the house next door, and I told her about Marilyn and Stu. How dreadful—she had read of such things, but thought they only happened among poor ethnic groups, people in tenements—not residents of Larchmont. We looked through the kitchen windows but the lights were off. After a few minutes the police car drove away, with the two policemen inside. I heard a scream and we went up to the study, she with some hesitation. "We really shouldn't; it isn't our business."

In their bedroom it was dark, they were only shadows against some hallway light. "Bitch. Call the police? Cunt. Twat. Call the police? Cunt. Cunt." I began to cry. "Call them again, cunt. Go on, what's stopping you? You rotten, fucking bitch." He was hitting her, not very hard, for she remained on her feet, but repeatedly.

"I don't want to watch. It's horrible. I won't look." She left the room, saying, "I don't know why you want to involve yourself with other people's misery."

Would nothing make her understand? Would I never stop trying to make her see that there is no life without misery, that if Stu hit Marilyn, she and I were being struck too? And how for God's sake had she gotten through so many years of her life without knowing this, that she had been struck, and struck again?

There is a muting effect in Larchmont, and other places like Larchmont. The trees, the green lawns, the lovely old faces of the houses muffle the sounds of despair. Those in torment hide as though torment is something to be ashamed of, to lock up in the attic like a mad relative. What will misery do to equity, to the neighborhood? What will despair do to real estate values?

Terrible things happen there, as they do everywhere else. People put bullets through their heads; they swallow handfuls of sleeping pills. They are borne off in the middle of the night in ambulances. Mortgages are foreclosed; alcoholics hide their bottles in the toilet tank; men leave their wives for younger women. What happens here happens behind closed doors, in the viper embrace of the family. Nothing shows on the street.

Husbands, wives, and children are thrown on each other more, perhaps, than in the city, where lives are inclined to branch outward, and more than they would in an old-fashioned rural community awash with relatives. Larchmont's appearance is deceptive. One assumes that the embrace of the village will supply warmth and support lacking in the family, and it doesn't. (It is, rather, those that have the warmth at home that can give to the community.) People move. The executive transfers are many, the old stay-puts few. Houses are owned on the average only five years. A high-mobile society, ambition, divorce, death, and despair put the houses back on the market. Wrote Vance Packard in *A Nation of Strangers*, "While mobility intensifies the emotional dependence of husband and wife on each other for human companionship, the loosely rooted life-style often creates immense strains that sour a love relationship."

Larchmont remains, however, a comparatively stable suburb. Its ability to muffle change, the very blandness of its surface are somehow consoling to those who do not like to be reminded of life's more disturbing aspects. A friend who lives there observed, "I'm struck by the contrast between Larchmont and Torrington, Connecticut, where we vacation. In the supermarket in Torrington you see blind people, obese people, crippled people, retarded people. In Larchmont there are no such aberrations." There may be one black family—nobody is quite sure. Now there are some Japanese and a sizable colony of French. But for the most part the population is as it always was—aged thirty-five to sixty-five and good-looking, often in tennis shorts and Izod T-shirts, and of that comfortingly well-balanced-sounding proportion stated with pride by the real estate ladies, as though it illustrated free-mindedness: one third Catholic, one third Jewish, one third Episcopal or whatever. I've heard there are a few gays who all live together in a sort of communal house on Chatsworth, but they don't bother anybody, and if they did somebody would write to the paper.

In the last ten years, only two issues, to my knowledge, have ignited more than a few people in the town: that of the retarded people's homes, and that of the crèche.

The question of the group homes is straightforward. Larchmont has not gone (any more than New York) for the actuality of having mentally deficient people in the community. Who needs retards? They'll drag down the neighborhood, pull down property values, ruin the equity. They don't belong in neighborhoods zoned for single-family homes. If all this sounds uncharitable, well, it's because the change is too sudden. You have to do these things slowly. Maybe five years from now.

They mean it. Of the six sites that have been under consideration for group homes in two years, each has magically disappeared off the market—sold privately. The one that exists is being slapped with lawsuits by the neighbors. You can imagine the pictures in their minds—drooling, crazy-eyed retards prowling into backyards, molesting children, eating the azaleas. Or just standing on the corner with weird grins on their faces. Who needs them anyway?

(It sounds strange, sitting now in Manhattan, where the mad, the lost, the demented wander the streets everywhere, where out my kitchen window the neighborhood bag lady, a sad and filthy creature, lies like a starfish on the steps of the Church of the Epiphany. If I don't love her, if I'm not truly Christian of heart, I know she has a message for me, possibly her only useful function. Her very existence makes me ashamed of what I call my problems. There but for the grace of God go I. Or there, or there, or there—for she has many sisters and brothers.)

While the homes-for-retards issue is a fairly straightforward demonstration of the anti-diversity, anti-change, keep-our-surface-clean forces that predominate in Larchmonts all over the country, the affair of the crèche is somewhat more complicated. The story began early in December of 1975 when Don Schanche, a newspaperman and, now, ex-resident of Larchmont (whose religious disposition I don't know, except that he attended the Unitarian Church in White Plains, said to be the church of choice for closet Jews and others of nonspecific religious persuasions), objected to the crèche which appeared annually on the lawn in front of the police station, a highly visible spot at the corner of Larchmont Avenue and the Post Road. The public display of specific religious symbols on municipal ground, said he, violated the historic principle of the separation of church and state. The village priest, rabbi, and Episcopal minister agreed, and for the first time in twenty-three years, the municipal green lay bare. It was decided to mount the crèche at the three churches on a rotating basis.

The village board meeting early in December which voted to accept the advice of the men of the cloth was attended by an enraged mob. A petition had yielded twenty-four hundred pro-crèche signatures. As documented by the Mamaroneck *Daily Times* (Larchmont does not have its own paper—the village is geographically enfolded by, and politically connected to, the town of Mamaroneck, which is larger and more diversified), the pro-crèches and the anti-crèches all behaved badly. "I have never seen an audience of any age or religious persuasion behave as some of those present did," wrote M. L. Berridge in an editorial (12/10/75). There were sinister suggestions of anti-Semitism, Larchmont's old skeleton in the closet. When the old guard Catholics, who had run the village for decades, talked of "nouveaux arrivistes," could they mean the Jews who moved up from the Bronx five years ago? They could.) The Catholics were feeling stung anyway by the impending closing of St. Augustine's parochial school (where, according to Phyllis McGinley, "everybody sent their kids in the old days"), because of dwindling enrollment.

The letters and accounts in the paper made diverting reading my last Christmas in Larchmont. One prominent Catholic lady wrote that she had seen a menorah through the window of the Senior Citizens' Center, and what about *that?* The head of the center replied that though yes, there was a menorah, there was also a Christmas tree, a crèche, and a cross. But the accusations of anti-Semitism were as shrill as the denials—it was mentioned that the Larchmont Temple had been desecrated that very year.

Though of course the Jews didn't want the crèche, a lot of non-Jews didn't either. Something else was going on. To lose the crèche would be "a terrible break with village tradition." The crèche, for those who felt strongly about it, symbolized spiritual values, the loss of the crèche meant the march of materialism. Why not the crèche? It didn't hurt anybody, did it? Wrote Patricia Gould O'Brien, a pro-crèche (12/6/75): "The rights of the many are being abrogated by a vocal and insistent minority. It would be interesting to analyze how long these protesters have lived in Larchmont . . . Twenty, thirty years? . . . Their whole lives? And how long do they plan to stay—only until their children are educated? . . . Two hundred years ago our ancestors fled from England to fight for freedom. Now too many Larchmonters are fleeing to Greenwich and not fighting."

Fleeing to Greenwich! Another conflict was here, perhaps the real one—the movers versus the stayers, those high-mobile, rootless, thrill-seeking members of a "loosely rooted life-style" so dear to Vance Packard, versus the stay-puts, satisfied with life's small things, willing to go on the line for their beliefs. Claudia McDonnell wrote (12/16/75): "[the defeat of the crèche is] victory for rebels without a cause . . . [who] represent no single religion, party, or race . . . united only by their fear of seeing the symbol of a conviction on commonly owned ground."

Meanwhile the Larchmont Crèche Society collected funds for a new crèche to be put on the roof of Leon's Taxi Stand, a particularly charmless building immediately visible upon getting off the train from New York. The old, banished crèche was placed on the lawn in front of St. John's Episcopal Church on Fountain Square, the first of the three rotation points. A week before Christmas somebody stole the Christ child, but a replacement was immediately supplied by the mayor's wife, who just happened to have one around the house.

The crèche became a political issue in the next mayoralty campaign a few months later; the Republicans were solidly pro-crèche, the Democrats anti-crèche, though the village board was split (in 1977, it went Democratic for the first time in modern history). In 1976, three Larchmonters filed a suit against Larchmont Village and the Town of Mamaroneck in U. S. District Court, challenging the constitutionality of the crèche; the suit was thrown out on the grounds that the crèche was a local matter, in which federal courts have no jurisdiction. Every Christmas since, the pro-crèches send their petition to the board, and every Christmas it is turned down. The crèche never returned to the lawn in front of the police station.

The crèche crisis (which had counterparts in other Westchester towns once the fever had spread) was a joke to some, but certainly not to the twenty-four hundred people—one third of the town's population—who signed the petition. Not the least strange aspect of the whole *mishegoss* is that anybody could get so worked up over something as ugly as an old-fashioned crèche, with rouged virgin, bland Joseph, and fat plaster baby. What would have happened if somebody produced a crèche by some abstract modern artist? Probably it would have been unacceptable, for what the pro-crèches want is tradition, and never mind the aesthetics; some link with the past and some other ugly crèche that to them, as children, embodied the miracle. To them it is beautiful—Mary and Joseph, the Christ child with its golden plaster halo, the shepherds and their sheep, the three Wise Men (I know, I used to carefully arrange ours under the tree every year). Certainly as a story, as a symbol, it's hard to beat. Probably those vacant maternal eyes, those dots of red on her cheeks, that ox and ass are part of it, for they are childish, and loved by children or by those who want to remember what being a child is like—and who would like to keep things the way they were then.

Though almost undetectable to an outsider, there is change in Larchmont as there is everywhere else. An article in the New York *Times Magazine* (3/16/80) by William Kowinski called "Suburbia: End of the Golden Age" says, "The suburbs are predicated on a way of life that is endangered in an era of two-paycheck families, childless couples, and frequent divorce. And now suburbia must also confront a new and potentially even greater danger—rising energy costs that threaten its very nature. The suburban era, in short, has come to an end." Schools, threatened by declining enrollment, close down or trim budgets to the bone. Student enrollment in the Mamaroneck schools, which include Larchmont, has dropped every year since 1976—now there are only 75 percent as many kids in the elementary schools as there were ten years ago.

A way of life orginating in the postwar baby boom has become inaccessible to those babies now grown up with families of their own. There is a critical shortage of affordable housing. According to a survey, "Young people cannot afford to live in the communities in which they grew up. Senior citizens cannot afford to live in the communities in which they raised their families. Municipal employees cannot afford to live in the communities in which they work" (New York *Times*, 1/4/81). However, the boom seems to have leveled off—now the three-hundred-thousand-dollar house that would have sold quickly a few months ago finds no takers (in such a house, the fuel bill can easily run to eight hundred dollars a month).

The suburbs are graying; the average daddy in Rye, which is comparable to Larchmont and just up the road, is in his fifties. There are fewer kids around, certainly fewer babies and tricycle generation. Those that do live there are more likely to be college graduates come home to roost before tackling the wide world, or teenagers home from Kent or Andover. (It is generally agreed that Mamaroneck High would work only for the strongest, most motivated kid—the shy child, the confused, the uninterested C student better go to private school, though Mamaroneck's Special Ed program is well regarded.) Violent crime has increased—one lifelong resident won't let her daughter walk around the streets of the Manor at night, and recently, coming back from an evening walk with a Larchmont friend, we listened to the crack of splintering wood as a burglar tried to force entry into his house with a crowbar.

Kowinski says, "In retrospect it seems that [suburbia's growth] was carried out with an almost willful lack of realism. Suburbia was an old dream in a form that fit its peculiar time. That time seems to be over. The dream must find new forms if it is to survive."

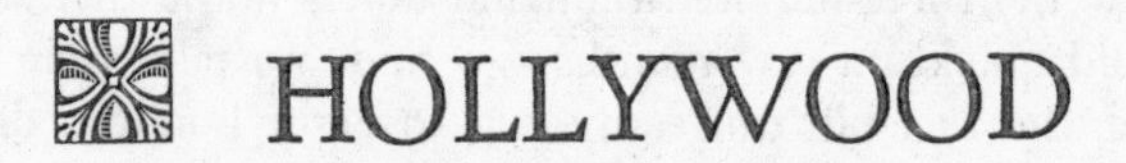

HOLLYWOOD

A Cottage on Vine

In the beginning I had two parents, and they went to Hollywood, where I was born. They (or my father after their divorce) lived in a total of seven houses in the flats of Beverly Hills, and so that was my first home.

Like Dorset, Beverly Hills is a six-mile square. Streets in the flats are wide and white, with manicured lawns or banks of ivy leading back to the houses. Behind are spacious alleys to accommodate the more homely necessities—garbage cans and delivery trucks. The streets are as silent and empty as those in Dhahran—the police sometimes question the lone pedestrian. Each has its own kind of tree; palms and petticoat palms alternate on Beverly and Canon, maples, of course, on Maple, lindens on Linden, magnolias, I think, on Roxbury; others I can't name but served as identification when I was a child. Camden, the summer my parents "tried again," had new saplings which are now full-grown. Rodeo had a bridle path down the middle, as did Sunset.

The houses freely embody the fantasies of the owners or builders. Swiss chalets, Georgian manses, Italian baroque, Dutch provincial, ultramodern, and Spanish adobe abut each other. I remember a small Japanese house on one corner, with mosses in the front yard and carefully placed white stones, and a tiny bridge over a tiny stream. Unlike communities in the east, with their caches of Tudors or Victorians, out here it's every man for himself. If you always wanted to live in a Rhine castle or a Bucky Fuller geodesic dome, and have the mills to pay for it, by all means build one. This is the land of doing your own thing.

This perfectly planned residential area is bounded at the north by Sunset, on the south by Santa Monica. The pink Beverly Hills Hotel fits neatly into the intersection of Beverly and Canon, where the foothills start. When I was small the hills were wild and dry, inhabited by coyotes and rattlesnakes, fragrant with anise. It was here the desert started. Now homes (they are always called homes here) jam the very precipices, line the canyons which fissure the mountain, and, lacking level land, hang out into space. There are homes on Mulholland Drive, the road that runs along the top of the Santa Monica range; from here you can see Beverly Hills on one side, the San Fernando Valley on the other. Homes are stuffed in behind other homes, overhang (on stilts) each other, sometimes—during mud slides—slipping down into each other's backyards. Though the hills are overloaded, the flats, for some reason, remain unchanged. Angelenos consider the hills more desirable because they are, more or less, above the smog. One must visit the place to understand the importance of having one's own breeze. The heavy brown-gold haze that hangs over the city is like a curse, or the eighth plague, God's vengeance (if you will) on this land of excess.

When you went down to Beverly, forty years ago, that meant south of Santa Monica, where the trolley tracks were, to the commercial area, which was then no more than a village. There were two movies, the Beverly and the Beverly Wilshire, and Will Wright's ice cream store, and Bullock's and I. Magnin's, and of course the butcher, the baker, the grocer, the dry cleaner. There was no supermarket—for serious food shopping you went down to the Farmers Market, that glorious bazaar of food shops on Fairfax. The streets were quiet and hot, and it was pleasant to take your ice-cream cone and sit in the shade of a tree in the park.

Going downtown—out of Beverly Hills, down the Strip, into the wilderness of L.A.—was a serious excursion. There were no freeways then, and it took over an hour to go to Union Station (where Nana and I alit from back East) or to Olvera Street, that spot of old Mexico, or to . . . well, there was nothing much else there, nor is there still, despite earnest attempts to turn that patch of urban blight, downtown L.A., into something stylish and compelling. L.A. is a city without a core, a loosely connected collection of suburbs which, as an area, can be better compared to Westchester than to New York. Its magnetic centers are the centers of the Industry, for L.A. is, both historically and at heart, a company town; the old movie studios (now "full of gypsy campfires" as my father put it), the TV studios, the watering holes of the great and famous, Le Bistro or the Polo Lounge of the Beverly Hills Hotel; within some of those homes that hang so precariously on the sides of cliffs, if they belong to the right people, the kind whose names shatter glass. These are the places where the hearts beat and the deals are made.

In the thirties there were Ciro's and the Trocadero, on the Strip, and there was always the Brown Derby, though that was more for the tourists. In the forties and fifties, when I went out to dinner with Pop, it was always to Chasen's or Romanoff's. I preferred Romanoff's because of Prince Mike, who said he was a member of the banished Russian aristocracy, a child of czars, and everybody pretended to believe him. He had white hair, a monocle, and he stood very straight, as befits a prince; and once when I ordered oysters there (in the wake of my father's shock that I had never tasted them), there was, in one of them, a lustrous pearl.

Like Larchmont, Beverly Hills looks like the kind of place where nothing bad can happen, where skies are always blue, faces smile, and bills always get paid. ("It has no hospital," Brendan Gill pointed out in *The New Yorker*, "because nobody is ever supposed to get sick there. It has no cemeteries because nobody is supposed to die there.") The tranquillity of the atmosphere belies the disaster-prone nature of the surrounding area, where mud slides carry away houses, brush fires destroy millions of dollars' worth of property within minutes, and the Big Quake ever threatens the lives of thousands. That such a city even exists where it does is remarkable, a man-made trick as impressive as Dhahran. No two places could be less self-sufficient. Both are forced blooms in the desert, dependent on incredible amounts of imported water. In both cases man struggles against the constant pull of nature to return the land to its natural state—particularly in L.A., where the gods seem to be getting angry, jarring the very earth and setting the hills afire, as though to destroy the human magic tricks that have created a city where one shouldn't exist. But those who live there believe themselves to be magically exempted. *Their* house won't slide down the hill, *their* canyon won't catch fire. How can they? This is fantasyland.

If Beverly Hills looks like dreamland, if it is, say, Sutton Place, Bel Air is the fanciest of all—Beekman Place—and Brentwood a notch lower on this celestial scale, like the East Sixties. I asked a couple of young filmmakers (one of whom is my daughter) to characterize the neighborhoods of their adopted city. "Those three are the top," said Marion and Lou. "They have trees, which don't exist anywhere else. On Rodeo Drive people wear flashy gym shorts and tinted glasses, and they drive around in Rollses and Mercedeses." Where would they choose to live? "Santa Monica. It's quiet, pretty, and near the beach. It has movie theaters, a few bars, and a lot of young people." What about Westwood—wasn't that the part of L.A. that tried hardest to be "back East"? "It's gotten very built-up and phony. Everybody's very preppy. They're all trying to be New York East Side—cool, in a chic way. In Hollywood people try to be cool in a punk way." And Hollywood? "Sleazy, full of junkies. West Hollywood is largely gay—leather-oriented—very nice. East Hollywood is Spanish." How about the beaches? "Malibu is the ultimate in chic, very hard to get into. Redondo, Manhattan, Hermosa—young singles, totally white. Everybody's blond and beautiful and drives a Porsche or a BMW. Marina Del Rey—plastic and nouveau riche. Too many health clubs and singles bars." Venice, the last resort? "Like Soho. Funky. Stuff goes on on the beach like in Washington Square Park. The artists took it over ten years ago. Now it's integrated, but it's the worst area for violent crime. El Segundo is black. Newport is posh, and Zuma's a nude beach." Are there any nice, dull areas for square people? "Culver City and Mar Vista. And Pasadena, very stuffy and old money." (I remembered my father saying, "We're not nouveau riche anymore, we've had our money for fifteen years.") How about the (San Fernando) Valley? They looked pained. "The pits. Dullsville. Hotter and smoggier than our side of the mountains. The big thing to do there is to go out at night in your car and cruise Van Nuys Boulevard. Gas stations are where everything happens. People cruise on Hollywood Boulevard too, for sex, drugs, and rock, but somehow everything that happens in the Valley is tackier." Lou presently lives in the affordable, integrated Wilshire district. "Lower middle class, a lot of young people, a lot of foreigners. Lots of Koreans and Japanese, who are very established. Mexicans, who are great, they'd never molest a woman."

And in conclusion? "L.A. has always been very turned in on itself because of its geography. It's still *Day of the Locust*. There's a sleaziness about everything. Six months is a long time there—that's the length of time it takes to make a movie. The whole place is very movie-oriented. People are attractive and easy to get to know. They have no roots, no neighborhood. They're into fads—nothing holds for too long, and anyway, the earthquake is coming. The 'new Hollywood' is morally and intellectually bankrupt."

L.A. lends itself to metaphor so well that one can't help wondering if it *is* a living metaphor rather than an honest-to-god place, put there to teach us something. It has the flimsiness of dreams, the easy come-and-go of something that flowers in a child's head. The people make fortunes manufacturing dreams and lose them as quickly. They build restaurants that look like hats and frogs, houses like flying saucers, movie theaters like Chinese pagodas. They venture the improbable and the unlikely. They wallow not only in their hot tubs, but in what, to the Easterner, appears to be unreality. To us they are like small children, believing themselves to be godlike in their ability to transcend the laws of gravity, of economics, of what we see as certain constants of human behavior. (They, on the other hand, find us stuffy, compulsive, obsessed with decaying values.) They live movie-set lives, they produce and direct themselves. Everybody longs to "have his own show." And, as though in warning, the earth rumbles, the fires course through the mountains, the houses, having been built on sand, slip down the hills and are destroyed; and still, somehow, it isn't any more real than barreling along the freeway at ninety or a noseful of cocaine or getting turned on in the Jacuzzi. Perhaps the only reality is one's own sensations. Everything else, to people so tuned to the visual, is something happening on a gigantic video screen that embraces everything and everybody except oneself.

More than any other place I've lived, and probably more than any other place at all, Hollywood is fantasyland, existing mainly in what its image conjures up in the mind. It is like one of the older, more plundered ruins of Europe—Mycenae, for instance, where you stand on a hill in the middle of nowhere, look at the remains of the Lion Gate and one or two other bits of rubble, and then, through half-closed eyes, try to imagine Agamemnon's armies crossing the plain, and the sentries lighting the torches, and Clytemnestra waiting in the palace with her lover. Touring Hollywood is a similar exercise in imagination. After I took my small sons there for a visit a few years ago, one of them said afterward, in some bewilderment, "But where was Hollywood? Did we go there?"

Well—we did. We walked along Hollywood Boulevard and found Grandpa's star—those brass stars set in the pavement that commemorate Hollywood's immortals, of whom Grandpa is one. We went to the Wax Museum. We went to Schwab's Drugstore—for Medicaid Spray, as I recall. We passed Gower Street, where the first movies were filmed. Ciro's and the Troc are gone, for Californians bulldoze their historical monuments faster than the Saudis. We put our feet in the concrete footprints at Grauman's Chinese. Even with half-closed eyes I had trouble. Hollywood Boulevard is almost as ugly as Eighth Avenue, and the Hollywood part of Sunset—the famous Strip—is a string of tacky eateries, topless bars, sex shops, a neon wilderness overlooked by huge billboard photos of rock musicians. At night it is acrawl with pimps, junkies, whores, and other human debris. There was something ridiculous about walking there anyway, or walking anywhere in L.A.

But in 1932 my parents had come there, and their first home was what my mother called a "cottage" on Vine; and that was what I wanted to see through the mists, that cottage, with those two in it. They were my Agamemnon and Clytemnestra, those armies had marched through my life. It was their myths that made me what I was—for like all children I had listened to them, watched them, and tried, by doing what I thought they wanted, to make them love me; and tried just as hard to punish them when I thought they failed. Now I was divorced again, a woman with four children and no husband; and like most of us at such moments of reassessment of our lives, it seemed necessary to go back to the beginning.

I've tried so often to imagine them in their cottage, from the little either of them said or remembered, for it seems to be the place where I started. I'll half-close my eyes. It's one of those Spanish-style bungalows, stucco, with a tile roof. Arched doors. A tiny patch of front lawn, a miniature driveway. Oleander. A mangy palm, the inevitable lemon tree. Inside, scratchy brown furniture, a Magnavox radio, framed prints—a Mexican in a sombrero asleep under a cactus, a coy senorita on a Disneyesque burro. Sleazy Navajo rugs on the tile floor. Dark and gloom. A small bedroom, a tiny kitchen with primitive icebox and oilcloth-covered table. Dented pots, a frying pan, a percolator.

In the kitchen, Marion, pretty, dark-haired, *zaftig*, yearning of eye, visibly pregnant. She wears a ruffled hostess gown and cuts up fruit for a salad. She loves Nunnally. Shortly she will have his child. He is brilliant, charming, talented, and hers. He is going to be rich and famous, which she never doubts. She has come a long way from Bayside, Queens, her sour, crabby mother, bossy sister, and two older brothers. She sings as she puts the dinner in the oven.

Nunnally comes in from his day at Paramount, where he is a fledgling scriptwriter. He is tall, slouch-hatted, blue of eye, with a weary, good-humored newspaperman's air. Women are always after him, but at the moment, he loves only Marion. He is both sharp and tender. At the moment he is amused, annoyed, fascinated by the studio and the people in it. She wants to hear every word. She sits on his lap while dinner burns. He talks and she laughs. "Today I had to write dialogue for a parrot," he tells her. He hands her his week's salary, three hundred dollars. Life is wonderful. They throw dinner in the garbage and go out.

They go to the Brown Derby, which is shaped like a brown derby. Since they are nobody they sit next to the kitchen. But some of the old newspaper guys from New York are there—Benchley, Mankiewicz, Arthur Kober, Sid Perelman. They're all on the gravy train now, but Hollywood's hilarious. They eat corned-beef hash and drink Jack Daniel's. Wit, wisdom, and boozy laughter fill the air. They go home very late—Marion drives, because Nunnally is rubber-legged. "I'm drunk, honey," he tells her in bed. "I love you," she says.

Dissolve to:

A much, much larger house on Bedford Drive in Beverly Hills. Meteoric success has started. I have arrived. Elegant furnishings and servants—Nana, a cook, a butler, a gardener.

It is night and Marion is in bed alone, wearing a maribou bed jacket. The bedroom is large and luxurious, with thick carpeting, a chaise longue, and a small gas fireplace, surrounded by shiny brass tools. A small kneehole desk by the window, paintings, and bric-a-brac. The mantel clock strikes twelve, but Nunnally, like Cinderella, is late. A tear trails down Marion's cheek, her lip trembles. As she dabs at her face with a lace hankie there is an ominous rumble. The room shakes. Pictures swing on the wall, silver ashtrays and monogrammed cigarette boxes slide across the polished table surface. An earthquake!

She leaps out of bed, puts on her bathrobe, and rushes into the hall, where terrified servants cower. "The baby!" she cries. She rushes down the hall and snatches me out of the crib, then runs out onto the patio to wait for the house to fall down. Nunnally appears, summoned by this earth's intimation of doom, heaven's punishment for his sins. Water sloshes around in the pool, lemons and limes jiggle on the trees, the patio stone cracks. It's the millennium! What are they doing here? They should have stayed in New York, where it was safe! As they prepare for their death, Marion looks at me. I am smiling for the first time in my very short life. "Nunnally, look!" cries Marion. "*She's smiling!*" Suddenly all is still.

Two years later. An elegant Hollywood party. Everyone is either beautiful, brilliant, or else very clever. Everyone is in the Business except the wives, who trail along like camp followers. Champagne, laughter, and wit. As usual Nunnally is surrounded by admirers. He looks homely and charming, with a slouchy, southern stance. He tells wonderful, funny stories, and the other producers and writers roar in appreciation, the starlets screech with glee.

Marion, sitting off with the other wives, half-listens to a discussion of the servant problem. She looks beautiful and forlorn. As she covertly watches Nunnally, she sees his hand rest on the behind of a starlet. She gulps down the rest of her drink and goes to the bar for another. And another. The room fades to a comforting pink blur, the faces all seem to smile, except Nunnally's, which is angry. They leave and drive home in their Cadillac.

Another elegant party. Again Nunnally is a star and Marion is left out. Again Nunnally's hand rests on a delicious starlet behind. This time, at the bar, a handsome young novelist approaches Marion. This time—for men have approached her before—she responds. He makes her feel desirable. They talk. He listens. He touches her. He wants her. Male attention clears her head, drives misery away. She laughs happily until Nunnally appears, angry and purposeful. He tells her to get her coat. Neither dares defy him, particularly the novelist, who idolizes him. They leave and drive home in their Cadillac.

A third party. Nunnally is away and Marion is escorted by their close friend, Joel Sayre. Shortly after arriving, Marion and the novelist spot each other from across the room, and very soon after that they leave together. Joel is appalled—his charge has disappeared. What to do? Much later that night

Nunnally arrives back unexpectedly and phones Joel. Where is his wife? Joel, grieved, tells what happened. Nunnally sets out to find Marion, and discovers her at the novelist's.

At home he says, how could you? And she says, but why can't you forgive me? They circle whatever is really going on —still as hard for me to find as the center of a maze, or the nut of some huge, deceptive fruit. I can only guess from the way I knew them. My father could be adorable one minute, sharp as a knife the next. He was subject to acute attacks of boredom, which descended between him and the world like a dark fell curtain. My mother was gallant and hopeful, with great powers of self-renewal, but with a coldness at her center, an inclination to withdraw. Neither believed in anger—it was not nice or amusing. She cared what people thought. He, a writer, stole people's hearts, plucked out their secret paradoxes to use as his clay, and loved them with the gratitude of a robber who loves the occupants of the house he plunders. But I only knew them as they affected me.

I don't remember my parents' living together, but I remember being in houses where they did.

A big, square white colonial on Beverly Drive, with columns, set back far from the street. Inside, acres of burgundy carpeting, a wine-dark sea. Silent rooms, very clean white woodwork. In back a big, deep lawn, a wire-haired terrier named Tippy. It is dusk, the magic time when my parents came home, my father from the studio, my mother from wherever she was, shopping or playing tennis. I am still playing on the lawn as it darkens, and now the light goes on in the kitchen. Through the window I can see Roberta, the cook, and Nana, and I can smell beef roasting. I am warm, almost burning with happiness, because all my people will be under one roof.

In my room, pictures swing on the walls, small china animals fall off a bookcase to the floor. The grown-ups rush around, very excited. I am thrilled at the trembling of the earth, at such connection with essential forces.

Another house, with a patio in back and a fishpond, on Maple near Carmelita. It is Sunday morning, and I sprawl on a rubber mattress on the stone patio while the adults read the newspapers. First my mother is there, and then she isn't. I whine to my father to read me the funnies. He promises to do so shortly. Nana disappears after my mother. I continue to whine—something makes me goad him. Unsaid things hang in the air. Already I dislike silences and departures, as though in premonition that my life will be full of them. I prod further, and suddenly he darts at me, his face enraged, and gives me a stinging slap on the thigh. We are both appalled at the red hand-mark that appears on the white flesh. Then I wail, wounded at this result of trying to break their silence.

I am in a glassed-in porch next to the living room in one of the seven houses, for they often run together. (Possibly this is the one on Camden the summer they "tried again"—my mother and I living at the house and my father coming for dinner, but not to sleep.) I have a bowl of guppies, one of which has lived for what seems to me an incredibly long time. I fail to understand why it doesn't die like the others. Something very bad is happening in the living room, behind the closed door—I don't know what it is, I don't really want to know. Instead I frantically draw pictures, trying not to hear my parents' voices. When my father comes in, I try to charm away his demons with a dozen masterpieces, but he rejects them.

I am five. In my room in the house on Beverly, I sulk. I am supposed to choose one of two dresses—a yellow satin or a blue silk—to wear to the studio to have my picture taken. I have told them I refuse to go. I hate having my picture taken. Nana tries to persuade me. "See, darlin'. You can pick whichever you want. Be a good girl." I crouch on the floor in my lacy slip and small white socks. Never will I go to the studio or submit to the forces of beautification. I will be as ugly as possible. Nana leaves and my mother comes. She's angry. I *will* be beautiful, she tells me, I *will* have my picture taken. No! I yell. She grabs the yellow satin dress and wrestles me into it. She wins. I still have the pictures, and my mother and I look like madonna and child.

I am at a large, elaborate child's birthday party. There has been a magician, games, cake and ice cream. Now three little boys and I are in the guest bathroom taking turns pulling down our pants. We do it one at a time, gravely looking at each other's behinds. (If we looked at each other's fronts, I don't recall it, though I know my analyst would say that this is conclusive proof that it happened.) Those pairs of little white globes all seemed alike. Then Nana opens the door—we are caught. I am riddled with guilt, as are the little boys, who flee. Nana tells my mother, but nothing else happens (though my analyst would say that this means something else definitely did).

I am going to the studio with my father. I meet him in a long building like a shed. In an outer office is his secretary, Dorothy. Within are his premises, a big room, furnished with casual elegance, a desk of pristine neatness, a typewriter on a stand. I throw myself lengthwise on the green leather sofa and eye the impedimenta on the coffee table, silver ashtrays and cigarette boxes. I love his office, I could stay there forever.

My father and I go down the hall to say hello to Mr. Zanuck, who chews a cigar, and other producers who appear out of offices. They are very polite and charming, and I am dazzled. Pop and I walk to the commissary for lunch. We pass two Louis Seize ladies with moles on their cheeks, a cowboy, a cop, and a handsome but very short leading man. We are greeted as royalty as we stroll along together. He wears slacks and a yellow sport shirt; I am all dressed up in a red plaid jumper. I cling to his hand, giddy with love.

In the commissary we order cold chicken, potato salad, and iced tea. More people come by to greet us, two bald men with cigars, a beautiful and famous actress who kisses my father and strokes his hair. I am torn between excitement over all this attention and a dark, stabbing jealousy that he is not, even on this special excursion, mine. He must always be shared. When we are alone with our food I try to amuse him, but a curtain has fallen between us and he looks through me as though focusing on something directly behind my head. I fail to interest him, he falls into bored silence, and I feel tears of misery press behind my eyes. The table blurs, a weight in my throat prevents me from talking or eating. A blond woman in a strapless gown comes toward us, crying, "Nunnally!" I know her; I have seen her on the screen, dancing and singing. For her he opens his arms, smiles the smile I so wanted for myself. They embrace. They both turn to me and smile, and his smile is as beautiful as the sun. Never mind how it got there, it warms me to the bone. I take it as though it were really meant for me alone.

After lunch we go to the set. We walk through the Western street, the Manhattan street, the French Quarter of New Orleans. My father talks of making movies, of tricks and artifice, of how the camera fools the eye. We walk through the saloon door and he shows me how there is nothing in back. I find these building fronts sad, almost frightening. I want to see life inside, watch the bartender slide a glass down the counter to the sheriff, but there is only dry grass and the construction that props up the set.

He opens a tiny door of the enormous sound stage where his picture is being filmed. Within this dark and cavernous place, one small area is brightly lit and crowded with people. On the floor is a spaghetti of black hoses. The red bulb is lit and he tells me to be quiet. I scarcely dare breathe. We creep silently over the black snakes and he lifts me up so I can see. From his shoulder I look down into a glaringly lit room, or part of a room, where a man and a woman stand. They are spotlit and vivid, like two animals in a clearing. Behind, in the gloom, are the ghostly figures of the crew, like forest creatures. "I don't believe you, Nicky," says the woman. "I'd like to, but I can't." "Fanny, you've got to," says the man. "We've been through too much together." As he walks toward her, a voice says, "Cut. Alice, honey, make it a little sharper. You're mad. This time you're not giving in. This time you're not taking his crap any longer. Okay?"

They do it again, and this time the director seems satisfied. "Print it," he says. Everybody relaxes and moves about, and Fanny and Nicky come toward us. "Nunnally," they say. He introduces me to them. "This is Miss Alice Faye and Mr. Tyrone Power." I have barely heard of them—my taste runs to Charlie Chaplin and Uncle Don. They beam at me and we shake hands. Am I enjoying the shooting? Would I like to look through the camera? Their beautiful faces smile, but I get tired of beautiful painted faces with their endless smiles. I prefer the plain homely faces of my father and Nana.

I try to be well behaved, but it's difficult, and I trip over one of the black cords and knock something over. I am borne off in disgrace, hot with shame. But my father only says, as he hands me over to Nana and the chauffeur, "You were so nice today, so lovely and well behaved. I was proud to be seen with you. Will you have lunch with me again soon?" I fling my arms around him, thrilled. No wonder he is so loved.

I am in one of the houses—Maple or Roxbury or Camden. I am waiting, hovering around the kitchen door, behind which Nana sits with the cook. "Poor little tyke," she says. "What'll happen to her?" I have been lying under the dining room table, tracing with my finger the lump made by the floor buzzer. I creep nearer the door. "I know for a fact," says Nana, "that *she's* the one wants to end it." The door is slightly open and I can see Nana, in her large starched white uniform, and Roberta, in her green one, sitting at the kitchen table with coffee cups in front of them. "Mr. Johnson says to me the other night, he says, 'Mae, do you think I'm a good husband?' Maybe he'd had a drop, but only a drop, and he'd come to say good-night to The Child. 'Lord knows, Mae, I love this little one. Does she love me too, Mae?' Lord, I coulda put my arms around him, standin' there so sad in the nursery. He sits down on The Child's toy chest. 'Oh, Mr. Johnson, she loves you better than anybody on earth, I swear she does,' I said to him. 'Every night she waits for you to come home. Of course, she loves her mama, but it's you she waits for. It's you makes her eyes light up.' He sighed and said, 'I only wish her mama's eyes lit up.' 'Well, sir,' I says, 'if she only had some sense.' 'I'm not a perfect husband, Mae,' he says. 'I've made a lot of mistakes.' 'You're a good man, sir. And that's what counts.'" Her voice drops, she whispers something to Roberta from behind her big hand. "Imagine," is all I hear, "poor little thing."

I stand up and walk into the kitchen. "Who's a poor little thing?" "Nobody, darlin'. Go play." "I *was* playing. What were you talking about?" "Never mind, now." She darts a look at the cook. "Good Lord. Little pitchers." But she pulls me onto her lap. "Here, now, take a bite of my doughnut."

1938. The Cadillac in front of the Camden house, loaded up. It is a melting, clear southern California morning. The roses and bougainvillaea are still damp. The eucalyptus trees whisper. Harold, the handsome Swedish chauffeur, flicks a chamois over the hood of the shiny black car. Marion, in a neat traveling suit, gets in the front, Nana and I in the back, Nana muttering disapproval. "She'll never find another like him," she says to Harold, sotto voce. "Good Lord." Marion consults a map of the United States. A red line crosses the country from Los Angeles to New York City. It loops around to include such interesting spots as the Grand Canyon, the Painted Desert, and Boulder Dam. I clutch a jar of lemon sour balls. Harold gets in and we roll slowly down the driveway, away from what I believe to be my home. My heart begins to tear, a long ragged rent which I have spent my life trying to mend. "It's all right, darlin'," Nana whispers. "We'll be back. Mr. Johnson will see to that." We roll through the quiet streets of Beverly Hills toward Sepulveda, which goes east.

In my mind my mother exists only in New York, my father only in California. Off his own turf he loses his authority. I see him at the door of our apartment on Sixty-sixth Street, where we lived for a year or two before moving into the brownstone. Nana opens the door, but the commander is there, my mother's dour new lover. "Oh, Mr. Johnson. *He's* here. You'd better come into the pantry." He follows her, a little unsteadily. "I'm better than that guy, Mae, aren't I?" "Oh, sir. Lord knows you are." She pours him a drink. "Have I got a chance?" "Would to God you did, sir."

Then, an apartment a few blocks away, with a sunken living room. My father is there, and my older half sister, Marge, who appears intermittently in my life. She is twenty. Another woman, not much older—Dorris, a young actress with golden hair. But again I remember rooms rather than answers, places where people were that seemed to resonate with mystery. Voices from behind half-closed doors, hints, clues that pointed nowhere. I lived behind a massive wall of protection.

"Your mother's cryin' again," Nana would sigh, her face dark. (But I never saw her cry.) "Your father's leavin'." (The sound of the front door closing.) And, "*He's* here again." The commander in full Navy regalia, braid and brass buttons. He and my mother sit in the living room, I am beyond in the study, in the big leather chair. (Did I really live behind closed and half-closed doors, or has my mind closed them against what I didn't want to see, muffled sounds I didn't want to hear?) In New York, my father is sad, pleading, and ineffective, my mother cruel and unforgiving behind her bright crimson smile, her upswept brown curls. "Your mother's a slob," Nana says. Her room is strewn with hastily shucked-off clothes, her dressing table strewn with rouge, mascara, spilled powder. She makes messes that other people have to clean up, strews her life untidily behind her without a backward glance. I don't trust her, she is careless. I resent her seizure of power over my father, who arrives and leaves so tantalizingly, so impotently. I resent my own helplessness and ignorance. (I must understand, if it takes the rest of my life.)

I longed for California, where I thought everything was perfect. I missed my best friend on Maple (even though she was given to biting me on the arm), the cool damp mornings, the clean white streets with their immense gutters where no water ever flowed; the clouds of purple bougainvillaea over the garage, the way the car purred along the quiet streets, the vast white beaches with their crashing breakers. I compared it all to New York and it always came out ahead of this dark, cramped, dirty place where I had been dragged against my will by my half-demented mother, who had put me in a car and driven me over mountains and through deserts to get here, without a word of explanation; a place where my father seemed to wilt, to apologize, to lose his glitter. I wanted him back in California, and me also; her if necessary, to keep life the way it had been before, and her under control, the harmless shadow she had been.

My family really was my father and Nana, those two plain-faced people whose love I felt sure of. I remembered them joking together (did my mother ever joke?) and their good-natured laughter was a domestic song. Sometimes my father would come into the kitchen for his nightly glass of milk, and peanut butter and crackers, and Nana and I would sit with him at the kitchen table while he ate. Sometimes the three of us went to the studio, or, in New York, to the Empire State Building or to lunch at Hamburger Heaven. We three were a multitude, a perfect if doomed trio, a pseudo-family more precious in its temporariness. I felt I looked like them, with my plain unpainted child's face; it was the beautiful women like my mother, with her furs and feathers and spike-heeled shoes, her stockings and gloves and chiffon scarves, her jewels and hairpins and hats, who pursued some mad course of vanity that seemed to exclude me, although, I was told, someday I would do the same—and which I resolved never to do.

Sometimes in Beverly Hills my half sister, Marge, came to stay. She is thirteen years older than I, and looked very much like her father. I admired her greatly for resisting the forces of beautification, whose snares had already caught me, for I was always dressed in starched pinafores and ironed hair ribbons, or else, at night, a fuzzy pink bathrobe and bunny slippers. But Marge was a frightening and admirable rebel. She was always in trouble, and she did strange things like locking herself in the bathroom and painting her nails green, or putting on a lot of weird makeup, as though in parody of her future. She ran away, she had a boyfriend with a motorcycle, she was picked up by the police and had to be gotten out of jail. I think of myself now as a child who never dared rebel, though old friends laugh at the idea; and that Marge thinks of herself as the most docile member of oppressed childhood is testimony to how little good, really, such acts of rebellion do for that deep pain we try to drown by distraction, like wounded soldiers who beat their heads against walls. She expressed herself as indirectly as all angry children do, without knowing her reasons.

Marge wanted to be a singer—the kind with a husky, jazzy voice who wears a long, strapless dress and clings to the mike in some smoky boîte. She had uniformed boyfriends, one of whom gave her flying lessons, and a small convertible with a rumble seat which she drove at incredible speeds. Once she drove me up the mountain to Lake Arrowhead to a cabin where we were to spend the weekend. It must have been in the late thirties, for Marge told me I should stop trying to prevent my mother from marrying Jo, the surly commander. "Your mother deserves some happiness," yelled Marge, as we scraped around hairpin turns on two wheels, narrowly avoiding the thousand-foot drops next to the road. "She doesn't want to marry Jo because she thinks you hate him." In my terror over the driving and the thrill of being talked to straight by Marge, and my own innocence, I didn't understand that the only reason Marge gave a damn one way or the other whether my mother married Jo was simply that if she did so, then she could no longer be married to Nunnally, which as far as Marge was concerned was devoutly to be hoped for; for then Nunnally might even remarry *her* mother, Alice; or failing that, would probably marry Dorris, to whom she was devoted. "But Jo is horrible," I said. "He brought a Christmas present to the dog and not to me." "Well, I don't think he's used to children," said Marge. "A woman doesn't want to be alone." "Well, she doesn't have to be alone. It's just that I don't like *him*." There was something sinister about the whole conversation—I knew, without knowing that I knew, that Marge would have dumped me over the edge if she could have gotten away with it. Since she couldn't, she took some limited pleasure in seeing me frozen with fear, which I desperately tried not to show. But why—wasn't she on my side? Didn't we share the pain, didn't we both fight the forces of beauty? But it was too late—now she was purple-lipped and green of eyelid, and all done up in sunglasses and bracelets, a silk scarf and long, curling hair which hung over one eye, like Veronica Lake, or whipped out behind her as we screeched around the curves.

In the Sixty-sixth Street penthouse, Nana and I watched and waited. My mother, in a blue pinafore, cultivated flowers on the terrace, handing me a trowel so I could help. Her painted face smiled as she hosed the planter boxes, then turned the stream on the concrete walls which enclosed my room, playfully, making huge loops and curlicues of wetness on the white surface. "Don't," I said. "Please don't. Mama, don't." The wetness would go through to the other side, curling and loosening the wallpaper in my room. It would fall off in damp spirals, and the wall beneath would be dreadful, damp and gray and crumbling; the dampness would seep through everything in the room, the bed, the books, the toys; my room would be an ashy grave. "Stop," I screamed. "Stop it. You're ruining my room." "No, I'm not," she laughed. "I'm just playing." "No, you're ruining it! Stop!" I tried to grab the hose from her hands, weeping terrified tears, and then began to scream, "I hate you! *I hate you!*" "But what did I do?" she asked, bewildered, as Nana appeared to gather me up, clucking with calming sounds. "Come, darlin', you can lie down in your room." "No, my room is ruined! She ruined it!" "I was just playing," my mother said. "It was all in fun." She seemed to be apologizing to Nana, who bore me off, muttering, "The woman has no sense, no sense at all."

Years later my mother said, "I wanted to have more to do with you when you were little, but Nana wouldn't let me." How strange that this woman who backed down so easily should have appeared to me a maddened tyrant. She tried, in fact, to please everyone, thinking this was the way to be loved; and the first strong and difficult act of her life, possibly, leaving a man who treated her badly, caused me to resent her with a sour little curled wisp of hate that never entirely went away, for all my subsequent attempts to understand her and sympathize with her. And I did, I did; years later I liked her, even loved her; I never thought for a minute she should have stayed with my father, and told her so. And all the time, like the little curled ash from a firecracker that remains on the lawn the next morning, my unforgiveness never melted with the rain or sank into the earth; it sat there to the end, a little gray snake, and we both knew it.

Nana and I waited by the fire in our sitting room, her feet in a pan of Epsom salts. Outside it snowed, and Gabriel Heatter was on the radio. I looked at Nana's poor corns, her swollen ankles and misshapen feet, usually shod in white nurse's Oxfords. I brought little doll's cups of hot water to warm her footbath and make her more comfortable. I would, if I could, trade feet with her, not forever, but just for a while, so she could run and play. Her calloused hands, her big rectangle of a body, her long horsey face with the bad front tooth meant love. Her little squiggles of permanented brown hair, her poor overweight body cruelly creased from what she called her foundation garment showed that even she could not escape. When she got all dressed up, for mass or for her day off, in her large magenta suit and black seal coat, it meant her departure for a few hours; when, later, she shed them for the white uniform, my heart rested again. We both longed for California, we didn't like it back East. Lord, it was cold, and dangerous—Hitler had taken Poland and now France was threatened. "Mr. Johnson'll make sure you go back. Here, don't spill that."

Then another news item. Nunnally had married Dorris that very afternoon. Nana's and my eyes caught in terror. "Good Lord," Nana said, "without a word of warning. Here, sweetheart, hand me the towel." She wiped her feet, while I stared numbly, and put on her slippers. "No," I said, "no." I had never imagined there could be such pain. "Here, darlin'. It's all right. Your daddy still loves you. Here, now, I better see to your mother"—her other child. My mother, who had a way of putting her two feet evenly together, like a little girl, and looking guilty; my mother who had played with the hose and destroyed my room; my mother who was, I was told, crying. "Now she's done it. Now it's too late. I told her but she wouldn't listen. How long could the poor man wait?" She went off to tend that crying grown-up. How could he still love me? How did I know I would ever see him again? Now Dorris had won, pretty, golden-haired Dorris. Now she had my father, she had California, she had everything.

Every June, Nana and I took the train to California, where we spent the summer with Pop and Dorris, and every September we came back again.

We traveled rather grandly in a compartment on the Chief, a place where I loved to be. As we hurtled through Kansas City or Wichita or Albuquerque, porters made up our bunks, served us dinner in the dining car, and joked around with us in their good-natured way. Through the tiny window in my upper berth, I watched cities and plains, tiny towns and cornfields go by. As we got farther west, the earth became dryer, more tumultuous; as we went through the passes of the Rockies, with their immense dark crags against the burning blue sky, I felt as though I was returning to my own land. I loved the hot, dry desert air—it seemed to fill my lungs as the cold, sharp air of New York never did. Emerging from the train at Albuquerque, where the Indians squatted in the sparse shade selling their wares, or at Needles, where the temperature was commonly around one hundred and ten degrees, Nana and I smiled with pleasure at coming home again.

The house on Beverly Glen, where Pop and Dorris lived for the first few years of their marriage, was, like all their houses, very grand. In front was a long driveway lined with rose trees which led up a steep hill to the house, and in the backyard was a pool and summerhouse. It backed up on somebody's tennis court, where the gentle ping-plop of the balls could be heard in the coolness of the morning. Within was a large, serene living room that nobody ever used and a curving stairway, meant for a bride, leading down into the front hall.

Beyond was a smaller, more casual sitting room, where interesting things hung on the wall; a mounted sailfish caught by Pop, a picture depicting Life's Choice—the straight and narrow or the primrose path of wine, women, and ultimate flames of hell. Staffing all this were the cook and butler, the maid, the gardeners, and Sue, the baby nurse, who came when Christie was born in 1941.

Dorris seemed very small, fragile, and slightly overwhelmed by the mini-industry that was her household. I was told she wasn't well ("Dorris is *frail*," my mother had said smugly, and indeed she appeared to be). I mustn't be too rowdy or make too much noise, I might disturb her. I remember her often in bed or walking slowly around in a bathrobe, her red-gold hair falling to her shoulders, her face, with its big hazel eyes, porcelain white, with a sprinkle of palest freckles. She spoke quite slowly and distinctly, and had a habit of pausing for a moment before answering a question, a moment in which I was afraid I had offended her.

"Now, I'm going to put you girls into this room," she would say to Nana and me. "Ordinarily it's Nunnally's but he's going to sleep in the small room down the hall for the time being. Right now it's still full of boxes but it's the only arrangement I can make. Sue has her own room next to the baby's. Some of Nunnally's clothes are still in the closet here so he might come in from time to time to get something. I've moved most of them but the closet in the small room is tiny and doesn't accommodate all of his things. We're still not organized and I'm afraid not very well set up for guests. The servants aren't flexible about extra people being here and things might not go smoothly at first." Thrilled at being back, I never noticed the elliptical nature of Dorris's welcome, and wondered why Nana muttered, "Well, la-de-da," after she left the room.

Sometimes I followed Dorris around, studying her secrets. Around the middle of the morning she would appear on the porch behind the house like a small, quiet ghost, then slowly make her way across the lawn, pulling off a dead flower or picking up some toy left out overnight, stopping to talk to the gardener or to Sue.

Her style was remarkably different from my mother's, as was her approach to running a home. My mother was inclined to be slapdash. She would canter down the stairs at 204 to where whatever maid we had was piling up laundry. "Send it all out, Emmy [or Ramona, or Marvella]. If you think the kitchen floor needs washing, this might be a good day to do it. The living room is a mess. If you need anything, order it from Mac's and charge it. I'll be back around five." Off she would skip, glowing and healthy, all done up in suit, hat, gloves, and fur coat. If, at five, the living room hadn't been really cleaned, she didn't notice—the living room was always dusty anyway. If Emmy or Ramona had taken her wages, plus some of the silverware, and left, she shrugged. "We'll get another one." She was amused that some people counted laundry before sending it out; she was gloriously unconcerned about the tidal flow of possessions from one owner to another, about loss or breakage. Ownership as such bored her, only activity mattered. "Oh, well. It can be replaced."

But Dorris gave her chores a grave and dramatic cadence that fascinated me, as I trailed her around the house or yard. In her long pink bathrobe she would slowly approach the Japanese gardener, who put down his rake and turned to listen respectfully. "John [or Henry, or Michiko], I've been thinking about these fuchsias, and I believe this is not a good place for them. I know it's shady but it isn't damp enough. I understand that fuchsias need a sandier soil . . ." She would go on for quite a while, while John stood on one foot and then the other, trying to get a word in. After the fuchsias, she would go on to the shedding of the eucalyptus and the pruning of the roses.

Then, with a small smile, she would move on into the

kitchen to talk to the cook. "Mildred, I think we'll have two of those chickens tonight, roasted. You can stuff them with that leftover bread from Sunday and some of the onions from the Farmers Market. Be sure to cook them slowly to that nice golden brown that Mr. Johnson likes, and use the juices for gravy. You could make a pan gravy and use up that little bit of broth here"—fishing delicately in the frig for a jar—"and the parsley and just a drop of sherry. With it I thought we'd have whipped potatoes, with plenty of butter. But whip them just before we eat so they're fresh and fluffy, and use half cream—use up the rest of this container—and half milk"—sniffing the milk—"you'd better start a new bottle. Sue will cut off a little piece of breast meat for Christie."

Mildred, Jenny, or Cecelia: "Well, Miz Johnson. I usually makes a gravy with water, and I cooks a carrot in the pan."

Long pause. "I'd rather use the broth up, Mildred. I don't believe we have any carrots, and I can't market till tomorrow. Then the fresh peas, just simmered briefly with a little water and butter. For dessert peach ice cream, served in the glass dishes, and the coconut cookies. Put a couple on each plate. Now about last night's dinner. The broccoli was a little overcooked, and Mr. Johnson mentioned it. Next time would you cook it for just ten minutes, and squeeze a little lemon into the water, to keep it green." The kitchen session took an hour or so, leaving Mildred obscurely frustrated, and Dorris would trail off to her room to rest.

(At dinner, Pop would take a bite and say miserably, "God, honey, can't she make plain old pan gravy? Is it really such a difficult thing to do?" and Dorris would reply, "I *told* her to, Nunnally. I explained exactly how to do it, and she did it her way. You have to understand about servants" [voice dropping]. "You can't expect things to be exactly the way you want. I gave her very precise directions. I can't watch her every minute of the time. She thinks I'm an ogre anyway. I have to rest for two hours a day . . ." Anxiety would creep into her voice. Pop: "I'm sorry, honey. Everything else is very good.")

Nana and I settled on the edge of this household, rather than really joining it.

In the privacy of our room, Nana dished out advice for negotiating my new double family, which had mainly to do with not upsetting the adults. I shouldn't talk about *him* (Jo) in California, *her* (Dorris) in New York. I knew my mother's face changed at the mention of Dorris; it stiffened and shrank in a strange way. She would stare at me defiantly as I plodded on (Dorris had twenty-eight pairs of shoes; she came from Tennessee; she swam sidestroke), saying nothing, her eyes growing ever more piercing, her back ever stiffer and straighter, her hands folded and tensed. She became a guardian sphinx at the gate of some vast censored area, a place of military secrets and arsenals of explosives. *Censored*, said my mother's face, like the blacked-out part of a wartime letter. It's not there. There is no discussion. Yet it was there, the black cloud of mystery ballooned behind her, bursting with its stifled thunders. The effect was so disturbing I gave up talking about the fascinating Dorris.

My father, when I mentioned Jo's name, responded with an interest bordering on actual fondness. An interesting man. A strong man. Rather quiet, a little taciturn. A talented artist, an impressive naval officer. Possibly a different sort of person than we were accustomed to, but full of good qualities nevertheless. No matter how forcefully I told him that Jo was a rotten, no-good stinker, no matter how much evidence I produced to prove it, he would patiently take my hand and tell me that my mother deserved some happiness, and that Jo was stable, serene, and steadfast, that he himself had found happiness a second time with Dorris and his dearest hope was that Marion would too.

Children, who want to know everything, soon discover that life, as seen through their parents' eyes, is less a bountiful landscape than a minefield full of hidden dangers. They don't know how wounded parents are, how ragged-edged and baffled; how sadly and inexpertly patched their wounds, how countless their self-deceptions. Those censored areas, seen by a child as tantalizing and dangerous, are more often only cover-ups for old hurts so sad, selfish, and trivial that revelation would be unbearably embarrassing to the adult who sustains them. Behind each evasion, every unanswered question, each lie told "for the child's good," is not some momentously important aspect of adulthood that is being held back for some excellent if incomprehensible reason, but rather an exposed and dwindled parent, a small parent-shaped person the size of a child who is barely able to hide some unbelievable hurt of often trivial proportions.

It appeared to me that some vast and terrible thing had happened to cause my parents to divorce, some unmentionable perversion of whatever was supposed to happen between men and women. I knew nothing of dailiness, of all the little nicks and abrasions that could weaken the fabric; of the small weaknesses and deceptions, promises and new starts that make up most marriages, for I had never seen one at work. It didn't really help to see my father living in apparent contentment with Dorris. Only my two people counted, only their history could educate me, and that remained sealed over—not, as I thought, because what had occurred was too great and terrible for my small understanding, and which I had to somehow earn the right to understand, but because they were too humiliated and confused themselves to even begin to answer their own questions, much less mine. I don't think either of them had the faintest idea why they did some of the things they did.

I believed whatever had happened between my parents to be my mother's fault. I saw her as wanton and destructive—a bad woman whose sexuality chewed men up—and careless, like Daisy Gatsby; my mother strewed, my father folded things and put them away. Under her spell, he had come to take her back, and she had refused him. He had gone on to another marriage, which I thought made him stronger, while she remained alone, taking up with this man or that one. That great black censored area behind her had to be guilt for the crimes she had committed on my father, which he, with his superior understanding, had been able to forgive. I saw aloneness as an admission of defeat and failure, marriage the great uncharted adventure whose success lay largely in the hands of the gods, but which was the only possible road to human fulfillment. (My mother said, "Marriage is so interesting that everybody should try it at least once.") Not venturing it would be like going to Baden-Baden without taking the baths, going to Monte Carlo without gambling, going to the ball without dancing the polka. You might lose your chips or trip over your skirt, but you were crazy if you didn't try.

Children of divorce sense, without really understanding, those discrepancies in their parents' explanations of what life is all about, those little hypocrisies created in the name of protection. The unanswered questions hang in the mind for years, refracted into little spots of nameless anxiety. But to question the covering stories is to risk expulsion. The family has proved to be breakable, and how dare one risk another break, which could mean abandonment?

So I accepted their explanations and covered up my own bad feelings; that they had indeed loved and had a happy marriage, but Nunnally had been a "bad husband," though my mother was blameless; they tried, for my sake, to work it out, but couldn't manage. My father had remarried happily, and my mother would too, if I'd just stop being so hostile to old Jo. Though it only skimmed the truth, barely touching the surface, it took care of my mother's hurt and my father's guilt, and it protected both of their deeper, unadmitted wounds—the wounds which were my legacy from them, my own stigmata which I dragged through my own life, which burned from lack of understanding.

I never really understood my father, so complete was his mask, nor, I suspect, did anyone.

He came from a small city in Georgia, of gentle and kindly people. He was not handsome, but was considered brilliant. He was loved and cherished, probably more than his younger brother. He wanted to be a professional baseball player or a foreign correspondent. He was surrounded by devoted kin. He didn't get into West Point because he flunked math, so he joined the cavalry, where he was an unremarkable soldier. He worked on newspapers around Georgia and then, at the end of World War I, came to New York. He was a successful newspaperman, short story writer, and eventually, screenwriter. Professionally he hardly knew failure. His first marriage, to Marge's mother, was brief. As I prod for areas that might give a little, like searching for weakness in a fabric, I would say that he fell too quickly into this marriage with a slightly older, more sophisticated woman out of need, being very young, inexperienced in city ways, and feeling very much like a rube. He had never really learned to take care of himself—his mother having done it for him—and was always extremely dependent on women and their offices. Here the fabric gives.

Still not yet divorced, he met my mother when they were both reporters on the Brooklyn *Eagle*, and, according to her, proposed marriage to her on their first evening together. Then followed a period of back-and-forth between Marion, his first wife, Alice, and one or two other women, while my mother vacillated between Nunnally and the man she was supposed to be engaged to. While Nunnally always sounds—in letters and from what my mother told me—very bereft and rejected, very quick to ask, "How can you do this to me?"—he was, in fact, rejecting to all of his women, sometimes in the most insensitive way; he made sure they knew about each other, he phoned them from each other's beds, and once married to my mother, he moved her into the apartment so carefully decorated by his previous girl friend, who had expected to live there herself. Later, at the end of the marriage to my mother, he similarly went back and forth between her and Dorris for years in what sounds like an acute state of indecision, whose result was, for both women, a kind of torturous teasing.

There is often a kink in the characters of those who rise quickly from a simple world into a complex and demanding one, spending all energy on work and leaving none to absorb the shocks of such change on the deepest self or to interpret their meanings. It almost sounds as though, in order to do what he did, he urgently needed to press a woman into immediate service. Strangely enough male helplessness has always been as acceptable as male power. Possibly Nunnally had to deny his profound helplessness and dependence by always showing he was free to go to another woman. I can get no closer to it than that, but maybe it's close enough. He married to be taken care of. And behind the enormous charm that made everyone forgive him anything, was a deep sadness that was part guilt and part the most profound and irremediable sense of failure.

He never confronted his own complexity, but remained baffled by the results of some of his acts as though they had been committed by some strange, cruel alter ego, which, in a sense, they had. If I ignore the fat of his nature, the quick intelligence, the engaging humor, the love for his children, the character and ability, and go straight for the bones, it's because they are what, in the end, move us. The mother who overprotects her child is only passing on a legacy of incompetence, a deep conviction that without another person to care for us, we are nothing. Perhaps she must do this out of her own deeply felt deficiency. That profound feeling that we lack, somehow, our very personhood, that we are at bottom useless, helpless, almost nonexistent, is passed on from generation to generation, in various disguises, like a wand in a relay race; we can work around it, cover it up, make it look like authoritativeness, lead useful and productive lives, even be generous to a point to those we love, but it is still there, flaring up like an old battle wound that throbs on damp days.

Dorris slowly gained authority as her health returned. Her quest for perfection was partly an anxious bride's attempt to please a difficult-to-please husband, partly a way to cope with her complex new Hollywood life, for Dorris had grown up a poor girl; but it turned out to be, as years went by, a deep inner drive of her own. With her meticulous attention to detail, she made homemaking into a high art. Her homes (the Johnsons moved to Mountain Drive in 1945, and to others after that) were, to my uncritical eyes, perfectly run; the food was good, the atmosphere serene; soiled clothes disappeared from the hamper and reappeared the same afternoon, clean and ironed; the children were impeccably dressed and cared for by Sue, the nurse. The house was spacious and elegantly decorated. It was remarkable that Nunnally could have stayed married to my mother, the strewer, for the ten years he did. Dorris took care of every detail of his life.

But the helpless person is not truly satisfied by finding another to care for him or her—no human equations are so neat. If Nunnally was, as I believe he was, contented with Dorris, his old habits died hard because he knew how dependent on her he was and had, occasionally, to try to deny this by seeking out other women. And Dorris for her own reasons quaked under her mantle of competence. She became harassed.

It was strange to me, bored as I was during those summers in California and never knowing what to do with myself, to find Dorris in the kitchen at midnight making soup, or, still in her bathrobe, organizing the linen closet before breakfast. When I got old enough to ask her why she did it, she smiled and said, "You'll find out when you have a home of your own to run. Then you'll see what little good education does the female. The demands are constant. Help is intermittent and usually incompetent. And your father, of course, expects perfection." I didn't believe a word of it. My father probably didn't even know where the linen closet was. Why didn't she relax and enjoy her luxurious life? She made me feel more idle and useless than ever. After Nana's final illness had sent her home to Chicago, where she ended her days, I would sometimes offer to help—really to have some palpable function in her household. Could I bathe the baby, make the salad, help with the shopping?

Dorris would pause. "Well . . . I have to go to the market later. I haven't had time yet to make a list. I want to take advantage of certain specials and to be sure to go to the place on Fairfax for produce. I have to stop on the way at the dressmaker's. My car isn't running right and I'm going to take the Buick. The decorator is coming at three and I have to be sure he leaves the samples for the library . . . while he's here I want to get some estimates for the new bedroom curtains. And if I don't stop at the fish place . . ." Like all the truly driven she hated to delegate work. I would wander off, find a book, take a walk up the mountain, go back in the pool for an hour. I had thought that if I helped I could lighten some of her responsibilities, which she later recited to Pop.

"Can't you have things delivered?" he would ask. "Won't

the fish store send things over? I don't have to have fish. I'll eat anything."

Dorris: Hah. Of a list of three.

Nunnally: As for the car, if it's giving you trouble, get a new one. It isn't worth it.

Dorris: It's not that. The regular man isn't there. He's the one I explained the problem to. The second man doesn't understand, but he refuses to admit it. He insists on taking care of it. The last time he fixed it . . .

The dressmaker?

Dorris: I have to have the dress for the opening on the fifteenth. You know it has to be right. It may sound silly to you but if I'm not satisfied with the way I look I feel uncomfortable. She's got it mostly finished but it's wrong. It's not a hard thing to correct but her ego is involved—she knows it's wrong but she won't admit it. It's gotten to be almost a battle of wills. If I could just get her to admit the side seams have to be opened up . . .

I lurked on the edge of my California family like an importunate guest. I waited for my father to come home every day, and when he did, ambushed him in the front hall. But he had many adorers—by 1949 I had two young half sisters and a half brother—and the competition was tough. When the children were small we would all gather in Dorris's room.

Her bedroom was large and luxurious, with thick carpeting, a chaise longue, and a small gas fireplace, flanked by shiny brass tools. A small kneehole desk is by the window, paintings, and bric-a-brac. The mantel clock strikes six, but now Nunnally is home. He sits in a small upholstered chair by the fire with his drink. I sit near him on the floor, wearing shorts and an old T-shirt. I am a dismal twelve-year-old, still carrying the sign of plainness and ugliness. The trouble is I don't like it anymore. I compare myself to Dorris, curled up on the loveseat in a pink and gold hostess gown. She looks beautiful and warmhearted. She kvetches charmingly about her responsibilities.

The little girls come in. They wear matching bathrobes with ducks hand-embroidered by Sue. They are very clean and slightly damp, and on the head of each is a topknot held by a blue ribbon. I look at my big, dirty feet, which hardly know shoes, and hairy legs, which I am not yet ready to shave. My hair separates into oily strands, my face has broken out in zits. I wear thick glasses; on my teeth is a pink plastic retainer which I can dislodge with my tongue. I am cold with hopelessness. My life is like a nightmare: I am trying to climb a mountain, but discover I'm the only one without rope; I'm about to play tennis but have no racket; I'm cooking dinner for many guests but have no food. In each dream I start out thinking I'm equipped, but discover at the last minute, foolishly, that I've forgotten the central item. How to predict? How to know what's coming? How to tie a string around my finger, so that it never comes off?

Nurse Sue, like Nana, is a harbinger of doom, and she feeds Dorris's anxiety. The bottled-water man did not bring the bottled water. The lock on the pool gate is ajar and small fingers might be able to open it. The cook is coming down with flu. The vacuum cleaner is broken. Something is always going wrong. Is this preparedness? How neat Nunnally is, how economical his life. He wastes no motion. He rises, dresses, eats his grits and sausage, spends some time with the kids. He gets into his car and leaves. At the office he neatly writes a script, three or four pages a day. Later he comes home and sits by the gas fire. He strolls through his life while around him the women, like Cassandra, cry their prophecies.

Nunnally, Nunnally! The cook will quit, the children will drown! The house will burn, the money will run out! The star will quit, the picture will flop! How to be like him? For he has fooled everyone into thinking he is serene. He sighs a little, he laughs. He is fearless. He tells a story and we all laugh.

He even makes me laugh at myself. "I won't tell what Nora got in Latin last term," he says, "but if Julius Caesar came up and spoke to her, she'd only understand forty-five percent of what he said." The laughter is like roses thrown onto the battlefield—they look pretty, but the bodies are still there. It is the noose by which we all hang ourselves. "Daddy," I screamed when I was younger, "*don't joke!*" "Nunnally," I have heard Dorris say in steely tones, "it's not funny." Maybe not—but what else is there? Said he once, to describe a woman's dingy dress: "It was the color of the bottom of Nora's feet." I would choke with the laughter that fought with a scream of rage. Anger, tears, panic, all were short-circuited into that orgasmic laughter. But without it we might have said nothing at all. How clever we all sounded, as that choked laughter became part of us. To coin a phrase was to win his heart. All of our expression was affected. Dorris once said that her slow, clear, deliberate speech was a direct result of trying to make herself heard through the dazzle of Nunnally's talk. As we all got older, what a bright place the dinner table was, what smart phrases we made. And always, just out of reach, neatly tucked out of sight, was whatever anybody felt.

During the early seventies, at the end of my marriage to Jack and after I had left him, I went back to California several times. The reasons were various—a book project was one, as were the weddings of my half brother and half sister. Once I took Justin and Jonathan to spend a little time with their mythic grandfather, who was ill and would not live much longer. I wanted them to remember a face and a voice, rather than a reputation, a name on a movie screen.

It was during one of those trips—the one which I spent partly in Santa Barbara, driving to L.A. in my rented car to stay for a couple of days with Pop and Dorris—that the idea crept into my head, at first soft as a whisper.

I think it was on the Ventura Freeway, to me, at the time, a place of unaccustomed joy—sweeping up the rise near Thousand Oaks, while beyond the Pacific waves foamed white on the beach. Or driving into the folds of those brown mountains, on whose slopes the green live oaks grew. Or else coming into Santa Barbara, with its sharp desert scent and streets lined with adobe buildings. Or lounging, at dusk, around a pool halfway up a mountain, listening to somebody's jazz from across the way and the whinny of somebody else's horse, with a carafe of wine nearby and no particular hurry to do anything. I had not been so free, and so alone, in many years.

The idea sharpened driving into Beverly Hills along Sunset, and turning up behind the Beverly Hills Hotel to Pop's and Dorris's house on Ridgedale. Here the fantasy became a little dangerous, for the Ridgedale house was the grandest of all the houses they lived in. It was on a large property with *gates,* and from the French doors in back, where the pool was and the line of matched cypresses behind it, no other human habitation was visible, and one had the sense of looking over a vast, many-acred estate. The lawn rolled down the hill to those scrolled, wrought-iron portals, leading out to the streets of Beverly Hills.

By this time Pop was mostly retired and he spent much of his time sitting in the small study reading or looking at TV with his old craftsman's eye, trying to pry out its tricks. But he was tired of writing. "I did it for fifty years," he said, when I pressed him to write his memoirs. "Isn't that enough?" As for Dorris, the modern world, with its attendant economy, had caught up with her. Now she did all the cooking, which of course was what she had wanted to do all along. She spent her days making aspics, pâtés, ham hocks, and butter beans. When he pleaded with her to leave the kitchen and sit with him, she said, "I've just started sautéeing the onions for the soup and have the other vegetables chopped. I've got the stock at a slow simmer. I'd planned to use the strawberries for ice cream and if I don't start it now I won't get it done. I must get the soup going before I run downtown to pick up the roast for tonight. He said he'd deliver it but can't promise it till six and I have to get it in before that. I thought I'd stop by the farm store for fresh corn . . ." Pop would sigh and pick up a book or else wander over to the window, looking out over his empty acres, for by now the children were gone.

It was simpler to be at their house now that I had stopped trying to be anything other than a guest. The pain I had suffered as a child by the knowledge, so hard to absorb, that California was not my home but a place I went on consignment, where Dorris must be thanked and not upset, had sunk like mud to the bottom of a pond; it was there, but I ignored it. It was too late for Dorris to make me or break me by not letting me help her in the kitchen; that particular helplessness she passed on (the wand) by her own driven nature was for her own children to contend with.

I watched my father in his chair, his head bent, his hair white, his feet in slippers, looking at the TV over his reading glasses—but not really looking at it, rather at something beyond; something, it seemed to me, that he had once wanted but knew now he would never have. As I looked at him the tears came. I saw a dozen Pops scattered over my life—the one whose hand I held at the studio when I was a child, the one who came to see me in the senior play at boarding school, the one who took me to Paris and bought me champagne at Maxim's. I saw him lounging in a chair reading the Sunday paper and climbing into a taxi in front of 204, while my mother watched from the doorway. He would never, probably, know how much I loved him, for I still couldn't say what I felt to him, about anything; in his presence, my mind obsessively buzzed the phrase rather than the feeling. Looking at that bent white head, I would have done anything for him, if only I had known what he wanted; what still, after his full life, eluded him. I was beyond bitterness at Dorris, for he loved her and needed her, and that was enough for me. She bore her own wounds, and if one of them was my existence, I thought time had taken the sting out of it.

One day he said, "One of the saddest things of my life is that you and I have always lived far apart. Do you know, I dream of having all my children and grandchildren under my roof at the same time?"

Ah—I understood that. Then, for a moment, he could pretend we all had common blood. Divorce is a luxury whose price is an unceasing, nostalgic longing—after a while one hardly knows what for. Our natures must crave a unit, for when it is broken, we wish for the very thing we once found unbearable. We shared this, he and I.

It never did happen. Five children and seven grandchildren were simply too scattered, and the call, somehow, too faint; by this time there were too many other voices. (Jack: I don't want to go to California to see Nunnally. Let Nunnally come here and see me. Dorris: Well, we could put Nora in this room, and the boys in the first maid's room. But that's where Scott usually sleeps. So I'll have to move all his things into the back bedroom, and when he comes we'll have to put him in Roxie's room. But Roxie's invited a friend so that won't work. We could put the boys in the second maid's room except . . . Any others: Oh, I'd love to come but I can't. I have to go to London/stay home and nurse a cold/audition for a part/live my life.) The closest we all came to being there together were those two weddings, and his own funeral, which probably shouldn't count except he was such a presence there.

But it was a mistake to take him so literally anyway. What good would one grand occasion do? He needed everybody nearby, going in and out of the house, sticking their heads in his room. He needed the voices of children outside his window.

I told Pop and Dorris I thought I would move to California.

Around the time this idea surfaced, Jack and I had arrived at a point of armed negotiation. I had accepted the fact that indeed it could happen again, I probably faced another divorce. But we were supposedly trying to solve our problems; and planning a move to California, with the children and without him, was not what the marriage counselor would have called a productive idea. It had been pointed out to me more than once that moving didn't solve your problems, you only took them along with you. They came with the luggage. They clung to the furniture like cobwebs.

But I deeply believed that it was impossible to solve our problems. They were as ingrown as a malignancy. The real question—why we had thought we could get along together in the first place—was even more painful than the ones the marriage counselor asked. The trouble went beyond the old stuff about why we couldn't communicate, why we couldn't express our anger directly, why we couldn't compromise. What was the matter with us, anyway? We were both intelligent. Our backgrounds were comparable. We'd both been analyzed. We must have had things in common that led us to marriage. And we weren't getting any younger. Did I really want to trail around broke, with four kids and no husband? Come on, now.

Jack and I were peculiarly unable to function together in everyday matters. We couldn't make a plan and stick to it.

Plans turned into fantasies, practical expectations turned into if-only discussions. Jack found it particularly difficult to reconcile his dreams with the realities that life dished out. The Prospect house had become a nightmare symbol of his disappointment. He, who had wanted a stylish life, was the unwilling paterfamilias to too many people and a falling-apart house in Larchmont. It was like the Yale dining room after the war; again the Spode had turned to tin trays. Feeling over-mortgaged and miserable with a life that was falling too short of whatever it was he had wanted, he lashed out in anger. And I didn't like anger; I'd spent most of my life avoiding it. It made me crazy—which, the marriage counselor said, was *my* problem. What he didn't know was that if I let out my anger, I might kill somebody, burn down the house, run up and down Prospect screaming. I might end up in the electric chair.

But—as in the case of the first marriage—I still didn't really, really understand. Something still eluded me, even though I could run through Jack's and my problems like the A student in a math class. We were two transplanted Manhattanites unable to function in the suburbs. We had the built-in split loyalties of the stepfamily. We still had not learned to handle money. Jack was a male chauvinist pig and my consciousness was rising by the hour. Besides all this we were passive-aggressive, hysterical, and full of Oedipal hang-ups. My father and Jack's mother had rendered us incapable of fully relating to a spouse, not to mention my mother and Jack's father. We hated each other for failing to be the mate of our dreams—I wasn't an idealized Marguerite and he wasn't a greatly improved Nunnally. Daily we lined each other up for the kill—I cooked things he didn't like for dinner, he promised to do things and then forgot to do them. Even when we strained to be aware of these unconscious transgressions and stop them, some mighty weight pulled us back into the same dirty old patterns where we felt most comfortable. The periods in which we tried desperately to anticipate each other's needs and do our best to fulfill them left us so exhausted we could hardly talk or eat dinner, much less pay attention to the children. It was rather like the way I felt in France after a day of not speaking a word of English.

It all seemed hopeless, and worse, it all somehow missed the point. Behind it all was some incapacity, some wound or frailty that explained our vast ineptitude—and I was too tired, confused, and wrung out by failure to try to understand. It was much easier to throw up my hands and start again with the dream of a new life—and where better than California, where I had always wanted to be? In the place of my sources I might find truth—or, failing that, a pleasant life free of problems, which I still thought existed.

To my surprise, neither Pop nor Dorris was overjoyed at my announcement. They didn't say, "Oh, what a great idea. You and the kids can stay here for six months till you get settled." They just kept eating their chicken, but their forks moved more slowly.

To help them along, I pointed out several things. For one thing I needed a change and the kids did too. I believed moves to be therapeutic, as long as they were well thought out. And this move would have many practical advantages. You could live a lot better for your money in southern California. Not that I'd live in Beverly Hills or anything like that. (Laugh.) But I could probably manage a garden apartment, say in Santa Monica. The boys would go to public school, the girls to UC.

What money, that I'd be living better on?

Maybe I could write for TV. If not, I made a perfectly respectable living. Rents here were half of what they were in New York. And you didn't need any winter clothes. And you didn't have to pay any fuel bills. No taxis—just a little Pinto or something. It was all remarkably economical . . . but what was all this about money? What mattered was the picture in my head. I saw us, the children and I, on a leafy patio at dusk, with pots of hibiscus and clouds of purple oleander growing over a trellis. The boys are doing homework, having just gotten back from the beach. The girls are home for the weekend. I bring out some nutritious bean sprout and brown rice casserole and put it on the table. We all wear jeans and T-shirts and we all have deep suntans. We raise a glass of wine to our new southland life . . . and of course we'd be around to pop in all the time. There would be a sense of family that had been lacking in the children's lives. The boys needed their grandfather . . .

What about Jack?

Well—Jack. The boys could spend summers in the East, as I had spent summers here. There were airplanes. It wasn't that I wanted to keep the boys from their father. Let Jack move here, too. He was always complaining about New York and dreaming of new starts. Why not? He too could have a garden apartment in Santa Monica.

Their lack of enthusiasm was puzzling—not Dorris's so much, but Pop's. Hadn't he said he wished we were around? But he seemed inordinately concerned with practical matters. He pointed out that I was pushing forty and TV was dominated by the young, besides which I had never written for TV in my life. He had tried it and been unable to do it, and he had written screenplays all his life. It wasn't as easy as it looked. Not only that, but the short story, my old form, was dead. And the novel was dying. A few people could sell them, but fiction as we knew it was terminal. You could only make a living writing highly commercial stuff which I didn't and probably wouldn't be any good at anyway. As for nonfiction . . .

This was all true enough, but there are ways and ways to present facts. I put most of what he said down to depression. It was like staying in the house all day for fear of being hit by a car. And Pop's and Dorris's idea of a minimum income was not mine. I didn't need Mercedeses or matching cypresses. Besides, I was obsessed with the idea of making a plan, a human function long denied me in the ambiguity of life with Jack. (Should we or shouldn't we fix the roof, take a trip, move back to the city, stay married? Should we be happy or miserable, live or die, love or hate?) I wanted lists, budgets, priorities, five-year plans. I wanted, for a change, to know, not to guess—I would live in a hut on the beach if it had a ten-year lease.

I had done a little research on how a person like myself might live in southern California. Santa Monica was not some rash idea, but a rather carefully thought-out conclusion. (I had started with Malibu.) I'd found my old Larchmont values about equity and the schools inapplicable in L.A. There wouldn't be any equity because I couldn't begin to afford a house anywhere I wanted to live. In Beverly Hills, Brentwood, and Bel Air, the lowliest shack was about one mill, and from there they went straight up. In less elegant areas they were five hundred thousand dollars or so. It wasn't that everybody was so rich (well, only partly), but they had a different system here. You put very little down and got an astronomical mortgage, which lasted forever and which you knew you would never pay off, but it was okay. Everybody was happily in debt. As for the schools, southern Californians, when asked, looked blank. What about them? They were great. The buildings were new and terrific. Many were near the beach. They had teachers in them . . . what exactly did I want to know? Well, which were the best? Did they get kids into college? College. Well, some kids went to UC which as I knew had a fine reputation. But what was the big deal about college? Look at the studio heads—most of them hadn't gone to college. Neither had most of the Hollywood greats. *Nunnally* hadn't gone to college. You didn't need a BA to write a great feature film. If you wanted to go into one of the professions, okay. But otherwise . . . what, really, was the point, especially for girls? How about acting school? suggested Pop. How about cooking school? suggested Dorris.

(Many weeks or months later, back in New York, I talked to a man who had moved with his wife and children from Westchester to L.A. "It's Santa Monica," he said, "P.S. so-and-so. It took me over a year to find out. They kept telling me the schools were all good, but California kids have to drop back a year when they come East." After patient searching he had found the closest thing to a Westchester school in L.A. "There's some busing but it still has a neighborhood atmosphere. The kids can *walk* there!")

I'd better admit, before going any further, that adding to the lure of southern California was another unsuitable man, who had appeared on schedule. I met him through friends in Santa Barbara, where I was working on my commissioned book project. He was unsuitable in his utter poverty, and the hints of dreadful money mismanagement—bankruptcies and the passing of bad checks—which haunted his background. Hugh's past, it was implied, was unsavory, possibly illegal. But in the mood I was in such matters seemed unimportant. He was very tall, like a redwood, with a custom-cut mane of silver hair, and a kind and battered face on which he wore rimless tinted glasses. On his feet were huge, polished, pointed cowboy boots.

Hugh set out to sell me Santa Barbara, which wasn't very difficult. The beach, the uncharted sea. Those soft black nights. Behind the city, those craggy mountains with their sharp resin scent. The wide white streets, the adobe buildings, the desert-dry air, clean because they were so ecology-minded no polluting industries were allowed in the town. He wouldn't live anywhere else himself. And it was cheap, you could rent one of those nice apartments down on the beach for less than two hundred dollars a month . . . Hugh thought I should bring all the kids to Santa Barbara and live *with him.* The trouble was he had no income to speak of. For reasons that were never clear (probably he didn't want them to be) Hugh, though college-educated, seemed to be unemployable. He did odd jobs here and there and was good at fixing things. He could do everything around a house and he was a terrific gardener. He knew what was inside a car and what made it run. When it came to kids he was Piaget and Mary Poppins rolled into one. He dug kids and they dug him. He had saved his stepchildren (Hugh was twice divorced) from padded cells just by being terrific with them. Think what he could save me in shrink bills! (And by the way, the schools, which I was so hyper about, were great, all new buildings and near the beach.)

This multitalented man could put on a three-piece suit, in which he looked wonderful, breeze into a classy cocktail party, and look like he belonged there. He didn't mind cocktail parties, they were fun once in a while. But what he really liked was to go home, get into his jeans, and putter in the garden or cook up a mess of scampi or something. He liked being calm, and cocktail parties were so hyper. Hugh equated hyper with Eastern and calm with Western, a viewpoint common among Californians. New Yorkers were so uptight, so driven, so competitive. And no wonder, living in that rotten climate, with all the noise and filth and the difficulties of living in New York. It was enough to make anybody crazy. And there was something weird about living in boxes all stacked on top of each other, without even knowing who lived in the other boxes. Life wasn't worth living if you couldn't go out and pass the time of day with your neighbor.

Hugh knew that his impoverished state might bother me, but I should look at it this way. I had been married twice and twice it hadn't worked out, and he thought, from what I said, that it had a lot to do with *roles*. He knew that *I* knew very well that there was no free lunch, and that being married to a guy who makes x-thousands a year had its price. Being financially supported by anyone—he didn't care who—created a minefield of hidden obligation and struggles for power. He who pays, says. And what irony for a woman like me who did her own serious work, and who had every right to spend her money the way she wanted. It was absolutely ludicrous that I had to actually ask Jack's *permission* to buy anything—but probably that kind of sexism all went with the East and competition and Jack was probably feeling so driven and crazy by feeling powerless in his own work that he had to come home and be powerful with me. (Out here we *like* women, Hugh said.) Anyway, it was perfectly obvious that I didn't need another scene like that. I needed plenty of time, peace and quiet to do my work, and somebody to take care of the everyday matters of life.

In other words I needed a wife.

It's difficult to evoke, one long, hard decade later, the power of such a statement in the early seventies. Each word was a cry from my heart. Never mind the inconsistencies or the slight gaps in logic. I would like to have bottled his words, to freeze-dry them and send them to my more downtrodden friends, labeled "Sisters—there's hope!" Never mind his track record with marriage—mine wasn't any better. Strolling through those soft, dark Santa Barbara nights, breathing that clean air (after a dinner for which I had picked up the check), I listened to this wonderful siren song, drank it like a parched traveler.

His last wife had happened to own a house, so Hugh had just moved in, fixing everything that was wrong with it and doing running daily therapy on the kids, while she went to work. (They had split over a slight difference about money.) Since I didn't own a house, I could buy a little piece of land (out here land is cheap, we have plenty of it) and Hugh would *build* one. He had never done it but he knew he could. He'd always wanted to and in his head were a hundred plans and ideas for the perfect family house, sunny but cool with a big patio and maybe a pool that snaked indoors, and how would I like a big tree growing right up through the living-room ceiling? On the beach, or in the mountains with a fantastic view? The kitchen I'd always wanted, plus gadgets unheard of in the backwater where I lived. (Out here we like to *enjoy* life.) Certainly a plot for Hugh to raise vegetables and herbs, which grew so easily here I'd freak out. A garage for all the cars everybody had to have. And a study for me—soundproof, if I liked, looking out into a eucalyptus grove or over the sparkling sea.

Of all the fantasies of home I've ever had, I think this is still my favorite. It still comes back like an absurd old song. There I am in the study, just finishing a day's work. I wear jeans, a T-shirt, and have a deep suntan. It's a Friday afternoon and the girls are about to arrive from Santa Cruz or UCLA or wherever for the weekend. Hugh has something wonderful cooking in the kitchen, a pearl of a place which looks over a counter into the rest of the living room, and the air is perfumed with garlic. I wander out onto the study level and look down into the living room where Hugh is sitting under the tree with Justin. "I know you're angry, pal, and I don't blame you," he says. "Do you want to talk about it?" Nearby Jonathan is doing his homework, asking Hugh an occasional question. The late rays of the sunset stream into the room, lighting up the outsized pillows and built-in sofas that are our furniture. (Hugh has made covers for them out of bright Mexican cottons.) Next to the big picture window, which looks out over Santa Barbara and the ocean, the big oak table is set for dinner, set with colorful peasant pottery and glassware.

Outside two cars roar into the driveway—the girls have arrived with their boyfriends, with whom they will stay in two of the six bedrooms (for we are not hypocritical, we know that sex is here to stay). Paula's car has something wrong with it, which Hugh immediately fixes. Marion has a problem in love, which Hugh and I discuss with her in the study, Hugh coming out with insights that set her mind immediately at ease. We all have dinner, which everybody helps to serve and clean up. Afterward the children go to some healthy, normal activity, like a night baseball game, and Hugh and I sit on the patio drinking a glass of wine. "How did it go today, honey?" Hugh asks. "Oh, pretty well. But you know having a book on the best-seller list isn't all roses. This one has to be *better*." "Do you want to talk about it?" Hugh asks.

But sometimes the old song has static. I hear my own voice rising nastily as I sit in the evening at the desk paying the bills. "My God, Hugh. I said it was okay to get a new suit, but a three-hundred-dollar one? And by the way, we don't have to live on lobster and filet mignon." Hugh, sitting nearby with a book, suddenly looks small (he is six foot four and weighs two hundred and thirty pounds). "The suit was on sale, honey. It was reduced from four hundred and fifty dollars." I flip through the stack of bills. "Fifty dollars to clean out the pool. Couldn't you do it?" "Well, I could, love, but it takes a hell of a long time, and I want to be available to the kids when they come home." "Look at this. Forty to fix the washer! Forty for the disposal! And the property taxes are going up this year—not to mention your Vidal Sassoon haircuts! What are we going to do when the money runs out? Do you ever think of that? You just spend it, but I'm the one who has to earn it! It's not easy to sit there and pull things out of my head—and half the time the kids make so much noise I can't concentrate. Don't you ever think of the way *I* feel?"

I can see my contorted face, hear my angry voice. I see Hugh shrink down until he is small and cowering, ducking his silver head, apologizing and suggesting new economies. I see my two little boys looking at us, from one to the other. Who is right? Whose side to be on? Hugh's dwindling and shrinking are the most infuriating thing of all. What's the matter with him? Hasn't he any guts? I know I'm being a pig. Why doesn't he stand up, all six foot four of him, and say, "Now listen here, babe. This is the deal. Clean the goddamn pool yourself. The taxes are on *your* property. Do you want to know how much this pad would cost you if you had to pay for the service you get from me?" (He whips out a list.) "Fifty thousand a year. Gardening—five thousand. Cooking—ten thousand. Shrinks—fifteen thousand, just for starters. Okay? If you don't like what I do, *hire* people."

In bed I worry because Hugh doesn't have an orgasm. I try everything under the sun but sadly he curls up in a large ball. By this simple device he affronts my femininity, which I've become terribly conscious of. I never thought about it much before but now it seems fragile and exposed, requiring all sorts of things to shore it up. I must have success and its symbols, money and the things it can buy, power and Hugh's orgasms. I'm a queen on a shaky throne, ever in fear of revolution, ever more tyrannical. The truth is I need him more than he needs me. Is this what I wanted? Did everything come back to those old issues of power and helplessness?

As it turned out the whole thing was solved by the judge in my divorce action, who forbade me to take the boys away from their father. When the decision first came I was crushed. But after I had accepted the idea, and planned to move back to Manhattan, I had the sense of waking from a lovely, silly dream. Better that California stay the *imago* it was meant to be.

When I saw myself living there, I had imagined myself younger than I really was, and successful in a field I had never tried. I imagined serenity and an easy adaptability I never had.

If I saw myself in *my house*, it was because no house there had ever been mine, or only, perhaps, the one on Beverly Drive where I played in the backyard with my dog, a small bright dot on my consciousness. The others had been filled with doubt and questions that were neither asked nor answered. After my father died in 1977, the place lost its meaning and appeal—for his death ended the possibility of ever going back to that long-ago dusk, when Roberta basted the roast, and Nana called from the door, and both my parents were coming home; or even before that, to the cottage on Vine, when they still loved each other and were more or less innocent. So the judge, unknown to him, closed the book on my childhood—to save, in his opinion, the childhood of my children, who needed both their parents—if not in the same house—at least in the same town.

Where was that judge in 1938, when I needed him?

THE INNERMOST ROOM

"I have sometimes thought that a woman's nature is like a great house full of rooms . . . and in the innermost room—the holy of holies—the soul sits alone." (*Edith Wharton*)

Now my mother has died and I have buried her.

Everyone secretly imagines their parents' deaths, as we imagine their sexual congress, never believing in the reality of either. Indeed they found us under a cabbage. But the most disturbing aspect of their deaths is the end of the possibility of further communication. There comes a time when all accounts are sealed.

As she lay in the hospital with an inoperable cancer, I found myself watching her face, looking at her hands and her thin body as though somewhere in her wasting flesh were answers to the questions I had never asked. Even though she barely knew me, even though she looked past me with opaque eyes, I waited for her to deliver me some final-hour information. "Nora," she might say, "I just wanted to tell you that you aren't Nunnally's child, but Jo's. That's why you're so fond of the sea." Or, "You aren't my child, but Dorris's. You were born when she was seventeen. That's why you're so fond of shoes."

Oh, Mom. You don't have to be so specific. Just tell me this—did you love me?

Of course. You were all I had. I admit there were times I didn't understand you at all. Sometimes I felt you wanted my blood, my guts. I didn't know what you expected of me. And sometimes you seemed hard, almost cruel. You have that mordant sense of humor. And you aren't much of a drinker, I'm afraid. You're like your father. He never could hold his liquor.

What were your mistakes? What would you change if you could do it over again?

Nothing. I had a good life.

Why do I have four children and no husband?

Good God. I don't know. Men are difficult, and you've never been exactly docile and obedient. As for the four children, much as I love them, I never understood that myself.

Why do I sometimes hate you?

I really don't know. I have a lovely disposition. I've always tried to please people.

Did you hold me in your arms when I was a baby? Did you cuddle me, and make little faces, and talk baby talk to me? Did you sing songs and tell stories?

Well, sometimes, but usually Nana wouldn't let me.

What was your mother like?

A crabby old bitch.

Did she hold you in her arms when you were a baby, etc.?

I don't think so. I was born during a typhoid epidemic. The other children were sick and my arrival was an afterthought. When the woman from the Board of Health came they hadn't gotten around to thinking of a name for me, so she put "Daisy" on my birth certificate. So that's really my name, Daisy.

What was your father like?

A sweet and darling man. He was Catholic, and every Sunday he took us to mass. My mother was not Catholic, and as soon as we got home she said, "What have they been handing you this time?" That's why I'm not Catholic. That's why you're not Catholic.

What were you like?

I was always an agreeable child. I did what was expected of me.

Why did you slap me in the face when I was eleven?

Because you were rude and impossible.

Why did you marry Rog?

Because I didn't want to be one of those women having dinner alone at Schrafft's.

How strange was the wasting of her flesh. I still thought of her as strong, glossy-skinned, a little overweight. Not really fat, but *zaftig*. Big breasts, broad hips, a tightly belted waist. Curved, swelling calves. Graceful plump arms. A straight back, erect neck and carriage. She always stood with her head thrust high, I suppose to make herself look taller and thinner.

I think of her in kitchens—the one at 204, the one in Dorset—or at a hundred dinner tables over the years. Tackling a steak on the terrace in Dorset, with the mountains beyond. Curling linguine around her fork at Louisa's on Fifty-eighth Street while Rog beamed at her. Plopping one of her casseroles on the table at 204—the one with yesterday's noodles and Thursday's chicken, tricked out with cheese, garlic, and wine.

A seaside restaurant in Cannes, in 1951, making her way

through bouillabaisse, spaghetti, steak, pommes frites, salad, liters of vin rouge, and to finish up, some fruit and Camembert, just before the money ran out. "I'll wire for more. We can't starve, can we?" There were four of us, and two other friends appeared out of the night, to sit down and eat their way through the same mountain of food. She only smiled as she picked up the check. "Oh, well. You only come around once."

Wiggins Tavern in Northampton, the day of my graduation. Rog, my mother, and Nunnally, me and a couple of friends. Many drinks, to get through it. It was one of the few times she hardly ate. Rog and Nunnally got along fine. Halfway through the weekend she left, taking Rog with her.

Thanksgiving dinner at her and Rog's apartment on Morningside Heights. Hamburgers she cooked by candlelight in our tiny rented house on Long Island, after a hurricane had extinguished the electricity. A diet dinner of pork, peas, and Pouilly-Fuissé.

In the last years of her life, her generous table grew more sparing, and her appetite, possibly because the cancer was already at work, grew smaller and smaller. In Dorset she would put a small roast chicken on the table for six people. "Isn't it enough? My goodness." "What's the matter with your mother?" asked an old friend. "She used to stuff us. Now she starves us." Going there for a weekend, I would try to head her off at the pass. "Please get enough," I would say on the phone. "It doesn't have to be roast beef. Get hamburger. But get a *lot*." I would hear my voice sharpen with that old anxiety—forty years later. I still didn't trust her. Had she forgotten the importance of food, with which she had, once, won my heart?

Had she forgotten the garden of our pension in Cannes, where the bottles of wine cooled nearby in the water trough, where Madame brought us the tiniest of green beans, silky with butter, served all alone? Or the magnificent quiche in

London later that summer of 1951, when rationing was still on, made with a dozen eggs smuggled in from Ireland? The chicken pies in Dorset; my first, lumpy cheesecake at 204; her Concord grape jelly which dripped from the ceiling in cheesecloth bags?

Had she forgotten the solitary dinner at 204 which she ate in her best clothes, because I had promised to be there with friends, and then failed to show up? Did she know I saw her through the window sitting there at the table in her low silk blouse with her glass of ruby wine, wondering why I had done what I had?

Lasagne verde in Florence? Scampi in Venice? Asparagus from the Victory garden during the war?

On her tray at the hospital, pot roast and potatoes lay untouched. She shook her head. Paula tried—"Come on, Grandma. Try to shove it down. How are you going to get better, anyway?" Propping her up, she put a tiny forkful of potatoes in her mouth, where they stayed for the next fifteen minutes. She would open her mouth for some infrequent word and the potatoes were still there. Her expression was pleading—did she have to? All right—the potatoes were no good. Fruit? Jell-O? Bread and butter? Nothing—she shook her head.

She had come down with whatever it was in Dorset, late in June. A cold, a pain in her side. It didn't respond to antibiotics, and she was put into the hospital in Bennington. After a couple of weeks the doctor told me he expected the worst. He'd done everything he could with the facilities at his hospital, and thought she should be brought to New York.

"I don't want to go to New York," she told me on the phone. Rog had gotten sick in Vermont, been brought to New York, and died there. "There's a lovely hospital in New Hampshire I'd like to go to."

"But why?" I asked.

"I just feel I have a better chance of getting out of the hospital in New Hampshire."

"Well, I think you have a lot better chance of getting out of St. Luke's. And when you're here we can all come and visit you every day."

The first day she looked thin but sprightly. She sat on the edge of her bed, picking at her lunch, chatting with her roommate, a pleasant black lady who had something wrong with her legs. The Plant building of St. Luke's is an old and particularly cheerless place, with high ceilings, elevators no longer in use, and small halls that curve around corners. Her room was tucked away in a back pocket, looking out over the roof of the building next door.

"I never put the gladiolas in," she said.

"That's all right."

"When I'm out of here we'll all drive up together, with the boys. I'll pay for the car."

"Fine. We'll go up. Now eat your lunch."

"I can't, it's awful."

After that she lay silent, staring at us as we came in, as though trying to figure something out. Who the hell are you? her expression said. One day she turned her face away as we came in. Her teeth were out and she didn't want us to see her without them. It took a few days for her to be able to face us without her teeth. There against the pillow was her little old lady's face with its sunken jaw. She looked a little fierce, which she never had in her life.

One weekend she packed up and tried to leave, before being captured, by a nurse, at the elevator.

"I had to," she confided to Paula. "You see I'd gone to a tag sale, and all the women there were dressed like cat burglars. The police came, and they said they'd arrest me if I didn't call them back today."

"Forget it, Grandma. I'll bet the whole thing's been lost in red tape. You know how those things are."

"Maybe you're right."

I said to a friend, "I don't know what I'll do if she asks me if she's going to die."

"Lie," said the friend. "Laugh at the very idea. Lie right to the end. They'd better lie to me."

One day she told me she'd been kidnapped, the day before, in the bathtub, of all things. With all her clothes on. Was the whole world going crazy? And Dr. McGowan had showed up, of all people. He wanted to take over her case and she was tempted to let him.

I said, "Dr. McGowan's been dead for twenty years."

"*What?*" She was fully there, possibly for the last time. Then her eyes grew remote again. "Well, maybe he wasn't here. But I thought he was."

By a curious coincidence old Marguerite was in St. Luke's at the same time, also dying of cancer, but putting up more of a fight. She craved Coca-Cola and Pepperidge Farm Goldfish, and if she didn't approve of the medicine, she threw it across the room. Her hair was long, white, and wild, her skin porcelain pale, her eyes a burning brown. Every once in a while a psychiatrist came in and asked her if she knew where she was. "I'll tell you where I am. The nerve. Now get out of here and don't ever ask me that again." She told me of plots hatched by male nurses. "But I'm onto them. They won't dare try anything with me. Do you know, that one" (indicating a fellow pushing a mop) "has been stealing my sheets?" She was armed with a particularly ferocious hatpin, which she had once stuck into a nurse whose face she didn't like. "The doctors in my family always had standards. They would never have put up with this sort of thing. When I had my appendix out I had a lovely private room and Mother brought me custards made with her own hands, with fresh eggs and country cream. There were linen sheets and of course I wore my own embroidered nightgowns." She too ate nothing except her Goldfish, which she picked up one at a time with her long, slender white fingers, the dozen silver bracelets rattling on her thin wrist. "Well, I have some regrets. I'd hoped to go back to Italy again. I should have married Alvin" (an old beau). "He would have done anything for me. I couldn't do it, I was loyal to Jack's father. Now I'm sorry."

Did Marion have regrets, had she taken wrong turns back at those forks? Now she was silent, her fierce little face staring from the pillow. Her hair, for the first time in her life, was straight, as it was meant to be, straight and gray. The trays came and went untouched, the roommates unnoticed. A particularly difficult biopsy really laid her out. "I don't know," the doctor said. "It's not like the movies. Maybe three months from now. Maybe tomorrow." She didn't seem to be in much pain—she seemed, rather, to be fading away, growing smaller and quieter and more shadowy each day. At the end she was, or appeared to be, unconscious most of the time.

I would sit by her bed, during those last visits, tidying up her few small possessions, sorting the get-well cards and refilling the couple of vases of flowers. Or else I just sat there looking at her. I touched her hand, her arm, her hair, moving it back off her forehead.

How little we had touched each other, she and I. The stiff little hug, the peck on the cheek or in the air next to it—the dinner-party embrace. Sometimes when I cried, she had put her arm around my shoulder and patted me on the back, pat-pat-pat, like the pendulum of a clock. I remembered no joyous embraces, no warm enfolding in a capacious lap—Nana had provided all that. What did she do with her warmth, with that lush, generous body she had? She had made love to men, but why hadn't she loved me? I ran my fingers over her cheek. Did I repel her? Frighten her? Was my skin coarse, did I smell bad? Was I hopelessly, incurably dirty? Others had seen their way to embracing me, including my children. Why not her? How often I had been surprised at the way men had loved my body, as though there was nothing on earth wrong with it.

Who was right, who was wrong? Or was she the one who was foul, as I had once thought, exuding a rancid sexuality that caught men like musk and made them crazy? Or, if we were both like that, why did it seem to me that she got the men and I lost them?

Her eyes opened, staring like silver coins somewhere around my left shoulder. "I'm here, Mom. Right here. Look at me." But she didn't. They closed again, and she went back to a rapid, shallow breathing that didn't sound good at all. How empty the place was. The nurses' station was around two or three bends, and was usually empty. I never saw a nurse in the hall, and in each room, it seemed, was some ancient, white-haired body, lying still as death. As the end nears we all begin to look alike, as we did in the beginning. I ran my fingers softly over her jaw and cheekbone, down her nose to her pale sunken mouth. Her illness, instead of repelling, made it possible for me to touch her for the first time in my life. When I got up to leave, she didn't notice any more than she ever had.

How many times had I left to test her, to see if she would ask me to stay, or done anything, to evoke a response from her? As I left for California, or Arabia, or wherever else I was going, would she cry at the airport, begging me to stay, or rage at me and tell me never to return? Only her bright red smile. "Good-bye, dear. Have a good time." Once, after she said planes made her nervous, I cabled her after every landing in the Middle East, Europe, anywhere else I went, in the joy of being worried about. Years later I mentioned it. "Oh, did you? I'd forgotten." Had I married, the first time, to see if she would stop me—to see whether she would praise or object? "Look, Mom. I'm getting married and going to Saudi Arabia, for God's sake. Are you going to do anything about it?" She smiled. "Good-bye, dear. Have a good time." Not quite fair—she worried a little about revolutions, dysentery, things I couldn't do anything about anyway. Years earlier: "My friend and I are going to spend the afternoon on the Bowery, making friends with the drunks. Okay?" "Well—I suppose I can't stop you. If they bother you, knee 'em—you know where."

Try to stop me, please. Lock me in. Tie me up. Tell me what to do. Forbid me *something*, besides sex and suicide.

Suicide was shameful—on that she was clear. A woman friend tried to kill herself by slashing her wrists. She lived, but had no shame. She never repented causing her friends so much distress. In fact her stay in the hospital was a perpetual cocktail party instead of the period of self-castigation it should have been.

Once, right after college, I thought I was pregnant. It was probably impossible, but I had been so drunk during the ensuing tussle in the car that I hardly remembered what had happened before a policeman appeared with a flashlight. When my period was two weeks late, I went to my mother, who froze with disapproval. She, in turn, went to Rog. How chill was the air at 204. Rog got the name of a woman doctor from somewhere and my mother and I went to see her. "I see no sign of pregnancy, but in such cases we recommend the girl have the baby." A few days later I got my period, all over a white dress in a restaurant, a common female fantasy. What did it mean? What did anything mean? That I was wanton, probably, redolent with sex, dangerous. I would be better off married, where my destructive potential would be neatly confined, where my overheated vagina would belong to somebody who would keep it under control.

"Why are you so *bad?*" my Aunt Margaret said to me when I was eleven. "Why do you cause your mother so much trouble? Why do you make her so unhappy?" Ah—if only I did. God knows I tried. I broke things. I was rude, messy, and dirty. I was always in trouble at school. For three months one summer I never took a bath. In the fall, at school, the gym teacher spoke to me about personal hygiene. I sulked and complained. Was she unhappy? I had no idea. How could you tell?

For years I trotted the boys or men I went with out for her approval, waiting for the tiny, stinging remark that would turn my love into a reject. "He's very nice. Does he have a job?" "Well, I suppose he's all right, but the tops of his socks don't meet his pants." "Funny you find him attractive—he seems unsexual to me." "Well—he's not our kind of person." Still only Nunnally passed. Why did I bother? Why did I care? I came to look for what she looked for in men—a hidden, almost invisible streak of cruelty, buried under a lot of charm and success. The helplessness behind the bluster. I was suspicious of warmth, I was accustomed, as she was, to another climate. We wanted confirmation of our own unimportance, a deity to serve and hate. Even our loving fathers couldn't counteract the need—it was mother, it seemed, who had the power. In my dreams, each man sooner or later appeared as a fanged dog, a simpering pig, a snake, or a crazed rat. Repelled by fear and disgust, I would have to move on to another. "He's not much—rather callow." (I dreamed him as a puny puppy.) "He reminds me of a boyfriend I had at your age, who slurped his soup." (He was a pig gurgling in the mud.) After a while I didn't need her judgments, I made them myself. What could I do to please her? Not get Nunnally—he was, in her mind, hers. Not find one as good as Nunnally, there was no such thing. Just keep on with my dogs and rats, for she must ever win the contest.

Or are these things all shadows, inventions of my own mind? For she encouraged me in everything, and was proud of my every accomplishment, praising a child, a published story, a new dress, a successful dinner party. Why do I pick out this dark thread among all the others? Are our minds so intertwined I can't separate them? How could I be so unsympathetic to her competing with me? For she dreaded age and the changes that came with it, always subtracting a decade from her age. (But why did she dread it so? What had been so terribly missing in her life, my serene, self-sufficient mother, who lived alone with such style, such panache? "I'm lonely," she said occasionally. "I'd like to marry again." But why didn't she *act* lonely? "I love Jo." Then why didn't she *show* it?)

I am rapping at the locked door of the innermost room.

"I want to go home," said the fierce little person in the hospital bed. She said it just once, while I waited as always for that terrible question: *am I going to die?* My answer was ready. "Of course not. Wow–that's crazier than the cat burglars. They have to find out what's wrong with you, don't they? Then we'll go to Dorset. We'll plant the gladiolas, and have a nice fat steak on the terrace."

But she never asked. By some merciful natural process the question had lost either its sting or its reality. I suffered and waited for it, but she only gazed at me with the flat stare of a newborn child. My mind refused to focus on the intense present but skittered around to the coming practical details. The Morningside Heights apartment. The house in Dorset. The car. The furniture. The banks, the insurance policies, the will, the name of the lawyer . . . she wasn't yet dead and already I was thinking of her possessions. No wonder she didn't love me. But I thought of all these things with dread–I was afraid I couldn't manage. (Is this the dinner party I can't cope with, the tennis game I can't play?) Really I wanted her alive, in the kitchen at Dorset. I wanted her as I wished her to be.

She died alone in the middle of the night, never breaking her silence.

The sad details of death have a certain dark humor. The ghoulish regality of Campbell's Funeral Home, though our man is a grinning jock. (There are no shirt sleeves showing below his black cuffs–do I excuse him his short-sleeved shirt, though it's mid-July? Do his socks meet his pants?) Wary of rip-off, I turn down the two-hundred-and-fifty-dollar cremation urn–I've been told to buy a jar at the Pottery Barn. I sign the papers that consign her to the oven.

In the evening, Paula and I go to identify the body. Campbell's is silent, the black-suited minions are mute. They show us to one of the draped, lamplit rooms, each with its single, silent occupant. The air is fragrant from the flowers. The person in our room looks strange, lying there covered with a sheet. The jaw is bony, the nose sharp, the chin juts out. Paula grabs my arm as we move across the room. "It's not her," I say irrationally. "It's a man." The face is that of an American Indian, taut, chiseled, the color of granite. She has reached some final androgyny. Then I recognize the straight gray hospital hair, and something familiar about the way it springs out above the forehead goes straight to my heart. Paula and I cling to each other, turn, and go out. Another day I pick up her shabby little suitcase from the hospital, her handbag, threadbare bathrobe, the get-well cards from friends. Her teeth. Her two pairs of glasses. Some undergarments, the dress she wore when she came in the ambulance. I look through it once, quickly, and throw it all out.

The children and I drive to Dorset to bury Grandma. (She may have misplaced her parents, but I will not misplace her—I will give her roots.) Our journey veers between majesty and comedy. She is in the trunk of the car in two containers—my Pottery Barn jar is too small, I have underestimated her remains. Actually there are quite a lot of them. The boys are torn between curiosity and respect. At every bump: "Be careful, she'll spill!"

The Dorset house is silent, dusty, too quiet. We all creep around, either speaking very softly or else hooting with nervous laughter. There is no center, no weight here. The owner has gone (but now I am the owner). We don't know what to do, we don't know who's in charge (but I'm in charge).

The Congregational minister comes to call. He is surprisingly young and freethinking. "Well, we're just about nondenominational by now. Do you have any ideas for the service? A favorite passage you'd like me to read, or that any of you would like to read?" The girls and I exchange panicky glances. Nothing whatever comes to mind. "I'm not very religious," I say. He laughs cheerfully. "Well, I'm not sure what that means." Is this Dorset? He suggests Kahlil Gibran, which we accept gratefully. After he leaves I sit staring into space. Not Jane Austen. Not John Cheever. Not Emerson or Erica Jong. My mind is a muddle of printed pages. This is supposed to be my business. Sylvia Plath? ("Dying/Is an art, like everything else./I do it exceptionally well.") A Nunnally Johnson script (Fade in—a pleasant middle-class living room. It is morning. A maid is vacuuming . . .) Shakespeare, Colette, Linda Goodman? ("Sag is one of those perplexing signs of duality . . .") Never mind, my mother is not literature, she is life.

Her tiny grave is under a maple in the Dorset cemetery, just beyond the eighteenth-century markers. It is a clear, breezy July day. Twenty or thirty people gather around. As I pour the ashes into the ground, having given up on finding a proper container, one of the boys says too loudly, "My God, Mom. Bones!" The minister (nice, but a little callow) moves in quickly with his readings. We stand silently on the grassy hill. The place and the moment are complete and crystalline. There is no better place for her. I have, at last, a sacred place.

Later that night I found the diary.

It was on her bureau, along with a clutter of pills and hairpins, combs, tweezers, and small framed pictures. Going into her room had always made me feel strange anyway—guilty somehow, and awed, as though I were in a hallowed place. It was very warm, very pink and white and fluffy. White bedspreads, puffy pink quilts. As always, many mirrors.

It was an old-fashioned five-year diary—a few lines on each page for each year, and it went from 1937 to 1941. I skimmed through it. Scenery, probably. What she had for dinner. Who was at the party, who wore what. Ah, no. This was something else. "Sick, depressed, cry at night . . . I've made a horrid scramble of my life, wasted opportunity, shattered so much that I might have preserved . . . I just keep thinking about N. and wondering how I can get him back . . ."

I had never known this existed. I had never known she existed.

". . . am going ahead with divorce . . . N. in today, to see Nora—he tried to make love to me, this being two weeks after his wedding—strange man . . . No word from N. Well, if he's gone, he's gone . . . Don't take everything out on poor Jo. He's been like a good doctor to you. Remember, you were in a bad way when he came along . . ."

God, I felt guilty—guilty as I had felt when, at ten or eleven, I used to go through her desk, reading my father's love letters, my face burning with embarrassment and excitement. None of this was my business—but whose business was it, if not mine? Everything was mine now, every pot and pan, chair and table, the house, the meadow, the grassy hill. Four and a half acres of Vermont were mine, along with every tax and debt and responsibility. I had no sister or brother to share the anguish and help make the decisions.

She could have burned the diary, and other journals I later found. She could have had a little bonfire, or buried them out in the field for the woodchucks. She could have left the diary hidden in the depths of some trunk or closet. Instead she had closen to leave me her life. If it came down to whether I was a daughter or a writer, that decision was easy enough to make. I had buried duty that afternoon. She had never been much for duty anyway, she who dreamed of being a star or a queen. She would have chosen to live on, and I chose to help her.

1937, BH (Beverly Hills): Jan. 1. "To Rose Bowl by bus for game—Sayres for dinner—dancing to 1915–1925 records." (I could hear the gramophone. There are Marion and Gertrude

Sayre, doing the Charleston, while Nunnally and Joel laugh. I am four, asleep upstairs. I am still safe.)

Then several entries which slope downward. "Shop–go to auction–market–ride Chico in Griffith Park–have hair done–Nora plays with friend–I'm sick, have influenza. Feel terrible in every way–N. goes away to work. Cry at night." Sometimes there is a barometric finale. "Frame of mind–fair. Frame of mind–terrible. Frame of mind–terrible in every way." When N. goes to Ensenada to work, frame of mind is desperate. When he phones, "mood–good." On an evening with N., "Chasen's for dinner, got drunk, felt fine." On a trip, "Mood–apprehensive. N. telephones, sounds ominous." On Feb. 8: "Made decision today to leave N. if he doesn't act better when I get home." At home–"N. a stinker at first–then at night changed, and was wonderful. He loves me, and I'm a dope if I can't make things go." Feb. 11: "Lucius Beebe's party at Troc–talked to Salvador Dali–N. wouldn't come home–I come alone in taxi, no coat, feel disreputable." Next day, "Awful hangover–no more drinks for me."

For the next few days she is despondent. "N. glum, and that sinks me . . . N. gives me hell for 2 hours in evening. Then changes completely, and is wonderful–says he had to get things off his chest." Mood improves but "N. goes out around 11, stays till 5 AM . . . to Marx's for dinner. N. never shows up–N. in pretty good mood, but if he doesn't change, I'm leaving August." In May she decides to divorce. "I'm satisfied there's no making a go of this."

In August she goes to Europe "to think things over." For three months she travels to Berlin, Vienna, Karlsbad (for a diet cure), Switzerland, Paris, London, Ireland, Scotland. It's all great fun–or is it? On Nov. 6: (BH) "Well, I came back and I'm sorry I did. Same old business, and I'm unhappy all over again." Nov. 17: "Am going ahead with divorce."

To read the stripped, bare bones of her feelings is as strange as to try and understand her without them. In the diary she sounds like a barometer herself, blowing hot or cold, happy or sad, according to what N. is doing. But N.–what's the matter with him? Ah–now I remember. He won't forgive her for the affair with the young novelist. She is waiting to be forgiven. If he forgives her they will stay married. If not they will divorce. (What about his affairs? That's different.)

Feb. 25, 1938: Day of Divorce.

By March we are in New York. "Have apt., about to furnish it . . . starting to write short stories–feel hopeful, ambitious." She is at Colony House, Nana and I are at my Aunt Margaret's in Great Neck. In April we move into the apartment on Sixty-sixth Street. "Now I can get to work in earnest." But Easter is blue, it's hard to concentrate. Then on April 21: "N. calls at night, in a desperate mood. Am mean to him and laugh at him." April 22: "I am sorry I was so mean to N. and write him offering my help." By the end of the month, she's moved into the apartment, finished a story, and been out on a couple of dates. "Wonderful mood. Happy over what I've accomplished in two months."

One might wish it stopped there. But on June 5: "Nunnally's been in town for two weeks. We're on very friendly and affectionate terms although I do get annoyed when he takes other women out to dinner–I told Ken to stay away until I'm alone." June 6: "I have a hunch N. is giving me the gate–he drops in every day, but always has urgent dates with other people–hasn't spent any time with me since Friday night."

Nothing has changed.

June 8: "N. now asks me every day if I will go back with him. Life is very dramatic right now, and so full of fun." June 20: "N. called twice last night about going back to Calif. with him–gosh I'm happy about everything–a roundabout way to reach this conclusion, but I feel very sure about it . . . if we marry again, by God, I'm going to be the best wife ever."

By the end of the month we are back in Beverly Hills for

the summer, in the house on Camden. "I am in a fine, relaxed mood—*must work* starting tomorrow . . . Things are going along very quietly, very smoothly. I am on wagon, don't smoke, work every AM, usually take Nora to beach in afternoon. N. comes in for dinner, we read, talk a little. Like married people." Aug. 3: "This funny, peaceful life marches on." Then, Aug. 23: "Think with Mr. Gallinshaw (?) I'm finally going somewhere with short story writing—gosh, what it would mean to me."

I have spent my life, like all children, judging my parents entirely on whether I thought they loved me enough, and never believing they did—always seeing the black thread. In this diary other threads of my mother's nature come into focus. Now I know she was a writer. Oh, she always wrote things, a short story course here and there, and her free-lance newspaper writing in Vermont, but always, as with everything she put her hand to, with a casual air. She wasn't a real writer like me and Nunnally. Now here she is struggling to master the short story, that difficult and intricate form.

I like her life this Camden summer—"a funny life, but not bad. Maybe it is leading somewhere, giving N. a sense of security. I hope so. It's hard to tell." Its only peculiar aspect is their method of "trying again"—as she told me once, Nunnally came every night for dinner but not for the night. Were they trying to do without sex? Did they think it was sex that tangled up their heads? Also, from what I know of both of them, it all sounds too peaceful—and in fact one can hear the ticking of a time bomb. Aug. 28: "SM [Santa Monica] Tennis —won singles—lost doubles—domestic situation has me stumped. I have to hold on to keep from breaking out. Hold on! You've set yourself till Oct. 3. It will take that long to start as a writer. That means *so much* now." Aug. 29: "Come back to this page in future when about to do something rash —I was in foul mood all day—ready to bust up everything—

Then all of a sudden, N. was so nice, I felt fine and think this PM's moods were ridiculous."

Certain threads take on color. When it comes to work they understand (he completely, she somewhat less so) about self-starting—they have the courage to attack the fearful blank page. When it comes to each other they become strangely passive, only reacting, it appears, to each other's acts. Nunnally is still reacting to Marion's old love affair two years before, which was in itself a reaction to *his* love affairs. Now Marion reacts to his reaction. Is this love? But Marion has a goal—"I hope I can be as firm as I intend to be at end of summer. No more seeing each other if marriage no go." Not only is she waiting for Nunnally's better nature to prevail over his "double standard," but she thinks, with intrepid female optimism, that marriage will solve it, even though it didn't before.

By September she is discouraged and worried about other women. "N. says he is afraid of me—others have said it—I should work on that." I know the stony stare, the erect carriage, the lifted chin. I admire his honesty—or I think I do. Is it really her he is afraid of, or his own judgment of himself? Does he understand why she is angry, or does she deny that she is? By October she feels "like a failure . . . now it is nearing time for me to leave—and I'll have to be brave all over again—what a mess I've made of my life!"

I can't help noticing, and regretting, what I've regretted often before, that the life she led in that mythic time and place sweeps by her unnoticed. She is in Hollywood in the thirties and she might as well be in Podunk—yet Hollywood is at least partly responsible for what's going on. It couldn't happen in the same way in any other place—the smorgasbord that is turning her husband's head is nowhere else so lavish, so exclusive of her. She hardly mentions the people she met, the parties she went to. Salvador Dali at the Troc whipped by in the wind. "Tell me about Hollywood," I used to say. She would shrug. "I was very unhappy there. I was very bored." I would beg for scraps. "Who did you meet?" "Oh, almost everybody." She was possessed by her own life. Now I long for more scenery.

At the end of October she and I, Nana and Harold, the chauffeur, leave for New York in the black Cadillac. We start off "gaily . . . all in good moods." Boulder Dam, the Grand Canyon, Gallup, the Painted Desert. Amarillo reminds her of "that awful night with N." She says, "I have a strong impulse toward security for Nora now—seeing her in the ugly hotel armchair crystallized it. Poor minx—" (I remember only the car, the Indians, the increasing strangeness.) The Ozarks, Little Rock. N. telegraphs every day. In Tennessee I am mildly ill, she regrets everything.

Back in New York she is "contented with this existence of no love, no gay parties—work—skating, cooking, reading, see lots of Nora, do just as I please. N. writes or calls often. By end of year I must *write story*." Soon she meets a man, Bill W. "Men like me, God bless 'em." But N. is coming "so I'm not going to start anything now." January 7, 1939: "Nunnally is here and being a stinker, as usual, so to hell with him." A couple of weeks later she's "got it bad" for Bill, who is stingy with phone calls. If only he were "more in love." She tells herself to get a job or get down to work—she is "frittering too much." Mood—good. She meets Lee, then gets rid of him in favor of the slow-moving Bill. To earn his love, she goes on small bouts of self-castigation—diet, no drink, no smoke. "Should be beautiful," she tells herself. "Bill's not going to ditch you for getting drunk, you did nothing bad, just stared, that's all." (I know that stare.) She rotates back to Lee, who is insolvent, but stimulating and intellectual. She goes off men for one day. She goes back on. She listens to radio shows, considers writing one. On February 25: "Der Tag [anniversary of divorce]—and I've been sad all day, sick and sorry about everything. Must do something—get a job, get into line, disciplined—this is a hopeless miasma I'm in. I need stirring—forget social life—Bill's gone—give up silly Lee, get to work."

A talk with her sister Margaret energizes her, and she starts investigating free-lance writing jobs. "Stanley W. [Walker] likes my NY on a Dime." But "No word from N. or Bill. Makes me feel bad—but job is important. The mere looking for it cheers me up. I know darn well I wouldn't be after one so hard if I had a man around . . . I get so restless and moody when my life is uneventful." March 3: "I am low & blue & lonely—no money, no job, no beau—I wish I was with Nunnally again." Life has never been duller except for that diet cure in Karlsbad, even though there are several job possibilities—a column for the *Herald Tribune*, *The New Yorker* food column, "You" feature, Condé Nast. Then "N. called at 6 this morning and wants to meet me in Chicago this weekend —I don't think I will, it's about time we broke off. Stanley called to say Wilcox crazy about Dime a Day idea and I'm walking on air. Damn Bill!"

She goes to a party with Anne Duffy. "I was so conscious of having no man with me—I couldn't leave fast enough after party." Nunnally persuades her to go to Chicago. "N. was darling and sweet and tender and no bad moments—nicer than we've been for years—we were very happy for 24 hours." Her divorce is final but she wishes she were married again. "Goal—next year—job, on way to marriage, social life. 2 yrs. —marriage." The *Trib* turns her down, Lee bores her, she is sunk again. "Life is a great big bust—I can only conclude that something is wrong with me." "Dime" idea turned down by *Trib*, *Times*, and *Sun*, and no word from Nunnally. She meets Ted, who is "stimulating."

April 9: "Three men have indicated in the last 24 hours they liked me, then I call Bill—that is perversity—Geo. Monnet took me to dinner. We talk about war & politics, at length he kisses me goodnight—I know he likes me—N. calls, we talk for an hour and a half—5:30–7:00 AM—says he loves me, no one else—wants me to go away with him—nix—speaks of remarriage—I don't believe it can work—Ted calls three times just to talk. I'd rather see Bill—"

April 10: "The answer is NO!"

April 11: "It's still NO!"

Indeed she is perverse. Doesn't she want Nunnally back? But turning him down so emphatically restores her good spirits—now life is fun, shows, dinners, exhibits, parties, drinks at Lillian Hellman's. N. comes to town, wants to remarry. He is very persuasive, and she packs Ted off. Then N. leaves and she hears nothing from him, sinks again. Another bout—diet, no drinks, no smoke. "A step up the whole dreary ladder again." A bitter letter from Nunnally discourages her, she tells him no go. But now Ted is gone. "That makes the third, and probably the last man I've lost because of N. I hope I've learned at last."

But nothing lasts, nothing sticks. Ted comes back, Nunnally comes back. When two more job possibilities fall through and Nana and I leave for California in June, she plunges into a busy social life. Her spirits, I am beginning to understand, depend on male attention. She is hungry for it, there is never enough, and nothing else really does the trick—though even when she has it she is inclined to punish the man who gives it to her. On a red-letter Sunday in June, Ockie and Ted come over, George calls twice, Ted once, and Nunnally, yet in love. A new one, Jo, surfaces. "I'm having fun, work & people & being irresponsible." She ponders the nature of strength; "health, steadfastness, honesty, serenity."

In the fall Nunnally comes to town with his final offer. November 3: "After wonderful summer with Jo, Nunnally comes to town, wants to marry me—for past month I've been frightfully upset—to hospital with nerves—can't make up my mind— In desperation, I take Santa Elena for South America —18 day cruise to think things over." Aboard ship, she broods: "Can't help being sorry about everything back home —poor Nora—I feel unsettled, unseated, awful, apprehensive, an awful frame of mind—I want quiet domesticity so much— Can I have it with Nunnally? Is it possible?"

But it isn't, I know now—quiet is the last thing she wants. Uneventfulness makes her chafe, threaten to "bust out." What terrible games my parents have been playing with each other. My mother wants to get herself into a position of power so she can twist the knife. My father does something similar. Each time she does it she is miserable. How incessantly they punish each other. They are both hooked on this futile and destructive game. Do they even call it love any longer? This was the Christmas Pop, Marge, and Dorris were in the apartment with the sunken living room, and Dorris was waiting to catch Nunnally, with Marge's help. How exasperating they all are, how infuriating. How easy for me to blame them all now.

In January (1940) Nunnally cuts down Marion's income. (It is strange that this tempestuous romance has been financed by alimony checks.) At the end of the month, on my seventh birthday, he tells her he plans to marry Dorris. "All day I feel my heart is breaking—Jo comforts me—Mgt and Geo [her sister and husband] scold me for having any sentiment over one who has hurt so much." February 4: "N.'s wedding day. He telephones me in AM, and we have a long emotional conversation—he says he can't get over me, but has to have someone, and Dorris adores him. He makes me cry."

Nunnally is back in two weeks, but by then Marion has started her characteristic ambivalence about Jo. "I'm getting tired of Jo and the uncertain future he represents." Other times she tells herself he is good and patient. She and Nunnally, she says, are still in love. "Things will work out—or do I go on forever like this?" March 13: "Still wondering what got into me to refuse N. for Jo. I must have been crazy—I like Jo and depend upon him, but N. is my bone and blood— there must be some way to get him back. There are no rules to our game, all is opportunism. Wait for the right time . . . I have a chance and I'll use it, by God. I always have had another chance with him." But when he does appear—"N. here last night just long enough to disgust me and make me know there is no life for him and me ever. I run to Jo like a plover to cover after an experience like that." (No explanation.) But shortly "Jo looks more each day like a mess of pottage—no job, no money, no immediate prospects. Incapable of supporting me, just 'wishes I wouldn't talk about it' when I speak of the future. I wish I had N. back, with all my heart."

How strange it is, as I read this diary, that I do not find my mother the "silly and useless woman" she somewhere describes herself, though once I would have been quick to do so. Though my parents' emotional fever chart borders on the ridiculous, I don't laugh, hardly even smile, for this is my history. I am stunned by her courage at presenting herself—if only for these small pages—in an unflattering light. Where is the vanity I knew so well, the control, the proud smile reflected in the mirrors that hung everywhere in her house?

On and on it goes, up and down. "N. came today around noon . . . I'm so fond of Jo, bless him . . . he's so low and hopeless but I'm pretty soft on him." A radio script falls through. She sees Nunnally, who "seems happy, I'm glad. He's entitled to it. I feel friendly but emotionally cool." Regrets again, if only . . . In May, "Jo off . . . talk of war everywhere—no hope of peace—good word about play from Maltz—wrote N. Trying to sell car, rent apt., sell some trappings, find new apt. & write story . . . started work at Red Cross today. Find I like myself a great deal better."

Then, a false rumor that Dorris is pregnant—"it hurts all over . . . I feel sunk these days—sure I made a wrong decision in not going back to N. I'll never get him out of my heart." July 19: "A number of things lately give life a brighter outlook; make the future seem more full of promise. 1. Getting solvent at last. 2. Jo's book to be done, his assignment for illustration. 3. N. writes often, and shows he cares, as if doors are not closed there. 4. I've made good at Red Cross. 5. Possibility of job on Sun. 6. Country house a possibility. I've gotten beautiful again—life really looks good." Then, more remorse. "If I knew we were ended I'd make my world entirely around Jo . . . so blue, I regret N. so . . . I get bored with Jo, and awed at the enormity of what I passed up for him, and probably blame him for it. Dope—I keep brooding all the time . . . it's been four years now of strife. Will I ever find peace?" She tells herself to thank Jo, the good doctor. "You were in a bad way when he came along, lonely, unambitious, and lacking in self-respect. He with his patient devotion, his steadfastness, his interest, has restored you to the semblance of a human being. You don't drink like crazy any more, you're calm, and looking forward—you feel cured now and ready to try your wings. You're beautiful, have a new job, have a new point of view, less introspective. Thank him!"

Then N. is coming. "I'm beside myself with joy . . . be lovely, Marion. Don't spoil it." He comes but disappears on Saturday night. Should she marry Jo just for protection? She knows it would be unfair—"N. would pop in and out of my life and make us all miserable." But love is not a logical condition. "Darling Nunnally," she writes on a Sunday in September, "I want you and no one else— And I'll suffer for you all over again—I want only you and I'll wait and wait and try and I know it will come true and we'll be happy . . . Nunnally just telephoned with the same wistful longing that he used to have—by God I'm going after him now. Nothing must stop me. Nothing will get in my way . . . a job won't hurt. It will make me feel better and act better and make me more interesting . . . So happy all day because I know Nunnally loves me and I him and I'm already putting us together in a house, maybe 204—sometime—" (so that was why 204 was a stage set). But as always her hope burns out at the whole discouraging business. She cautions herself: "Don't despair for N. *He has always come back.*"

In the fall Nana and I return from California and we move into 204. N. comes to town. Though he's friendly, he seems involved in his life with Dorris. Even Jo is not one hundred percent dependable, he breaks a date. As always, when feeling insecure, she makes resolutions: "I'll start on a beauty program at once–hair–exercise–clothes–etc. get rested, read books–work hard–see friends–train Nora by being with her–train dog–get Edna [maid?] in line–cultivate N.–and see what happens."

It's heartening to hear the dog and I will be trained. It's remarkable–I'll try to say it without bitterness–how little role I had in her life, or in my father's either, since when Nana and I are in Beverly Hills, he is in New York half the time chasing my mother. It's not really that they don't love me, or so I'd like to think. My mother, when she mentions me, seems sorry when I depart for California, glad when I come back. I was, at seven, an attractive child, doing all right at school, keeping my woes out of sight. But my parents were both simply too involved in their hot and hectic dance to have much time or energy left for a child. They had a certain amount of guilt about me, especially Nunnally, but it wasn't guilt that kept him trying–to put it bluntly–to get into her pants. I just didn't have much to do with any of it–a perversely consoling thought, for children of divorce often think that it was their bad natures that broke the marriage. (I would –I think–rather have it this way.)

In June of 1941 Marion goes to Bermuda, where she is depressed and listless. "I have no life of my own in New York, just none." She resolves to get lots of rest and exercise –tennis and horseback riding, for my mother was a firm believer in the cult of the body. She resolves to get a defense job or at least sell a story. In August she hears that Dorris is indeed pregnant. "It depresses me–do I still want to wait for

N.—to see him thru this with the chance that he won't want me later—with more of his emotional tie-ups than ever? My heart doesn't bleed any more, I just feel tired." There are no entries till November 23: "How my small history repeats itself! Nunnally has been here for a few weeks and we have had a most lovely time together. Then last night we parted once more, and it hurt all over again and I've been way down in the dumps ever since. And I have so little hope—Dorris is having her baby early in March, how can I compete with that? And he seems well satisfied with all that. Not pulling at the traces at all. Have I any hope at all? Any?"

The last entry is in March of 1942: "I have hunch Jo is going to ask me to marry him before month is out—he is slated to leave NY for Cape Henry. Hates to leave me, is so affectionate, so disturbed about going away—I'll marry him, of course, and we'll be so happy."

Well, she didn't, and she wasn't. Probably the war kept her going for a while with Jo—his arrivals and departures, the whole hopped-up atmosphere of New York during those years. Then after the war was over there was some unfortunate episode about money; my mother bought a house on Center Island, Long Island, in which Jo shared, or lived in part of the time; I remember him painting there. Somehow he got the house, which she had money in, and got her car, and married somebody else. I heard he was living in that house, and he'd treated her badly, and there was nothing she could do about it.

Nunnally kept turning up for years, as late as the 1960s, when she was living with Rog in the apartment on Morningside Drive. She told me that on that last occasion, she turned him down. I suspect he only stopped because he got tired, and after that kept her as a fantasy. In California a year or so before he died, I showed him a picture of my mother and the children. He looked at it for a moment. "Who's that?" he asked, pointing to the gray-haired lady in the picture. "My mother," I said. He looked utterly amazed. "Oh, my God."

He had not recognized her.

It's hard to say which aspect of this remarkable document stunned me more. I had no doubt my mother, assuming she had recently re-read it, found it foolish and silly. We are all ridiculous when we are in love, and embarrassed later over the lengths to which we went. What wasted time, and for what? I can see her sigh, shake her head. If it hadn't been for her feeling for Nunnally, who knows what she might have done? Gotten a wonderful job. Become a successful writer. Even been a more useful person. Married someone else, for to her, not being married was a waste of time too. All the little tries, new starts, resolutions, that came to nothing, that only put her back at the start of that dreary ladder she fell off so easily.

But what she probably saw as sad foolishness—and of course I can only guess—I read with awe and admiration. The diary supplied the last pieces of the puzzle, the tiny key to that room. At last I knew what she had felt for my father, and sensed what he had felt for her. Truly they were my king and queen, the tenants of my Mycenae. They had not disappointed me. Oh—of course they had, in a hundred ways. But in a grander, finer way they had not. I had been born of a pair of lovers and until now I had never really known it.

I wondered if it really made any difference. There are all kinds of marriages and all kinds of children result from them. Children are conceived when parents are drunk or unmarried, making up after a searing fight or offhandedly when one of them is thinking of somebody else. Often they get along well and love their children, perhaps better than they love each other. Or they make a clean break and start again with an understanding new mate. There are no rules.

And perhaps I was clutching at a straw. It was undeniable

after reading this diary that two people in the heat of such a romance had little energy or emotion left for their child. They were too caught up and baffled by their effect on each other to ever explain to me, as I grew up, what had been going on, for I doubt they understood it themselves. To them both, to the end of their lives, I was a symbol of the other. Oh, I've no doubt they both developed a certain fondness for me as a character as time went on, and a certain pride in what I did. But I wonder if my mother ever looked at me without seeing Nunnally, or if he ever watched me cross a room without thinking of her. (Once, near the end of his life, Pop reminded me of some school story he said I'd told him years before. "It wasn't me," I said. "It was Mom. She told me that." He stared at me for a moment. "Oh. I guess I forgot.")

In these days of sharpened female consciousness it might not seem fair or correct to consider a woman's marriage and love affair the material of her soul; her feeling for a man the embodiment of her most private self. What about her work, her identity? Wasn't he in fact distracting her from that, keeping her from what might have been a finer discovery of herself? Well—maybe these days, maybe some women. But not this one. Not the way she was brought up. She followed him to the end of the earth—not a bad description of Hollywood—with head high with pride. She wanted nothing more than to sail in his wake.

She was not the first woman to be defeated by Hollywood, the town where wives, as Dorris once said, "are about as welcome as venereal disease." In New York, where they had both worked on newspapers, she had found his unpredictable roamings and his occasional disappearances easier to take. And there they were not rich, they had to struggle a little. But the life of a big Hollywood producer did her in. Ladies' luncheon parties and antique auctions were not enough; idleness dissipated her energies. As always the place exacerbated the problems. Back in New York, things didn't really work out. The action was still there, the excitement crackled as it always had. But all the job possibilities fell through, the stories didn't sell, nobody bought the great column ideas. She couldn't get the knack of radio writing. And always, to her, it was secondary. "I know darn well I wouldn't be after one so hard if I had a man around."

I read of her professional failures and disappointments with amazement. Never had I known, never had she told me. Once I asked why, after her divorce, she didn't go back to newspaper writing, her first skill. A shrug. "I guess I was afraid of failure." She never told me how hard she had tried and how disappointed she had been. She may have made little cracks about my boyfriends, but never about my work. She was all praise, all encouragement. I was good. I would make it. I had (Nunnally's) talent. She jumped with joy over a story sale or a book contract, told all her friends. (Could I be so generous, if one of my children were a writer?) I thanked her for a lifetime of letting me do what I had to do, without ever interfering or begrudging me success. How could I have spoken to her so sharply about that prostrate consciousness of hers, when in fact it had benefited me?

But something still eluded me. Why was she so miserable? What was this "miasma" she lived in for all those years, while giving the appearance of being so cheerful, so in control? I had always admired her ability to find contentment in whatever life dealt out. How did these two people fit into one—the carefree girl about town who could make a party out of nothing, who thought things took care of themselves, who never counted the laundry, and the obsessed woman of the diary, rocked by her moods and passions?

I'll jump ahead to another journal I later found, this time about travels with Rog in Europe. In August of 1962 they were in Dublin where Rog mostly, and Marion secondarily, were tracking down their ancestors' graves, plus doing a little sightseeing. My mother's old friend Florence was with them. One long entry will do:

(A trip to Killarney, which is turning into) "one big fizzle—it rained, Rog got balky about going in a jouncing cart. So we hired a car and went to Ran [?] Castle, had a look at the lakes, a walk in woods to see a waterfall (nonexistent) and a long walk to see a large house, stony & cold, and not allowed in—but could see gardens, not as pretty as Phoenix Park—Rog was furious with us for walking to see this last sight. Back to hotel for a drink, & Rog had to have a third double Bourbon & left his hat and coat at hotel—I had to go back and get it. At last on train, then tea plus sandwiches & fruit which we brought with us. Rog started drinking and I was miserable. He was so hostile to Florence and me, kept bothering us and annoying us, like, as Flo said, an idiot child. We finally got to station & I hoped home, but no, we went to Davy Byrnes for drinks we didn't need. Rog talked to everyone, embarrassing me.

"Next AM Rog felt terrible & stayed in bed. Flo and I went to town . . . that night to the Russell for dinner, but not until I had thrown the book at Rog. I was really disgusted about his behavior the previous day . . . [description of sightseeing] Rog met us . . . after a day of delving into Quaker records. We went to Royal Hibernia, agreeable until Rog got indignant about the price of drinks, and created a diversion . . .

"Sat. Rog and I went to Amer. Exp. where Dr. Murphy's blood report was waiting for him. It looked bad. Rog spoke of going home at once. Said 'one of these days I'll get it.' I said we all would. He even spoke of flying home, unheard of, & had me call Amer. Exp. to see if they would charge plane fare. Said his pressure had been up ever since we started to travel. At last he quieted down . . . [later] Flo & I sat in sun on the porch, nodding & chatting—we are so comfortable together, & understand each other so well—she said Rog, like Tommy [Florence's ex], gets bored and creates a big fuss over nothing to get his wife's sympathy and be the center of attention. I went out & got some peanut butter & Rye-Vita, and Flo came in for an hour for a drink of Irish, peanut butter, cheese, fruit etc.—this was our dinner.

"In evening to Intercontinental hotel in Ballsbridge. Rog got angry because the hors d'oeuvres had salt on them. I got so upset at his rising voice that my appetite went, I picked at a sardine, could not eat the steak. I don't seem to be as tough as I used to. Back at Montrose House Rog accused me of being so unsympathetic with his salt free diet that I felt misunderstood, mistreated & alone, & decided to leave, then & there — He decided if anyone was going to leave it should be he. So he packed, called a taxi, then called it all off. But I hardly slept & today feel as if a steam roller has passed over me."

In London, staying at a friend's flat: "I am determined to do the best I can about R's diet while we are here—[at Harrod's] bought entrecote steaks, wild strawberries from France, Devonshire cream, salt free gruyere & other delicious things . . . this is a happy place and I feel our emotional troubles are over, for the time being . . . Read '4th of June' about adolescent boys at Eton, about beatings & masturbation, about homosexual relationships, bullying & snobbery, about immoral mothers & arrogant dukes. It's really a nasty book."

It's nice to see her writing about food, which didn't seem to exist in 1940. It also confirms what I know from her diaries and other stories she left—that she was a real writer. What she writes—except the dutiful travelogues—you keep reading. It's not so nice to read about Rog's all-too-familiar antics.

Why was this woman who was willing to turn herself inside out for a man so unhappy with the ones she had? And why did they treat her so badly?

I believe that a happy marriage is largely a matter of luck. I don't think, as some do, that we are drawn again and again to those walking wounded who will be our opposite numbers in the infantile games we are compelled to act out. In my experience men have never lined up before me with neat rundowns of their pathology at the ready, so I can reject the healthy ones and go straight for the sickie. In fact they have never lined up at all. They have appeared at the most unlikely times—at the party I almost didn't go to, at somebody's house when I've dropped by, at a publisher's meeting—and usually when I have not been looking for them. There have been as many and more whom I never did meet—the ones at the dinner party to which I didn't go and the blind dates who came down with the flu or suddenly had to leave town.

Whether or not we have taken up with each other has had more to do with circumstance than fatal perversion. The timing was right. Christie, when she was two or three, had a duck that followed her around the lawn on Beverly Glen. The duck had been taken from its mother at an early age, and Christie had happened to cross its path at the exact moment when nature impelled it to follow some larger being. I have followed men, and they have followed me, like Christie's duck—because the moment was right.

My mother fell in love with my father's charm, as many other women did. She believed, like most people in love, that she would improve his nature, he would give up all those other women for her. With her devotion he would no longer need them. There are few strong enough to fight this illusion, and such noble characters deserve points for insight, though they may never marry. The other men she knew bored her, and she made a trade-off—she chose the love, the excitement, and the risks over the security. (If she didn't, she would never dance the polka.) As for Rog, he was certainly the best one who had come into her life since Nunnally—far better than the shy, depressed Jo, whom she had tried to talk herself into for so long. She knew Rog's health was not good and she probably would spend years nursing him, but she accepted this (even though he never helped her with the dishes, as he had promised). And she loved him, no doubt about it. He made her, most of the time, happy, glad to bring him his slippers, his pills, and his Old Fitz. If she suspected his weaknesses—and I imagine she did—she took them as part of the package. Should she—at fifty-two—have turned him down? She couldn't know that he would drive away her friends, infuriate me, and make her, from time to time, miserable, for the darker side of his nature only surfaced after they were married. Even if she had known she probably would have married him anyway. For her—a woman who needed a man badly—what else was there? Darling grandchildren and more rejection slips would not be enough to satisfy her. Why not? And whatever their marriage, I don't think she ever regretted it.

But she carried with her, as Rog did, and Nunnally did, and Jack and I did, and many others, a kind of fatal flaw, a certain deficit of nature that, given the right circumstances, could turn a decent prospective union into a nightmare. All of us married to be taken care of. All of us, on some profound level, felt ourselves to be helpless, useless, almost nothing as long as we were alone. At the same time we resented the power that came with protection, we bit the hand that fed us, we resented our own dependency. At worst we hated the person who dared to love us, rotten kids that we were.

Though my parents' marriage was far different from mine and Jack's, there were certain unsettling similarities—the lining up for the kill, the tries for power, the peculiar embracing of misery, the retreat when closeness threatened. Nunnally disappeared and went to other women; Jack was given to spectacular rages. My mother and I, branches from the same tree, had more devious methods—I saw Rog get as frightened as I did when she suddenly got up and left, or cooked the wrong kind of food. I'd watch Jack's hidden fury escalate when I forgot to tell him something till too late, made a promise and didn't keep it.

If Marion Byrnes, in 1925, had chanced on a more secure man than my father, she well might have stayed married for the rest of her life. But the one that crossed her path got frightened to death at her little rejections, her little snipes, and went barreling off after starlets; which frightened her further, and then she had to pay him back. And the next one was so truly terrified of illness and death that no amount of attention was enough, for God knows she was devoted to him. And because he abused her, and threatened to leave her, because she believed him every time he said it, she had to pay him back—oh, in such tiny ways.

It's remarkable how many of us have this brand of fear, this wound in our natures that makes us so dependent and so exasperated by our dependency. Everywhere I look I see people frightened of love and its demands. We either remain essentially alone, venturing into love and sex only as transients, or else we suffer in unhappy marriages and relationships.

For fear—if you've had it long enough—becomes a familiar condition. I know that there was hardly a time when I *wasn't* afraid. The circumstances of my life seemed terrifying. My mother was absent or removed from my feelings, so absorbed was she in her own. How could she be reassuring to me when she was so frightened herself? Now I think the reason I was so angry at her was not that she left Nunnally, but that I didn't believe her to be strong enough to steer the ship herself. Really that was the gray snake. I grew so used to the quiet, dark chord of fear that I didn't know what it was like to be without it.

She gained a lot of strength as the years went on. But she didn't have it when I needed it—and so, needing a protector like the duck, I was inclined to follow the first large being who came along. I was programmed not for choice, but for circumstance. As it happened, the large beings who crossed my path had similar fears; and since we expected each other to fill a gap that could never be filled, we were, inevitably, dreadfully disappointed, crushed, full of bitter rage.

The thirst for love deep as an addiction—that's the wound. A thirst so deep we will do anything for it, go anywhere, try to drag love from stones; marry too fast, expect too much, hang onto the dead marriage that was made because of it in the first place. We long to relinquish responsibility, to curl up and let somebody else take care of everything; and having done so, we accuse our protector of tyranny, rattling the cage we entered so eagerly. We confuse love with fear, never having experienced it without; and if we do encounter love alone, we cover our eyes to hide from a light too bright to look at.

BACK TO TOWN

New York, 1981: still the town everybody loves to hate.

It's amazing the way it lumbers on. The streets are full of holes, the plastic garbage bags are piled in mounds on every block. The dog shit is back. The subways, having far surpassed anybody's wildest nightmares of degeneration, continue to grow even worse. They are shrieking, rattling coffins of doom, covered with spray paint. There are not enough police, which explains in part the steadily rising rate of violent crime, but not the plentitude of tickets stuck on cars in midtown. A woman I know was held up at knife point in the dry cleaner across the street. Another woman was shot in the eye by a burglar in a nearby apartment building that has one of the most elaborate security systems in town. Everybody has a story. To be without a mugging experience is a little like being a virgin, an unusual, rather quaint condition. I remain chaste but my sons have been dipped in the waters. One lost his coat to a couple of muggers one rainy afternoon, on Fifty-ninth Street between Lexington and Park, which I had considered safe territory. Now Dry Dock Country is out, which is probably why you never hear it mentioned anymore.

True to prophecy, the city is becoming a crime-ridden, deteriorating wasteland dotted by the fortresses of the rich. I live in an apartment whose exorbitant rent is a bargain, in a building whose income requirements I could never meet since they stiffened a couple of years ago. Though we have a pretty good security system, all my jewelry was stolen. I took it hard—I loved my jewelry. Most friends weren't very sympathetic. "Oh, mine went years ago," or, "It happened to me twice." We have developed calluses we never asked to have. My children, having lost their innocence, fear the city in a way I never did. They go along certain well-worn paths but never wander off to explore. Should we go or stay? Stay in the city or move to the country?

I don't approve of regret in others, all the headshaking about how things aren't the way they used to be, but I indulge in it like a secret vice. Behind the 1981 city is that old 1945 or 1950 city, shimmering around the edges like the corona during an eclipse. Through half-closed eyes I can see the El train rattling up Third, sending down showers of snow; and below the trolley with its woven wicker seats, sending out sparks from its electrical connection. Mac's, the Armenian rug dealer, the shoe repairman on the corner, and all the itinerants of Sixty-second Street—the man with the vegetable truck, the one with the knife sharpener, the organ-grinder with the monkey. I can hear the wild Italian tenor voice that sometimes cascaded between the buildings of our canyon; and superimposed on the bland brick front of the high-rise on the corner is the red-brick face of 204, like a paper cutout, steps going up to that black front door with the old brass knobs.

The place that once seemed so simple and clear is now full of paradoxes. If the population of Manhattan steadily decreases, why do there seem to be more crowds? Why, if there are fewer people, is there an apartment shortage? Why is there an apartment shortage if so many have been built in the last twenty years, if new neighborhoods are constantly created? There didn't used to be any SoHo or TriBeCa. Most of the West Side was slum. The Village was for the young and adventurous. Even York Avenue, where I live, was a wilderness. But now every corner is used, people live everywhere, and there still isn't enough room. Is it the economy? The baby boom? Divorce, the new chastity, the old sexual revolution? What was once comprehensible has gotten immensely complicated—or am I talking about myself?

Real estate is an obsession in the city. The subject of apartments is more compelling than sex, which has lost something of its mystery and shine. Those who have them don't move, but arrange their lives in order to keep them. Those who don't, move out of town or to another borough, an equally drastic psychological removal. The way to survive is to stay in one spot for decades, to have been able to predict the current predicament twenty years ago. The planners survive, the spontaneous pay—and the cost of mistakes, like everything else, goes up all the time.

There is still a remarkable optimism about this city. In my neighborhood tiny shops open, last a few months, and disappear. Then another one comes. Little places that sell cheese or ceramics, antiques or knitting wool or candles. Around the corner there is one that seems to sell nothing but potted orchids. There are tiny coffeehouses and Korean vegetable stands. Many don't make it, but knowing the rents they pay, it's remarkable so many even try.

The Orwellian vision of mass production now seems quaint as the organ-grinder's monkey. Now the variety is so infinite the head spins. Thirty years ago we knew nothing of kiwis or pâtés, croissants or bean sprouts or tabouli. Once cheese was either Swiss or Cheddar—now I could drown in Brie, l'Explorateur, feta, Saga, and Morbier, all casually sold at the corner deli. Wasn't home decoration simpler, and wasn't there less choice about what to wear? Once I could spot a Claire McArdell or an Anne Fogarty from across the room. I knew which shoe departments had what. Clothes told you a lot about the wearer. But I can't sort my way through capes and leg warmers, knickers and tunics and multicolored stockings and a thousand kinds of boots. How can you tell who's who? Kids wear Grandma's mink, Jersey housewives wear down vests. Bag ladies wear Argyle socks, tiny mites wear high heels and punk haircuts. It must be one reason I feel so dazzled. What do I put on, and who am I, anyway?

But part of the city's stimulation is such mysteries, its refusal to submit to easy explanations. I used to think that I understood it, or would have if only I had never left. But now I know I never did, and if I had it wouldn't have remained stubbornly in my head as the place I was always going to go back to.

I still occasionally daydream about a house in the country. Not Dorset—that's my mother. *My* dream house, my perfect place. I love other people's stories about the old farm in Putnam County, the house on the banks of the Connecticut River. Willows moving at night in the light from the windows. A lawn going down to the water's edge, the cry of a loon. A stone fireplace with burning pine logs. The safe place, or the place I believe will be safe.

In the meantime, from my apartment, I look out at the city lights, which sweep across my horizon in a wide belt broken only by a church spire and the Department of Sanitation, buckled by a small square of the East River at one end. It's foolish to still be excited by it, I suppose, and by the pictures it conjures up in my mind—of hope and glamour and possibility, of better worlds than mine. By now you'd think I'd know better.

Though I know my hopes really lie in my own hands, I'm still looking through other people's windows.

NORA JOHNSON is an accomplished writer of novels, nonfiction, and drama and a popular critic and reporter for major magazines throughout the United States. Her novel *The World of Henry Orient* was made into a successful film and musical play and her most recent book, *Flashback*, the memoirs of her life with her father, the famous filmmaker Nunnally Johnson, received excellent reviews.